Gospel Music
Encyclopedia

Gospel Music Encyclopedia

Robert Anderson & Gail North

Introduction by Don Butler
Executive Director, Gospel Music Association

Sterling Publishing Co., Inc.   New York

Oak Tree Press Co., Ltd.
London & Sydney

Contents

Preface   6

Introduction   11

Acknowledgments   16

Encyclopedia Listing   17

Pictorial Encyclopedia   21

Dove Award Winners   191

Members of Gospel Music Hall of Fame   197

Radio Stations   207

Television Stations   221

"In Concert"—A Photo Album   225

A Sampling of Christian Music   249

Amazing Grace . . . Statue of Liberty . . . Blessed Assurance . . . Go Tell It On The Mountain . . . Bringing The Sheaves . . . Nobody Knows . . . Down By The Riverside . . . Rock Of Ages . . . I Love To Tell The Story . . . Swing Low, Sweet Chariot . . . In The Sweet By And By . . . Are You Washed In The Blood? . . . Shall We Gather At The River? . . . In The Garden . . . The Old Rugged Cross

Major Recording Discography   271

Gospel Music Association—Officers, Board of Directors   314

Index   316

Picture Credits   320

Preface

Gospel music is a ministry with a big message. The people who make up the "who" of Gospel music—the singers, songwriters, musicians—are spreading the word, the good news, their personal testimony to an audience of millions every day.

The extraordinary popularity of gospel music is rooted in a singular concept: this music can touch the heart and soul of the listener like no other music can! It brings solace in times of sorrow, inspiration in moments of despair and offers strength when life seems to have sapped the remaining remnants of courage and conviction. In short, gospel music offers an inspiring sanctuary—it is the gut-level communication of the Christian message to all souls.

As old as America itself, gospel music is as much a part of this country's history as the Declaration of Independence. According to Melvin B. Shestack, author of *The Country Music Encyclopedia,* "a gospel group sang at the inauguration of George Washington; Stephen Decatur led his sailors in singing hymns before naval battles; and Jeb Stuart would insist on singing two hymns before chasing the enemy. Even George Armstrong Custer prided himself on his deep voice and favored songs praising God."

Of course, the first gospel music was the Psalms of David singing praises to the Lord. Later, hymns were developed for church congregations which encompassed more melody, and gospel lyrics were then added to some of the songs. Black singers purportedly used their own work songs as a foundation, adding lyrics which turned their songs into gospel.

Early in the 1900s, gospel music began to expand its boundaries—it moved from churches to schoolhouses, to new settlements—but was still confined to the rural areas of the country where singing conventions and Sunday-night gospel sings were held. At that time, traveling was limited to around three hundred miles from home, so concerts were held in cotton fields, stadiums or any place where a large crowd could gather.

Music conservatories and music publishers played an important part in the gospel music revolution. The establishment of music and singing schools led publishing houses to gear up their presses and turn out printed pages of music. In order to gain exposure for their songbooks, publishers invited local singers to work for them as demonstrators. Most of the singers were glad to do it even though they held full-time jobs and only sang on weekends.

In the late 1930s and early 1940s a number of gospel performers had their own radio programs. It was an exciting era of live performers and live radio. This exposure led to a rise in bookings and radio listening, and eventually the early groups and individual singers were able to support themselves by their singing and give up other jobs. When the first recordings were made, it was the same music that was sung in churches which launched the vocalists' sales.

Rhythm and blues and country music were spawned to a large extent by gospel music. Black and white gospel, in the present era, appeals to a cross-sectional audience. However, both developed from two separate cultures. White gospel, the strongest in the South, developed with country music and country performers. It began with a gospel content, expanded and developed into country music. Many established country singers ultimately went back to their roots and began performing gospel again.

Black gospel grew up along with rhythm and blues. Rhythm and blues also began with a gospel content, then expanded and evolved into the pop market. But the gospel content is never far from the music.

According to The Reverend James Cleveland, one of the most well-known black figures in gospel music,

Andrae Crouch has bridged the gap between black and white audiences. . . . The white artists are very interested in the more soulful type of gospel music. . . . In the contemporary sound of gospel music, many black musicians are now embracing the contemporary sound. There is a great upsurge of white choirs that sing like black choirs, and the blacks have always tried to excel and perfect performances relating to sound, arrangement and instrumentation. Orchestrations and the like bring us closer to what the white man has been doing all the time. . . . So they're coming our way, and we're going their way. Somewhere in the middle of the road we're bound to run into one another!

There was another development in the gospel music revolution that made a deep imprint on the contemporary gospel sound. Rock and pop music acted as the springboard for a generation of people who did not have ties to the church, the old hymns or any of the old traditions. In the late 1960s and early 1970s, many disenfranchised young people were drawn to the Christian experience, to the cohesiveness that gave their lives new meaning. Desirous of a music they could relate to, they applied their own language and their own rock melodies and beats and created what is known as Jesus rock. The influence of the contemporary Jesus music is now felt all over the nation in the form of both white and black gospel.

Today, whether it's black gospel or white gospel, Jesus rock, traditional, quartet style or Christian blue grass, the ministry of gospel music is carried all over the country with a message that is uplifting, positive and soul-inspiring. It is the dedication and commitment of the many talented performers that seem to ensure a continuation of loyal audiences.

The authors of this book recently attended a gospel concert in Tennessee, and after the performance engaged some members of the audience in conversation. We asked, "Why do you go to gospel concerts? Is it because of religious conviction?"

A woman in her mid-thirties, who had attended the concert with her husband and two children, told us what we believe to be the general feeling among gospel fans.

"First of all," she said, "there aren't many things the whole family can do together these days and gospel music is certainly family entertainment. The kids love it as much as we do. And, to be entertained while praising God, well, that's just something that really makes you happy!"

The combination of entertainment and religion is what makes gospel music so spectacularly powerful today. Henry Slaughter, one of gospel's most popular musicians, is overwhelmed by the acceptance of gospel music as entertainment. "It's the same music as when we sang with only piano," he says, "but one style of music has an effect on all others; country influences pop, pop rock, rock gospel. I was playing for a church youth choir in Dallas recently and have never been so challenged to play rock gospel in my life. And I enjoyed it.

The message is the same, but the young folks relate to it more."

Gospel seems to have expanded, becoming accessible to more people as the new changes were incorporated. Jim Hamill of The Kingsmen feels that the newer songs are actually more relevant than the old vaudeville-style gospel of the early days. "They're deeper," he says, "not as cornball. It's a change to music that is not only more entertaining, but more uplifting."

Reflecting the spiritual and social revival going on in the United States today, the private lives and the public performances of many of the entertainers mirror each other with amazing accuracy. Sherman Andrus, who was initially a member of Andrae Crouch and The Disciples, a black gospel group, spends much time working with young people and believes that "we are all Christians singing Christian music." The members of The Rambos, a major recording group, say that they sing to "communicate truth," while The Lanny Wolfe Trio's members say that they are "excited about what they believe" and this excitement is expressed in their music. Performers like Keith Green run halfway houses and evangelistic street ministries, along with their full concert schedules, and The Reverend James Cleveland believes that "music is one of the most perfect magnets you can use to draw people to church."

Why gospel artists actually perform is another truthful reflection of their lives and their art. Henry Slaughter says, "It's a call of God." J. D. Sumner says, "It's my way of Life," while Jim Hamill says, "It's the thrill of knowing you are blessing someone; you are making someone happy. Our reward is the same as a preacher's—we can retire in heaven."

Retiring in heaven may be a most important consideration to gospel music performers, but retiring on earth seems to be a more immediate possibility. Crowds for gospel music are doubling, tripling and quadrupling. New record companies are sprouting up every year and all the standard record labels now produce gospel albums of their own. Concerts by The Blackwood Brothers and The Florida Boys sell out the house in South Carolina and Missouri, while Andrae Crouch packs them in at New York's Madison Square Garden. Evie Tornquist is a regular performer on such shows as Merv Griffin and Johnny Carson and resists offers to go "pop." Gospel is "pop" enough for Evie and her records sell well. The music business now considers gospel an integral part of its makeup and the activities of gospel performers consistently make news.

Gospel groups like The Stamps or The Happy Goodman Family own luxurious tour buses that could be called showmobiles. They provide home and transportation for groups who may travel one hundred thousand miles a year or more and play at least twenty dates a month. "To be a successful champion of the Lord," J. D. Sumner says, "a group has to operate as a business. But that doesn't mean that the message is lost."

And the message is rarely lost. Don Butler, executive director of the Gospel Music Association and the author of our introduction, believes in the "message" as a priority goal of the GMA. He says that

> acceptance of the gospel of Christ is the number one goal. . . . To see men's lives change and to elevate people to a level just a little higher than the mundane things of life. This is the prime purpose. . . . Secondly, the effort is to educate, and by educate, I mean to make people knowledgeable of the great heritage of gospel music and then to better equip people to have a better style, a better professionalism, a better manner in which they present this music, through workshops, seminars or whatever. . . .

The Gospel Music Encyclopedia is the very first book to bring together almost all of the great gospel artists. These people are some of the most interesting, talented and unusual men and women this country has ever produced. They have stimulating lives, good ideas and philosophies worth knowing about. We have tried to include as many individual performers, groups, songwriters and musicians as possible in this volume and to share some of their personal visions. However, since so many new groups make their mark every year, we haven't been able to include everybody. But rest assured! If we've missed any of your favorites, the situation will be remedied in the first updated volume.

In the meantime, God bless you all.

BOB ANDERSON and GAIL NORTH

Introduction

Within the pages of this encyclopedia, I believe you will find the "who" of gospel music. It will be more difficult to answer the question, what is gospel music?

There is no easy definition of gospel music.

To me, music is music and what makes it gospel is the lyric content which contains the message of Good News, Hope, Promise, Faith and Assurance.

Any song containing such a message, regardless of who sings it, is gospel. There are many artists in the recording industry who perform pop, jazz, classical, country, rhythm and blues, etc., on a regular basis; occasionally they record message songs of gospel music.

Gospel music has become popular in the last decade because people are tired of negative messages; they want to feel better from having heard a song and they like a style to which they can relate. Also, the quality of recorded gospel music has improved considerably.

Gospel music has become a big business in terms of sales, distribution and consumer acceptance. Gospel music is not new; it is and has been often referred to as a sleeping giant. Gospel music has grown to such a degree that ABC bought Word, Inc., one of the largest gospel companies in existence. MCA, another large corporate entity, has announced plans to enter the gospel field.

The question has been asked about a line between entertainment and religion. Why does there have to be a separation? Who decreed that religion could not also be entertaining? Is it imperative that religion be sad, somber, reserved? Or may it be alive, vibrant, vital and electrifying?

Some have said it is becoming "show biz."

Well, there is a streak of ham in most preachers and certainly the choral productions along with special music and drama are entertaining. I have attended very few that did not have a touch of show business. I believe that we should use whatever method will best reach those who are without hope and dejected.

Gospel music at one time was most popular in the Bible Belt states. The Bible Belt has moved or expanded, and migrating families have brought the appreciation of gospel music to a national and international status. It is featured regularly in concerts throughout the United States, in all major cities, and on a tour basis overseas. The marketplace has really expanded in the past ten years.

Gospel music performers are different from other show business persons in very few ways. I would not suggest that only gospel music performers are sincere and devout because I think this is untrue. They are really a big family and travel primarily the same circuits; they are a lot like the old vaudeville performers or summer stock actors or jam session jazz musicians. They have a feeling for each other. So, the difference—other than that previously expressed about the message —is one of size of market and amounts of money commanded for recording contracts and concerts.

In past years gospel music was identified by the simple chord structures and plaintive message. Social statements were not made, and if you heard an oboe, French horn or strings, it was pop, classical or some other style of music. Not so any more. The quality of recordings and stage performance has improved tremendously through outstanding arrangements and orchestrations. The message has become more in tune with the issues of life rather than just pie in the sky.

The word pop comes from popular. How could anyone think that the gospel message set to music could become too pop? The more acceptable a tune is musically, the quicker the attention is drawn to the message.

Gospel music is more than just a means of livelihood for me. I enjoyed, embraced and worked for gospel music long before I was able to earn a living from it. Like many others, I enjoy all types of music and my personal library contains not only gospel music but the classics, jazz, rhythm and blues, country, and pop. I am exposed to rock and roll, folk and show tunes, but I do not enjoy a steady diet of any one of these. Neither do I have a steady diet of gospel music. I enjoy a mixture. To me this is why gospel music is such an im-

portant segment of my musical needs. It offers an alternative somewhat in style and definitely in lyric content—an avenue of escape from the more mundane things of life, a confirmation and reaffirmation of my faith. Gospel music appeals to all age groups and I think this is the primary reason—it enriches a life rather than perpetuating a con job on one's spiritual and intellectual being.

I have been fortunate to have an opportunity to work in an area that I truly enjoy. Given the same set of circumstances, I most definitely would choose gospel music as my field of endeavor. There is a challenge and much potential for gospel music and a wealth of satisfaction in realizing just a minute bit of progress in the warmth of a smile or the set determination in the eyes of a listener truly touched by the hope and promise of the gospel as set to music.

I sometimes wish that I could predict with great accuracy the future of gospel music, but since that is impossible I only can say that I have hope and faith for continued improvements musically, professionally, spiritually, and financially. Taking into consideration the outstanding growth and progress in each of these areas over the past twenty years, I certainly think that the 1980s will see a further expansion and, yes, even an explosion of gospel music throughout the world.

In all honesty, I do not predict, as some have, that gospel music is going to be as popular as any other form of music or entertainment, although it already enjoys record sales which surpass those of some other forms of music.

I believe and am firmly convinced that gospel music has only scratched the surface in sales of product and acceptance. Antiquated marketing and distribution are rapidly being replaced with up-to-date, sophisticated methods. Persons with advanced business acumen are becoming involved in gospel music, and results are beginning to show.

As I stated earlier, the quality of gospel music performances is improving and the message is now couched in a language which is easily understood. Timeworn clichés and rhetoric are giving way to a more specific and definitive style.

This new sophistication is not tearing away or destroying the message and sound enjoyed by our ancestors; it is serving to enhance and make it more palatable.

Gospel music getting too worldly? No, the gospel message will always remain the same because it is truth. The presentation may well take on the appearance of something too contemporary, but Luther and his compositions were said to be too contemporary during the Reformation. As each new generation has come along, new ideas and expressions have become the contemporary.

We deal with human beings and we live in a complex society; thus, we must endeavor to reach the masses with the best and most acceptable means possible.

Gospel music is truth and this truth is spoken through lyrics —lyrics that contain no pornography, no expression of illicit love affairs, no sexual promiscuity, no suggestion of drug involvement or experimentation. Instead, it puts forth pure love undefiled, brotherhood of man, respect for one another, and honesty with God and your neighbor. This is good for mankind.

For the most part the people who make up the "Gospel Music Industry" are like a family with kinfolk stretched around the globe. Like a family, the members have made great sacrifices in order to continue in this family. They are a dedicated group that will respond in time of need; they will give of their time and talents to each other in the form of benefits, to help churches become established, in community and civic affairs, and in charities nationwide. They are like any other family; they have their differences of opinion; they have their different areas of involvement, different likes and dislikes, but they are family and all have a common bond that runs like a golden thread, and that is the message.

There are many unknowns and unsung heroes in the world of gospel music and although, as in any other field of endeavor, some receive recognition in their lifetimes, others will help lift their hands and will applaud them for their accomplishments, knowing full well that if they study, train, create, and give cheerfully of themselves, their day will come sometime—somewhere.

DON BUTLER
Executive Director
Gospel Music Association

Acknowledgments

The authors and publisher would like to extend thanks and gratitude to the following people who helped make this book possible:

Don Butler—Gospel Music Association

Bill Gohring—Word Records

Marvin Norcross—Word Records

Norman Odlum—SESAC

The Benson Company

Charlie Monk—April Blackwood Music

Ralph Carmichael—Lexicon and Light

Linda Miller and Associates

Hoyt Sullivan—H.S.E. Records

Milton Bingham—Savoy Records

Herman Harper—Don Light Talent

James Bullard—Roadshow Records

Great Circle Representation

Billy Ray Hern—Sparrow Records

Donald H. White (for his patience and tenacity)

Natalie Parness

Betty and Becky of Century II Talent

Cody Barnard

Duane Allen

William Golden

Richard Sterban

Melvin B. Shestack

Joe Bonsall

Also a special acknowledgment for enduring support to Jessie and Carlo. And to Charles . . . for his vision.

Encyclopedia Listing

A

Andrus, Blackwood & Co.
The Archers
Ayala, Bob

B

Bagwell, Wendy
Banks, Bishop Jeff
Bethlehem
Bethlehem Gospel Singers
The Blackwood Brothers
The Boones
Boone, Debby
Boone, Pat
Bridge
Brown, Scott Wesley
Burgess, Dan
Burton, Wendell
Byron, Jon

C

Caesar, Shirley
Camp, Steve
Candle
Carson, Martha
Cash, Johnny
The Cathedral Quartet
Cheré, Tami

Children of the Day
Christian, Chris
Clark, Terry
Clawson, Cynthia
Cleveland, The Reverend James
The Continental Singers and
    Orchestra
The Couriers
Courtney, Ragan
Crouch, Andrae
Culverwell, Andrew

D

Dalton, Larry
Danniebelle (Hall)
Davis, Jimmie
Dino and Debby (Kartsonakis)
The Dixie Echoes
The Dixie Melody Boys
Dixon, Jessy
Dogwood
Douglas, The Reverend Isaac

F

Farrell & Farrell
Field, Fred
Fireworks
Fischer, John
The Florida Boys

Fong, Oden
Ford, David
Ford, Tennessee Ernie
Found Free
Francisco, Don

G

Gaither Trio, The Bill
Gaither, Danny
Gilbert, Jim
Girard, Chuck
Goodman Family, The Happy
Gospel Seed
Grandquist, Nancy
Grant, Amy
Green, Keith
Green, Lilly
Grine, Janny

H

Hale, Robert
Harris, Larnelle
Hawkins, Walter
The Hemphills
Herndon, James
Hibbard, Bruce
The Hinsons
Holm, Dallas
Honeytree (Nancy Honigbaum)
Howard, Tom
Huffam, Teddy and The Gems

I

The Imperials
Ingles, David
The Institutional Radio Choir

J

Jackson, Mahalia
Jeremiah People
Jerry and The Singing Goffs
Johnson, Mike
Johnson, Phil
Jones and The Modulations,
    Glenn
The Jordanaires

K

Keaggy, Phil
The Kingsmen
The Klaudt Indian Family

L

Lafferty, Karen
Lawrence, Doug
Lee, J.J.
The LeFevres
The Lewis Family
Lympic & Rayburn

M

Mann, Johnny
Mann, Lynn
McGuire, Barry
The McKeithens
McSpadden, Gary
McVay, Lewis
Meece, David
Mercy River Boys
The Mighty Clouds of Joy

N

Nelon Singers, Rex
Nelson, Erick
Netherton, Tom
Nielson and Young
The Norman Brothers
Norman, Larry
Nutshell

O

The Oak Ridge Boys
Oldham, Doug
Omartian, Michael
One Truth
Owens-Collins, Jamie

P

Pantano/Salsbury
Pantry, John

Patillo, Leon
Paxton, Gary S.
Pope, Dave
Powell, Sara Jordan
Presley, Elvis
Preston, Billy
Price, Flo

R

The Rambos
Rambo, Dottie
Rambo, Reba
The Rebels Quartet
Rettino, Ernie & Debbie
The Revelator Quartet
Riley, Jeannie C.
Robinson, Bishop
Rogers, Roy and Dale Evans

S

Sandquist, Ted
The Scenicland Boys
The 2nd Chapter of Acts
The Sego Brothers and Naomi
The Sensational Friendly Four
The Sensational Gospelaires
The Sensational Harmonizers
Sharalee
The Sharretts
Shea, George Beverly
Sheppard, Tim

Slaughter, Henry and Hazel
Smith, Connie
Snell, Adrian
The Soul Stirrers
The Speer Family
The Statesmen
Stonehill, Randy
Stookey, Noel Paul
Sumner, J.D. and The Stamps
Sutter, Lynn
Swaggart, Jimmy
The Sweet Comfort Band

T

Taylor, Danny
The Telestials
Thomas, B.J.
The Thrasher Brothers
Tornquist, Evie
Turner, Norris

V

The Voices of Nashville

W

Walker, Albertina
Wall, Alwyn Band
The Wall Bros. Band
Ward, Clara
Wilder, Dean
Wilkin, Marijohn
Willard, Kelly
Wolfe Trio, The Lanny

Y

Young, Ovid

Z

Zimmer, Norma

Pictorial Encyclopedia

ANDRUS, BLACKWOOD & CO.

Sherman Andrus
Terry Blackwood
Karen Voegtin
Bill Egtlin—Keyboards, Vocals
Bob Villareal—Guitar, Vocals
Tim Marsh—Drums
Rocky Laughlin—Bass

When Sherman Andrus and Terry Blackwood made their debut in the con- temporary Christian music field, they created an upward surge on the charts that prophesied a very exciting future. Formerly with The Imperials, Sherman and Terry became good friends and, as fellow musicians, experimented in some new musical areas, both in the studio and on stage. Their collaboration helped to shape The Imperials into a major force in the gospel music arena.

In 1977 Greentree Records, a division of The Benson Company, released their first album, *Grand Opening*. Their second

ANDRUS, BLACKWOOD & CO.: *"We are all Christians singing Christian music"*

THE ARCHERS: *"Too much going for them to miss"*

album, *Following You,* features songs by Phil Johnson, Tim Sheppard, Reba and Dony McGuire.

Terry lives in his hometown of Memphis where he and his sister, Kaye, pursue a duet-performance schedule. Sherman lives in Oklahoma City with his wife, Winnie, and son, Sherman Jr. A frequent soloist on college campuses, in churches and in community concerts, he feels that his calling is with young people of all races, and has worked with them extensively. Sherman's feeling about gospel musicians is that "they have been superkind. We are all Christians singing Christian music."

THE ARCHERS

Tim Archer
Steve Archer
Janice Archer

Sharing God's great message of love for all mankind, The Archers—Tim, Steve and Janice—pursue their dedication to Christian music by traveling wherever they can to spread the gospel message. The Archers come from a family where everyone was involved in the ministry. They are but three of the five children of Lee and Neoma Archer; their

23

father spent thirty years as a minister; their brother, Gary, is a pastor in Ventura, California; their brother, Ron, ministers in Holland.

Beginning their own ministry in 1965, Tim and Steve sang in their father's church and then expanded to other churches in the Northern California area. By 1967 they had added members and instruments to their ensemble, and over the next few years received enthusiastic encouragement from their friends Ralph Carmichael and Andrae Crouch.

In 1972 they recorded their first album, *Any Day Now,* on the Charisma label which was later purchased by Impact Records. Subsequently, *Any Day Now* was re-released as *The Archers.* The favorable response to and widespread exposure of this album led to The Archers' performance at Expo '72 where more than 500,000 Christians assembled in Dallas for the week-long event. That same year they were also featured in a film with Pat Boone as well as a series of Boone concerts and performances.

By 1974 they had become one of America's leading contemporary Christian groups and released their second album *Keep Singin' That Love Song.* Their third album, *Things We Deeply Feel*, was their first for Light Records; their fourth, *Fresh Surrender,* received outstanding recognition across the country, was nominated for a Dove Award, and was followed by a fifth album entitled *Stand Up!*

The most significant event and highlight in the history of The Archers was the addition of Tim and Steve's sister, Janice. The contribution of her rich soprano voice, and its impeccably harmonious blending with her brothers', gave The Archers their tighter, more exciting vocal dynamics.

Their ever-growing musical accomplishments and popularity give credence to *Billboard* magazine's acclaim for this special group: "The Archers have too much going for them to miss."

AYALA, BOB

Bob Ayala feels that his ministry is to rejoice with those who are rejoicing and to comfort those who are in need. From the reaction to his music, he most certainly does just that!

A tremendously talented musician, singer, composer and performer, he decided in 1969 to turn those attributes into a Christian ministry and began performing at the Salt Company, a Christian coffee house in the Los Angeles area. Since that time he has leaped ahead personally, and so has his music. Revolving around the spiritual problems of young couples, moral issues and inter-personal relationships, his songs are memorable, enjoyable and brightly expressive—his lyrics are messages that pierce the heart and soul of the listener with great intensity. Like so many of his Jesus Music contemporaries, Bob Ayala gets very involved with his songs. They are a part of him, an expression of his innermost feelings, and are inspiringly represented on his Myrrh album *Joy By Surprise.*

Although legally blind, Bob still enjoys baseball games, painting, and relaxing at his home in Whittier, California, with his wife Pat.

B

WENDY BAGWELL & THE SUNLITERS [Wendell Lee]

Wendy Bagwell
Jerri Morrison
Jan Buckner
Charles Beatenbo

Wendy Bagwell was one of the first gospel performers to have a million-seller and to sing in New York's Carnegie Hall. According to author John Pugh, Bagwell is "possibly the most talented, versatile, prolific, multi-gifted, many-faceted artist on today's gospel circuit." Although extremely diverse in both his musical interests and lifestyle, Bagwell is probably best known to both gospel and country audiences as the man who does the snake song. *Here Come the Rattlesnakes* is the biggest selling gospel record in history and when it first appeared on the charts, Bagwell received myriad offers to cross over into pop music. "But I've been a gospel trouper for almost twenty years," Bagwell says, "and I plan to go on singing the good news 'til the good Lord carries me off to a better place." Few gospel singers have as identifiable a trademark song as Bagwell. At least five requests for "the snake song" are made at each of his public performances. Bagwell says he doesn't mind. He loves the snake song as much as his fans do. Here are Bagwell's own dramatic words about the origin of his hit:

"We average 150 shows a year and as many churches as we can. If we're off on a Sunday we'll try to make a church after a Saturday night. This little church in Kentucky had been after us for about six months. Finally one night we figured we are as close as we were ever going to get, so we drove all day across the state and came to this little place over by the West Virginia border.

"We did our show and noticed these boxes off to one side, but didn't think anything about it. Nobody told us this was a church that handled snakes. As soon as we finished our show, we found out plenty quick. They opened those boxes and brought out five or six of the biggest, ugliest, meanest rattlesnakes I had ever seen.

"We were trapped up in the pulpit area with no way to get out, and for the next fifteen minutes we's as skeered as we's ever been in our whole lives. That's when I came up with that line, 'Geraldine, look around and find out where they got a back door.' And Geraldine says, 'I already looked and they ain't got one.' And I say, 'Where do you think they want one?' Another woman offered to let me take her snake. I said, 'Lady, there ain't a greedy bone in my body. [Appropriate pause] Give mine to Geraldine!' Afterward the preacher explained that they took up the snakes to show they had the faith. I said, 'You know, I had a feelin' those snakes knew you people had the faith and wouldn't harm you. [Another

WENDY BAGWELL & THE SUNLITERS: *The man who does the snake song*

pause] I also had the feelin' they knew I didn't!'

"It was another two, three years before we recorded it. The preacher up there has always told us how much they liked the record, and that we're the best advertisin' they ever had. Where it goes over biggest is up North: Illinois, Pennsylvania, places like that.

"We've always done funnies along with our gospel show. We started out singin' in our church in Smyrna, Georgia. I wrote a song called 'Pearl Buttons' and it was played on some New York radio stations. After two, three years we wound up playin' Carnegie Hall. We's skeerder there than we was in the snake church. I told some funnies, we closed with 'Pearl Buttons' and the people came out of their seats, all five tiers of them. I thought they was fixin' to leave. I never thought they were goin' to give us a standin' ovation."

The Bagwell group has been going strong for over twenty years. Wendy's backup singers are called The Sunliters and they are still Jerri Morrison and Jan Buckner. A few years ago, Charles Beatenbo joined the group. Bagwell makes a point of never taking money from churches, not even a love offering. "Some people think Christians shouldn't laugh," he complains. "I don't know what kind of religion they got. If anybody should have laughter, it's the Lord's people."

Among the songs Bagwell has written are "I'm Looking for Jesus," "Good-Bye Devil," and "Little Country Preacher." He is a frequent guest on national TV programs. He lives with his wife and family in his home town of Smyrna, Georgia, and generally records for Word, Inc.

BANKS, BISHOP JEFF

As a gospel preacher and an artist of music, Bishop Jeff Banks searches for new avenues in his life where he can contribute and share the good news of Christ with mankind.

Born in Pittsburgh to the late Anna and James Banks, Banks spent much time playing for churches and gospel singers. He was an accompanist for The Byrdett Singers of Detroit, Michigan, the late Mahalia Jackson, and he sang with The Mary Johnson Davis Singers of Pittsburgh. Later, he and his brother, The Reverend Charles Banks, traveled and recorded as The Banks Brothers. Together, they organized the famous Back Home Choir, and in 1956 the Banks Brothers appeared in Rhode Island at the Newport Jazz Festival and presented gospel singing—the first time in history that a gospel concert was heard there! That appearance catapulted the Banks Brothers to Carnegie Hall, Madison Square Garden and Hunter College. They recorded "Lord I've Tried," which earned a gold record, and then went on to record the album *Master Mind Is He*.

BETHLEHEM

Danny Daniels—Acoustic & Electric Guitar, Lead Vocals
Dominic Franco—Pedal Steel Guitar, Vocals
John Falcone—Bass Guitar, Vocals
Randy Rigby—Vocals, Keyboards, Lead Guitar
Dan McCleery—Drums, Percussion, Vocals

"It is our desire that the love of Jesus would come through us to feed the Body of Christ and to save the lost. We want Jesus to be seen and heard in us and in the music He has given us to share." Those are the words of Danny Daniels, Bethlehem's lead vocalist, who, with his musical colleagues, hopes to bring the message of Good News all over the nation.

In 1974, from their roots in Orange County, California, the ministry of Bethlehem began. Since that time, with their mellow sound of country-rock, Bethlehem has crossed the land from the Pacific Northwest and Southwest many times and taken the Lord's message in song onto college campuses and into prisons, bars and churches. Dedicated ministers of the Word in music and song, they now hail Boulder, Colorado, as their home base and regard touring as an integral part of their desire to reach out to people, in any place they may gather.

THE BETHLEHEM GOSPEL SINGERS

James C. Mclean
Mrs. Lorraine P. Mack
Mrs. Retha Mack Smith
Mrs. Mary Rachel Mack Nicholson
Mrs. Mary Lou Mclean
Francis Rogers
Sandy Moore Jr.

In the late 1960s The Bethlehem Gospel Singers were organized at the Bethlehem Baptist Church in Laurinburg, North Carolina by James Mclean. The group gained their fame singing spiritual songs at the morning worship services. Since 1962 they have been heard and seen on many television stations throughout North Carolina, South Carolina and Georgia.

Members of the group include Mrs. Lorraine Pagues Mack and her two daughters, Mrs. Retha Mack Smith and Mrs. Mary Rachel Mack Nicholson, along with Mrs. Mary Lou Mclean, Francis Rogers, Sandy Moore Jr. and James C. Mclean.

THE BLACKWOOD BROTHERS

James Blackwood
Cecil Blackwood—Baritone
Jimmy Blackwood—Lead
Pat Hoffmaster—Tenor
Ken Turner—Bass
Tommy Fairchild—Pianist

Without a doubt, the name Blackwood Brothers is one of the most preeminent in sacred and gospel music, and the group's exciting sound is recognizable around the world. They have sung to more people, sold more records and traveled more miles than any other gospel group. The Blackwood Brothers were chosen as the only musical entertainment provided for the 1978 Presidential Prayer Breakfast in Washington, D.C., attended by 3,500 dignitaries and, of course, President Jimmy Carter. They were also selected by the Billy Graham Association to participate in the Memphis Crusade which was attended by over 400,000 people.

The Blackwood Brothers have been re-

THE BLACKWOOD BROTHERS: *Their sound is recognizable around the world*

cording records for thirty years and have sold 15 million albums—an average of 500,000 albums per year! The group first achieved national prominence in 1954 as winners on the *Arthur Godfrey Talent Scout Show*. Shortly after his triumph two group members died in a tragic plane crash, but, rebounding from this disaster, the group returned to the Godfrey Show in 1956 and won again. The National Academy of Recording Arts and Sciences has nominated The Blackwood Brothers among their top five for the best Gospel Album of the Year Award every year since the awards began. They won Grammy Awards in 1967, 1968, 1970 and 1974. In 1973 and 1974 they won the Dove Award for the best Male Gospel Group from the Gospel Music Association. In 1975 and 1977 they won the GMA Fan Award as the favorite gospel group. In 1977, the National Quartet Convention Association voted them Favorite Group.

James Blackwood, who is known as Mr. Gospel Music, has enjoyed over fifty years in gospel music, and is the only one of the original four who began singing in 1934 in the clay hills of Mississippi. James is a seven-time winner of the Gospel Music Association's annual Dove Award for the Best Male Voice in Gospel Music and has been enshrined in the Gospel Music Hall of Fame.

Cecil Blackwood, the baritone, master of ceremonies and manager of The Blackwood Brothers, has won honors from *Singing News* as the Favorite Baritone Singer in gospel music. He started his career at a very early age and as a teenager formed his own gospel group with such friends and singers as Jim Hamill of The Kingsmen and the late Elvis Presley. When his brother, R. W. Blackwood, who was The Blackwood Brother's baritone, was killed in an airplane accident during a trial run on the airfield, Cecil joined the family full-time as baritone. He's the nephew of James and the son of the late Roy Blackwood, the original tenor for the group.

Jimmy Blackwood, James' oldest son, started in gospel music at a very early age with The Junior Blackwood Brothers. He later joined The Stamps Quartet and then, in 1970, joined The Blackwood Brothers full-time. He is now the group's lead singer.

Pat Hoffmaster, the newest member of the group, is one of the highest, smoothest first tenors in gospel music. He achieved the honor of being voted Favorite Tenor by 350,000 fans and received the 1977 *Singing News* Fan Award.

Ken Turner is perhaps the most popular crowd pleaser to ever sing with The Blackwood Brothers. His low-note trombone imitations always bring down the house. Ken is also a songwriter.

Tommy Fairchild, acclaimed Number One pianist and arranger, has played the piano since he was a child. Indeed, his famous technique is the secret behind the marvelous Blackwood Brothers sound .

The Blackwood Brothers set a record in having the Number One song, "Learning To Lean," on the Top 40 charts for the longest period in history—fifteen straight months.

THE BOONES

Cherry Boone
Lindy Boone
Debby Boone
Laury Boone

One of the most powerful sources of consistently good Christian music in the industry today, The Boones, four attractive and talented young women, display a zest for performing and a message of faith to share. Their success and warm reception by audiences are well-earned, all a direct result of their superlative performing which, of course, has long been a tradition in their family—they are the daughters of Pat and Shirley Boone, and the granddaughters of the legendary country and western singer Red Foley.

The Boones made their debut in 1970 when their father and the then little-known Osmonds were touring Japan. Their interpretation of "What The World Needs Now" caused a sensation, opening a new phase in the Boone Family. *Variety* called their act "one of the most talked-about shows of this or any other season," and the *Los Angeles Herald Examiner*

THE BOONES: *A zest for performing and a message of faith to share*

reported that the group was "enthusiastic, effervescent, with a fine perception of their music."

Cherry, the oldest, is married to Dan O'Neele, an author and youthworker.

She is a talented songwriter and instrumentalist. Lindy, the second oldest, is married to Doug Corbin and has two children, a son and a daughter. Debby, of course, is well known as a solo per-

DEBBY BOONE: *"You Light Up My Life"*

BOONE, DEBBY

Debby Boone's recording of "You Light Up My Life" outsold every single of 1977, more than three and a half million copies for the Warner/Curb label. Her first solo effort, this recording held the number-one position on the Billboard Pop Chart for ten consecutive weeks, making this the longest-running top-of-the-charts single a Warner Brothers label has ever had.

Debby was born in Hackensack, New Jersey, the third of four Boone daughters (the others being Cherry, Lindy and Laury). As might be imagined, there's always been a whole lot of singing going on in the Boone family—whether at impromptu home gatherings, at church or on tour. Debby's earliest memories of family singalongs center around her dad Pat's career. Her "big break" occurred when Pat headlined a bill in Japan with the then unknown Osmonds. It was decided that the girls could accompany him to Japan. The song they came up with was "What The World Needs Now Is Love" and the singing Boones have been a welcome staple on musical circuits throughout the world ever since.

Her strong voice and serious interest in music established Debby as the lead singer of the girls early on. Once she decided that she wanted to make her career in show business, she discussed her ambitions with her parents. "My father

former as well as being a member of the group. Her single, "You Light Up My Life," shot straight to the top of the charts, stayed there for two months and earned a platinum record. Laury, the youngest Boone, has a variety of interests including songwriting, piano and photography.

Their first album, *The Boone Girls*, gave gospel enthusiasts a taste of their potential, and their second, *First Class*, includes a selection of songs fresh from their concert tours.

told me it was a hard life for a girl, but he never did say, 'Please don't do it,' " remembers Debby.

Since the success of her single and LP of the same name, Debby has been very busy guesting on major variety and talk shows. Her popular single, entitled "God Knows," is a beautiful love song written and produced by Brooks Arthur; her second album is entitled *Midstream*.

When her time isn't spent rehearsing or traveling, Debby fills her days learning the piano, writing music and making the Boone name a household word for a whole new generation.

BOONE, PAT

The original "clean-cut," "all-American" image of Pat Boone has taken quite a beating over the years. Certainly, there have been those in the past who have doubted an artist's ability to retain such high standards and still achieve success in show business. Undoubtedly, they misjudged the character and beliefs of the majority of Americans and the seriousness of this man's conviction.

Pat Boone is not only a success now, but has remained a star for two decades and he has done so while continuing to proclaim the importance of a personal relationship with Jesus Christ.

A descendent of Daniel Boone, Pat was born in Jacksonville, Florida in 1934 and is one of four children. His family moved to Nashville when he was three years old. Performances on local amateur shows and a stint as a master of cere-

monies for a high school talent revue on radio led to honors on the *Ted Mack Amateur Hour* and, subsequently, the *Arthur Godfrey Talent Scout Show*.

In the fall of 1954, Randy Wood, founder and president of Dot Records, signed Pat to an exclusive contract. Pat went to Chicago to record the single "Two Hearts, Two Kisses." An immediate success, it was followed by his first million-seller, "Ain't That A Shame." Subsequent hits included "I Almost Lost My Mind," "Friendly Persuasion," and "Don't Forbid Me."

Pat met his wife, Shirley, while they were both students at David Lipscomb High School in Nashville. They were married and relocated in Denton. Although his success was meteoric, Pat's desire for learning continued. In 1958, he graduated Magna Cum Laude from Columbia University with a B.S. degree in Speech and English. By this time, he and Shirley were the parents of four girls—Cherry, Lindy, Debby and Laury—currently known as a musical aggregation themselves, The Boones.

In 1956, ABC signed Pat to his first television series, *The Pat Boone Chevy Showroom*. It was produced by Boone's own TV production company, Cooga Mooga, Inc., making him the youngest performer on television with his own network show. He followed this half-hour series with a daily ninety-minute syndicated series for Filmways. In the same year, he signed a million-dollar contract with Twentieth Century-Fox and starred in fifteen motion pictures. These included the box office hits, *Bernadine, April Love, All Hands on Deck, Mardi Gras, Yellow Canary,* and *Journey to the Center of the Earth.* Pat also starred in *The Cross*

PAT BOONE: *Clean-cut, all-American image*

and the Switchblade, a film based on David Wilkerson's novel.

Pat Boone set the all-time popularity record by staying on the charts for more than 200 consecutive weeks. He has had no less than 60 songs on the charts with 15 hitting the Top Ten. "Love Letters" remained on the charts for 34 weeks—a record for a single—and remained Number One for 5 consecutive weeks.

Pat has sold more than 50 million records, has 13 gold discs, 2 gold albums and a platinum album denoting 3 million sales.

BRIDGE

The concept of their director, Jim Van Hook, this dynamic young ensemble, featuring eight musicians, six vocalists, a road manager and soundman, is composed of talented young people from all across the country. They travel from coast to coast appearing in concert halls, on college campuses and in churches, sharing their contemporary musical sound and personal testimonies.

BRIDGE: *Talented young people from all across the country*

SCOTT WESLEY BROWN: *Writes songs born of his own experiences*

Bridge has released three albums on the Impact label entitled *Bridge, Peace In The Midst Of The Storm* and *Bridge —Live with Bob Benson*. These albums feature songs by such gospel songwriters as Phil Johnson, Lanny Wolfe and Dallas Holm.

BROWN, SCOTT WESLEY

"I can only take others as far as I am myself," says Scott Wesley Brown. "If my relationship with God is straight and together, if I am nurtured by the Word and led by the Spirit—God can use me so much more in the lives of others."

Scott is one of the young performers for Jesus who writes songs "born of my own experiences, especially my struggles and the needs I see in the body through my travels." With three albums to his credit—*I Am A Christian, Scott Wesley Brown and I'm Not Religious, I Just Love The Lord*—on Sparrow Records, he embarked on his first live, in-concert album, joining a thirty-five-piece orchestra and band.

DAN BURGESS: *Specializes in Christian choral work*

BURGESS, DAN

Dan Burgess quickly earned a reputation as one of the finest contemporary and traditional music writers and composers in the country specializing in Christian choral work.

For five years, he was a director with The Continental Singers and for several seasons he also auditioned and selected talent for that group.

Burgess has served as a church choir director and worked on the staff of Lexicon Music, where he represented the company with choral directors from many denominations and backgrounds.

His three choral songbooks and records include *Thank You Lord, Songs You'll Want To Sing* and *Celebrate His Love,* all on Light Records and Lexicon Music.

Dan is a frequent and valued participant in music seminars, choral workshops and Christian camps.

BURTON, WENDELL

Wendell Burton's number-one priority is to serve the Lord in whatever direction he leads. Yet, his life hasn't always had this unswerving focus. Raised in Texas, Oklahoma and California, he attended Sonoma State and San Francisco State College, where he majored in political science. It was through a public speaking course at Sonoma State that Wendell was encouraged to try out for the theater department's production of *Oh Dad, Poor Dad,* in which he played the male lead. After that success, he auditioned for and got the part of Charlie Brown in the San Francisco production of *You're A Good Man, Charlie Brown* at the Little Fox Theater. After starring in *Charlie* for over a year, he left the cast to accept the leading role opposite Liza Minnelli in the Paramount Pictures film *The Sterile Cuckoo.*

Subsequent to this big break, Wendell starred in various television series, including *Medical Center, Love American Style, The Rookies,* and *Dr. Kildare,* as well as such TV movies as *The Red Badge of Courage, Go Ask Alice,* and *Journey from Darkness.*

But after achieving such tremendous success so quickly, Wendell soon discovered that there was considerably more to a happy life than merely being a star and impressing people. He thus embarked on a spiritual quest for God that culminated in a trip to India which unfortunately deepened his confusion and despair. Six months later, however, he discovered and met the person of Jesus Christ.

Since then, Wendell has served as vice-president of the Hollywood Free Theater, a nonprofit organization whose goal is to provide professional entertainment and theatrical instruction free to the public while glorifying God and proclaiming the Gospel of Jesus Christ.

Adding to his long list of achievements, Wendell made his debut gospel recording on Lamb & Lion Records in an album titled simply *Wendell,* which features ten of his own songs. Two special favorites are "Brand New Life," and "Good Ol' Gospel Feeling."

JON BYRON: *"My education was in the scriptures"*

BYRON, JON

Jon Byron, one of the few contemporary Christian performers with a Master of Divinity degree, is very definite about his calling. "My education was in the scriptures," he says. "That's what God wanted to teach me and that's what I show in my songs."

He graduated in 1975 from Westmont College in Santa Barbara, California, with a Bachelor of Arts degree and in 1978 received his Master of Divinity degree from Fuller Seminary in Pasadena, California.

Byron, who played guitar and sang in church choirs from an early age, grew up in a musical family where music was part of daily life. He actively began writing songs as a sophomore at Westmont; he has now written more than fifty.

With his folk-soft-rock approach to his personal brand of Christian music, Jon appeared in concerts all through his years at Fuller Seminary as well as at many discipling seminars throughout the country.

His first album, on the Light label, was *Portrait of Love*. "My message is how an individual relates to Christ in an attitude of praise and how God leads us into a family," he says. "It's also important to explain clearly how we relate our new relationship to other people through love."

Jon and his wife, Francie, have one daughter, Erin Marie.

— C —

CAESAR, SHIRLEY

At the age of ten, Shirley Caesar began her career as a member of The Charity Singers in Durham, North Carolina. Known then as "Baby Shirley," she toured churches throughout the South, appearing in concerts with gospel greats like Clara Ward and Mahalia Jackson. Shirley later joined The Caravans, one of the top female gospel groups in the country. After eight years with The Caravans, she was ready for a solo career.

Shirley Caesar has been awarded three gold records and was the first black female gospel singer to win a Grammy. *Ebony* magazine has given her its annual Best Female Gospel Singer award three times. She has been in the vanguard in introducing contemporary gospel, using her powerful voice to communicate a unique sound that transcends gospel and takes on a universal dimension.

CAMP, STEVE

Born and raised in Wheaton, Illinois, Steve Camp grew up in a strong Christian family. Beginning his musical career at a very young age, he started his first band in the sixth grade and later, while in high school, was a member of The Campus Life Singers.

Steve's personal involvement with music through his own songwriting talents did not emerge, however, until his years in college. It was then that Steve realized

SHIRLEY CAESAR: *A voice that transcends gospel and takes on a universal dimension*

it was much easier to communicate his faith to many people through a song composition than by talking one-on-one with an individual. Because of his own personal shyness, his music became the medium for sharing his testimony of Christ.

The event that most affected Steve's musical personality was the death of his father. Through this very personal experience of loss, Steve began to compose songs that were reflections of his own deepest feelings. It was after his father's death that he wrote two of the songs on his debut album, "Let Not Your Heart Be Troubled" and "Song For Mom."

Steve's further involvement with Christian music includes his work on Petra's *Come and Join Us* album and Scott Wesley Brown's *I'm Not Religious.* Several of the songs on his new album were written with Larry Norman, with whom he shares a close friendship.

Describing his music, Steve says: "The style I try to write in is a pop-Jamaican type of rock with a reggae kind of feel. I try to make my songs middle-of-the-road, easy-listening pop. I want my music to appeal to the young and the very old alike."

CANDLE

A captivating group of men and women, Candle has appeared in live concerts on college and high school campuses, coffeehouses, churches, television and radio. Frank Hernandez is one of the chief song writers for the group. Prior to his acceptance of Jesus Christ, he appeared regularly in various night clubs on the West Coast. Georgian Banov was a rock singer in his native country of Bulgaria; now, he is vocalist, flutist, drummer, violinist and composer for the group.

Candle has recorded *To The Chief Musician, Part 1 and Part 2, Music Machine, Within the Gate* and *Bullfrogs and Butterflies,* which was recorded with the entire Agape Force Prep School.

CARSON, MARTHA

Best known as a songwriter and singer, Martha Carson has written over one hundred songs, including "Satisfied," "I'm Gonna Walk and Talk With My Lord" and "I Can't Stand Up Alone." Her albums include *Gonna Shout All Over God's Heaven, Get On The Heavenly Road* and *Shepherd Of My Soul.*

CASH, JOHNNY

From the rugged terrain of Kingsland, Arkansas, to his first musical experience while stationed with the Air Force in Germany, to his initial recording contract with Sun Records, through a shattering personal experience, to his current status as super-star, Johnny Cash has always remained close to the music that he loves. A prolific composer and tireless performer, he has never forsaken his roots or his religion.

CANDLE: *A captivating group*

His compositions, such as "I Walk The Line" and "Folsom Prison," have placed him in the top rank of composer-singers. He has recorded such hit gospel albums as *The Gospel Road, The Holy Land, Hymns By Johnny Cash* and *Hymns From The Heart*.

THE CATHEDRAL QUARTET

Haskell Cooley—Pianist, Arranger
Glen Payne—Lead Singer, Manager
Roy Tremble—Tenor, Sound Engineer
George Amon Webster—Baritone
George Younce—Bass, M.C.

THE CATHEDRAL QUARTET: *They sing of the hope, love and happiness in Christian life*

The Cathedral Quartet is a group of talented men dedicated to spreading the gospel through their music. They sing of the hope, love and happiness found only in the Christian life. Their purpose in performing is to help others know the real joy of living in and for Christ.

Musically, The Cathedral Quartet has always combined individual talent with a unique "togetherness." Theirs is the ultimate in smooth, rich harmony. They sing a wide variety of music, much of which is composed by Quartet members.

Finalists in the competition for the Gospel Music Association's Dove Awards and the *Singing News* Awards for Best Male Gospel Group, The Cathedral Quartet's recordings on the Canaan label are consistently among the most popular songs on radio across America.

CHERÉ, TAMI

"Every now and then I meet a very special person," says Ralph Carmichael, president of Light Records, "one who seems to have a combination of gifts rarely found in the possession of one individual. When I met Tami Cheré, I knew she was one of those 'special' people."

Tami Cheré has come a long way— from a farm girl in northern Michigan to a Light Records recording artist with a busy concert schedule. Tami was born in 1963, the daughter of Magdalene and Delmar Gunden. When she was three years old she joined "family sings" in the home where her uncle, arranger-composer Danny Lee, was a frequent visitor.

TAMI CHERÉ: *"A sensitive and caring Christian"*

Prior to accepting Christ at a Christian summer camp when she was ten years old, Tami frequently sang solo in church, at PTA and other gatherings. Subsequently, with the encouragement and help of Danny Lee, Bob MacKenzie and Gary Paxton, she produced a small seven-inch record with two songs on each side which, in conjunction with her promotion appearances, sold several thousand copies. With the four songs from the first record, plus six more, she produced her first custom album, *Little Flower*.

In 1976, when Tami was thirteen, Danny Lee arranged for Tami to record her third album. Lee felt the album was so good that he arranged for Light Records president Ralph Carmichael to hear it. Carmichael signed Tami as his young-

est artist, and released her first album, *Keep Singin' That Love Song,* in 1977 as well as her second, *He's Everything To Me,* in 1979.

According to Carmichael, "Tami is a sensitive and caring Christian with a burning desire to share her Christian experience with people around the world."

CHILDREN OF THE DAY: *"Things happen after we leave"*

CHILDREN OF THE DAY

Russell Stevens—Bass, Vocals
Marsha Stevens—Guitar, Percussion, Vocals
Wendy Fremin—Guitar, Vocals
Kit Freeman—Piano, Drums

Children Of The Day is one of the oldest of the Jesus music groups of the early 1970s still going strong today. Organized in 1970 and still averaging 150 appearances a year, the group is consistently invited back for concerts because, says Russell Stevens, its business manager, bass player and vocalist, "things happen after we leave."

Along with Stevens, regular group members include Stevens' wife, Marsha, on guitar, percussion and vocals; Wendy Fremin on guitar and vocals, and Kit Freeman, the sound and road manager, who also plays on backup piano and drums.

In their early years, as they drove an hour each way to church, they began singing the simple songs of their new-found faith. Following church concerts, they received an invitation for their first concert of six songs. They drew their name from a favorite line of scripture: "You are all children of the light, and the children of the day."

Between concerts the group has recorded six albums:

Come To The Waters, With All Our Love, Where Else Could I Go, The Children Of The Day Christmas Album, Never Felt So Free and *Butterfly*.

CHRISTIAN, CHRIS

Unlike many of today's contemporary Christian musicians who spent much of their lives apart from Jesus, Chris Christian has always been in close and abiding contact with the Lord. Chris was reared in a Christian atmosphere and regularly attended church in his hometown of Abilene, Texas. He became interested in all kinds of music at an early age—he formed his own folk group during his college years at Abilene Christian College and made small-concert tours throughout the South.

After graduating with a degree in Business and Investment, he moved to Nashville where he played banjo in the Opryland Dixieland Band. Later he joined popular nightclub singer Wayne Newton and played lead guitar, banjo and harmonica.

In 1974, after leaving Newton's band, Chris returned to Nashville, began writing his own songs and playing guitar with Jerry Reed. By 1975 he was head of the Nashville division of Twentieth Century-Fox Music Publishing Company. Not content with that position, he went on to form his own companies: Home Sweet Home Productions, Home Sweet Home Jingles and The Gold Mine Recording Studio.

Music buffs recognize Chris from his songs and appearances with stars like Elvis Presley, Olivia Newton-John, The Osmonds, Jeannie C. Riley and Debby Boone. Working with these artists, Chris has appeared on *Midnight Special, American Bandstand, Wide World of Entertainment* and *Music Hall America.* A

CHRIS CHRISTIAN:
*"Close and abiding
contact with the Lord"*

highly respected producer, he has produced recordings for Pat Boone, Honeytree, Dogwood, The Imperials and B. J. Thomas' *Home Where I Belong.*

Chris' first Myrrh album, *Chris Christian,* earned him a reputation not only as an excellent producer but as a talented artist. Several of the songs on the album became instant favorites—"Great, Great Joy," "Mountaintop" and "Get Back To The Bible." His second Myrrh album includes a brand-new crop of Chris Christian tunes like "Lonely Man," "I Waited So Long" and "Now I See The Man."

CLARK, TERRY

A native of Texas, Terry Clark has been involved in the growth of contemporary Christian music for several years.

During the early, pioneering days of Jesus music, Terry was part of a group called Children of Faith which recorded one album. Although the group never became widely known, it was a stepping stone in the development of Terry's current ministry.

After Children of Faith disbanded, Terry and his brother Duane were offered the opportunity to join the Myrrh recording group Liberation Suite for their 1975 European tour. It was during that widely acclaimed tour that Terry became good friends with Chuck Girard—a friendship that resulted in Terry's eventual signing with Good News Records.

Terry started to work closely with Chuck on several projects. He became a member of Chuck's own band, an opportunity which brought Terry's own music before audiences all around the country. He co-wrote "The Warrior," a very popular song on Chuck's album *Written on the Wind.*

After being a part of several group ministries, Terry presented his music as a solo artist. An expert musician, accomplished on keyboards and guitar, Terry came forth with a progressive work. His first solo album, *Welcome,* on Good News Records was produced by Chuck Girard.

CLAWSON, CYNTHIA

"Cynthia Clawson sings from her soul; she will cause you to hear from your heart." So says Buryl Red, Cynthia's producer, who knows that her nearly four-

CYNTHIA CLAWSON: *Sings from her soul*

octave vocal range transcends all musical barriers, giving her the ability melodically and emotionally to interpret lyrics that touch the spirits of all who hear her.

Since the age of three, Cynthia has been working to develop her exceptional singing voice. A 1978 finalist for Best Gospel Female Vocalist, Cynthia's combination of artistic dedication and deep spiritual commitment has generated excitement among television and music industry personnel alike.

The daughter of a Southern Baptist preacher, Cynthia has been the featured soloist at many Southern Baptist convention meetings.

Cynthia has recorded jingles and station announcements for the Radio and Television Commission of the Southern Baptist Convention and numerous radio and television commercials for stations across the country.

Cynthia has made several guest appearances on the popular Christian Broadcasting Network television show, *The 700 Club* and *The PTL Club*. Other television accomplishments include her initial nationwide exposure on the Carol Burnett summer replacement show. She's been a guest on many syndicated series, including that of evangelist James Robinson, and on a Southern Baptist series, *At Home With The Bible*.

An equally prolific recording career has produced four solo albums, including *In The Garden* and *The Way I Feel* on the Triangle Records label.

Cynthia is married to writer/actor Ragan Courtney and she and her husband frequently collaborate on songwriting.

(See more about Ragan on page 52.)

CLEVELAND, THE REVEREND JAMES

Recognized as the reigning superstar of gospel music throughout the world—they call him The King of Gospel—The Reverend James Cleveland's background contains all the ingredients that make up the experience of gospel music.

Born of poor Christian parents in Chicago, Cleveland was introduced as a child to gospel music at the Pilgrim Baptist Church there, where the "Father of Gospel Music," Professor Thomas A. Dorsey, was music director.

During his young, formative years, Cleveland performed with many great gospel groups. Combining the best of these groups with his own unique and creative genius, he organized the Cleveland Singers—still the group which travels exclusively with Cleveland and a dynamic force in the world of gospel music.

Cleveland's first recording hit resulted from the collaboration of Cleveland, The Reverend Charles Crain and The Reverend Leslie Bush at Detroit's Prayer Tabernacle. The three young men organized the church with Cleveland as minister of music. The one hundred-voice choir, The Voices of Tabernacle, recorded "The Love of God," for an unknown label, Hob Records.

On the Savoy recording label, Cleveland has earned six gold albums: *Peace Be Still, I'll Do His Will, Lord, Do It, I Stood On The Banks, Lord Help Me,* and *Jesus Is The Best Thing.* His *Amazing Grace* album with Aretha Franklin has sold over two million copies. He has been the recipient of an honorary doctorate degree from Temple Bible College, winner of the Grammy award, *Billboard* magazine's Trend-Setters Award, *Ebony* magazine's Artist award, the National Association of Negro Musicians' award, NATRA's award as best gospel artist and the *Billboard* award for Best Album and Best Male Singer in Soul Gospel, for *Live At Carnegie.* Cleveland has performed all over the world and has recorded a total of fifty-four albums.

Cleveland is pastor of the Cornerstone Institutional Baptist Church in Los Angeles, and founder and president of the Gospel Music Workshop of America, a convention of singers from all over the country. The Reverend James Cleveland, the apostle of gospel, makes music as elemental as faith, hope and love.

THE CONTINENTAL SINGERS AND ORCHESTRA

The Continental Singers is an independent, nonprofit organization founded by Cam Floria in 1967, and dedicated to musical evangelism and the training of young people interested in the field.

THE CONTINENTAL SINGERS AND ORCHESTRA: *Dedicated to musical evangelism*

THE COURIERS: *Donating their time and talents*

With sixteen full-time staff members in the home office located in Thousand Oaks, California, they handle arrangements for tours by nine Continental Singers and Orchestra, and one Continental Orchestra in the summer, plus two permanent full-time groups—Jeremiah People and Act One Company. They also provide support and assistance to a sister ministry in Great Britain, Continental Singers, UK.

Since Floria organized the first unit, various editions of the Continental Singers and Orchestra have made more than 4,500 domestic appearances and over 1,200 foreign appearances before more than three million people.

Each unit of the Singers includes 25 vocalists and a 10-piece orchestra; the Continental Orchestra involves 36 instrumentalists with a full string section and 8 singers.

The Continental Orchestra has recorded one album on the Impact label, while the Continental Singers and Orchestra has recorded three albums for New Life as well as twelve for the Word and Light labels.

THE COURIERS

Dave Kyllonen—Bass-baritone, M.C., Manager
Duane Nicholson—Tenor
Neil Enloe—Vocals

If it were possible to describe The Couriers in one word, it would surely be "ministry," and the ministry of the gospel is the all-important motivation for their very existence. It is a carefully guarded priority with The Couriers. This fact is further reinforced by their donating a month of their time and talents each year to the needy mission field at no cost to the missionaries.

Their songs are selected almost solely on the basis of their message. Their arrangements are meticulously designed to best portray that message. The Couriers hold back nothing when they sing their songs. The result is that the message comes through strongly. Although Dave, Duane and Neil have vigorously pursued their musical craft, it isn't what you *hear* when they sing that makes them outstanding, rather it's what you *feel*.

Dave Kyllonen, the bass-baritone for the group, is manager, emcee and preacher. Of all Dave's duties, he most enjoys preaching. Usually he's called upon to give a ten-minute closing after an evening of music.

Duane Nicholson's tenor voice is one that perhaps most exemplifies the Courier sound. Born a preacher's son in Iowa, he knows the inner workings of the church as well as its music. He has inherited the "pastor's heart" from his minister father.

Neil Enloe's role is largely that of providing the musical material. He has composed over forty gospel songs and hymns. Songs such as "The Joy Of Knowing Jesus," "He's More Than Just A Swear Word" and "The Cross Is My Statue of Liberty" are among his better known compositions.

Through their forty-five long-playing record albums their songs daily bring faith, comfort and strength to thousands. Their weekly telecasts find their way into the homes of not only the Christian community, but also the unchurched. Their personal appearances number more than three hundred each year.

RAGAN COURTNEY: *Turns simple words into literary masterpieces*

COURTNEY, RAGAN

A writer of plays and poems, an actor and busy concert artist, Ragan Courtney's list of literary and performance credits is long and varied. His versatile writing style is communicated through a variety of mediums—books, records, stage and choral productions.

Noted composer Buryl Red has collaborated with Ragan on many varied projects. They have written such musical dramas as *Hello World, Celebrate Life* and the praise concert *Beginnings*. Ragan wrote and narrated the 1971 CBS Christmas Special for which Buryl was musical director, as well as Red's work entitled *Acts,* which was commissioned for and premiered at the 1978 Texas Baptist Convention.

With his wife, Cynthia Clawson, the accomplished singer and songwriter, Ragan has completed *Bright New Wings,* a musical dealing with life's transformation that comes through Christ, and *Angels,* an exciting children's musical using puppets. Ragan and Cynthia have co-written several selections for Cynthia's albums on the Triangle label.

Ragan has the ability to turn simple words into literary masterpieces, reflecting his own experiences and heartfelt beliefs. The sensitive sharing of his life's journey and Christ's guiding role leaves a gentle impression of religion's deeper meaning on all who are exposed to it.

CROUCH, ANDRAE

Andrae Crouch is a gospel singer of a special kind. He knows his roots and whereof he sings. The whole spectrum of the black gospel experience—the holiness churches, Thomas A. Dorsey, Mahalia Jackson . . .

About his music he says: "I believe the lyric of a song and the actual feel of the music are two different things. For example, by taking the infectious beat of Motown, the well-produced, innovative Philadelphia Sound, the simplicity of

ANDRAE CROUCH: *"The laid-back laboratory of the Lord"*

Nashville or Muscle Shoals, and attaching it to the Lord's message, a lot of people are going to listen."

Andrae Crouch and his group, The Disciples, are a road group—a traveling band. They tour both in the United States and around the world. Crouch has filled Carnegie Hall, Madison Square Garden and even Nashville's country-music shrine, the Grand Ole Opry. His audiences are among the most varied and mixed for any gospel group. He has played before presidents and also makes it a special point to include prison concerts in his hectic itinerary. He works in what he calls the "laid-back laboratory of the Lord."

Crouch, who lives in Woodland Hills, California, is a genuine son of a preacher man. His father, Benjamin, was a "bootleggin' street preacher" spreading his gospel from the sidewalk level to anyone who would listen. Eventually he organized a congregation in Los Angeles which is where young Andrae got his first taste of and feeling for the music.

When not quite in his teens, Andrae began playing regularly in his father's church. He also began writing gospel songs for the youth choir there. Today he has had his gospel material performed and recorded by artists like the late Elvis Presley, The Imperials and The Jessy Dixon Singers.

Yet, while listening to the late Mahalia Jackson and all the other great traditional gospel singers and groups, he had his ears open to many others. It began to show in his music—he moved away from the roots of standard gospel fare and turned it into a unique fusion of rhythm and blues, country, jazz and Latin rock.

"I have one question when I write a new song: 'Does it reach you?' I feel the feedback from an audience if the song is working. I know what is real—that's what I get being raised in the church, before those congregations," says Andrae Crouch.

In the gospel world, Andrae is called a trend-setter. He is a Grammy Award winner, records for Light Records and has appeared in concert with Billy Preston, and Santana, as well as Johnny Cash, Pat Boone and Billy Graham. In terms of music and audience, he's hard to pin down. He attracts white and black, "born-again" converts and those who come just to hear the force of his music.

CULVERWELL, ANDREW

Some years ago in a shoe factory in England, Andrew Culverwell offered this silent prayer:

"Lord, I feel you have something special for me to do. If I'm to do it here in this factory, I'm willing to stay. But if it is to be somewhere else, then I know you will open the door, and I'm willing to go."

Soon afterward, Andrew's career as a touring soloist began its ascent. Starting out at seventeen, Andrew spent his evenings and weekends traveling throughout Great Britain with a contemporary gospel group called The Four Kingsmen. During his four years on the British gospel circuit, Andrew grew into a skilled singer and songwriter. He was signed by an English record producer, and his first solo album, on Polydor Records, was *Where Is The Love*.

In 1973, when Andrae Crouch brought him to the attention of Manna Records, he entered the American gospel scene. He recorded his next three albums for Manna: *Andrew, Born Again* and *This Is The Song*. There were a number of songs on these albums that were picked up by other contemporary Gospel singers such as Evie Tornquist, who recorded "Born Again" and "Come On, Ring Those Bells." *Take Another Look* was his first

album on the DaySpring Label, a division of Word, Inc.

Rapidly becoming a contemporary gospel star of international magnitude, Andrew has given concerts in eight countries on four continents. He has been seen on TV many times and is in demand as a concert headliner and Christian entertainer by churches representing a wide range of denominations.

Andrew currently lives in Atlanta, Georgia, with his wife, Sue, and their daughters, Sarah and Annabelle.

— D —

DALTON, LARRY

Composer, arranger, conductor, concert pianist and singer, Larry Dalton has done more already than most people do in a lifetime. Born in 1946 in Big Stone Cap, Virginia, the eighth of nine children, he was the son of a minister-storekeeper. He began playing the piano at the age of three, studied piano technique at seven and became a church pianist at nine.

While a senior in high school, he wrote original music and adapted traditional Appalachian music for *The Trail of the Lonesome Pine,* one of America's most famous outdoor dramas.

In 1965 he entered Oral Roberts University and, while still a student, became organist for the Oral Roberts crusades which traveled the world.

While living in Tulsa, Dalton accompanied various visiting artists including Evie Tornquist, Pat Boone and Dale Evans, as well as playing for Richard and Patti Roberts for many years on television and in concerts.

In 1973 when Ralph Carmichael left the Oral Roberts television shows, Dalton stepped in to direct all music for *Oral Roberts Presents* and *Oral Roberts and You.* He wrote music for more than eighty half-hour and hourly special television shows before he resigned in 1975.

His albums for Light Records and compositions for Lexicon Music include *Build A Bridge* and *The Living Sound,* plus a choral book and album—*The Great Praise Meeting* and *Sing Around The World,* a compilation of choral songs. His Light Records solo album is called *Brass, Strings, and Ivory,* and features his piano with full orchestra.

LARRY DALTON: *A church pianist at nine*

DANNIEBELLE [Danniebelle Hall]

From the time she was twelve, Danniebelle played the piano at her church but had no idea that God was preparing her as a gospel singer. It wasn't till she was eighteen and made a visit to Los Angeles that Danniebelle learned she had a special gift as a communicator.

She had already spent one year at a Catholic college, where she learned two vital lessons—she found she didn't want to study home economics, and black girls were not included in all the activities of the other girls. Before that, she hadn't really felt the sting of prejudice.

With her father, who worked for the railroad, Danniebelle came to Los Angeles for a planned two-week visit, but from the moment she arrived Danniebelle had a feeling that she was destined to stay.

A friend asked her to play piano at their suburban Los Angeles church and then, quite unexpectedly, Danniebelle was asked to sing her first solo—a request that rapidly became more frequent. For soon many Los Angeles area churches heard of her special qualities and asked her to sing for their congregations.

This same friend introduced her to Charles Hall, who quickly became her biggest fan and married her six months later. Danniebelle's first venture into professional singing was in 1967 after she had been married for eleven years. At that time, she formed her own group, called The Danniebelles, who cut an album and toured the country for four years. Then, in 1973, Danniebelle joined her favorite gospel singing group, Andrae Crouch and The Disciples.

DANNIEBELLE: *Sharing her love with people who are hurting*

Looking back, Danniebelle feels her years with Crouch were wonderful and very fulfilling. She was able to develop and grow professionally, learning techniques and timing to enhance her career. She is deeply indebted to Crouch and feels that she should pass her skills on to others.

When Danniebelle sings, she peels the cover off her audiences and looks into their souls, where color, denomination and financial status are immaterial. She enjoys sharing her love with people who are hurting, through a musical marriage of sound and meaning.

Her album *Let Me Have A Dream,* was a beautiful showcase for the talent God has been nurturing so carefully. Her warm pop-lullaby "Ordinary People" touches even the coldest of hearts with a ray of hope, while "He Can Work It Out" reflects her deep humor and breadth of human experience.

DAVIS, JIMMIE

"My roots in gospel are deeper than in country music," explains Jimmie Davis. "Back home we always went to church and there was a lot of singing. Our own church was held every third Sunday because we couldn't afford a full-time preacher, but we attended some church every week. And, on Sunday afternoon we'd gather and sing. We learned a lot of gospel songs and hymns my grandparents sang. My parents were Christian people. My neighbors were Christians and it was a wonderful thing to have been exposed to that type influence early in life. It means so much."

Most all of those songs, "back then whether you could sing good or not," are the same ones Jimmie Davis continues to sing today. While music was a major part of life, it was writing that interested him the most. While teaching music in Shreveport, he was given the opportunity to perform once a week on radio singing— sometimes his own compositions. A recording executive heard him and he cut his first song, "Nobody's Darling But Mine." Shortly thereafter, Gene Autry came out with his version of that song, and later, in 1939, Jimmie's big one came out: "You Are My Sunshine."

During the mid-1930s, his popularity and fame gave him tremendous exposure. The people demonstrated their confidence in him by electing him to public office. Soon after that, he was nominated as the Democratic candidate for Governor of the State of Louisiana. He held that office from 1944–1948.

Jimmie's believability and credibility, exhibited in his singing, were the same qualities he brought to public life. One music critic claimed that Jimmie had "the God-given talent to make yesterday come alive and to fill tomorrow with hope." This held true for both of his career areas.

During Jimmie's musical career, he was recognized as a country singer and songwriter. He sang sacred songs but they were not his main thrust. In the 1950s he changed all of that and his nearly 30 albums since then have all featured gospel songs and hymns.

His wife, the former Mrs. Anna Gordon, an original member of The Chuck Wagon Gang, continues to record and joins her husband in his personal appearances in churches around the country.

Jimmie Davis has received honors by the hundreds for his achievements. He is former President of the Gospel Music Association and, in 1972, was inducted into Nashville's Country Music Hall of Fame.

JIMMIE DAVIS: *A God-given talent*

DINO AND DEBBY: *They blend their talents*

DINO AND DEBBY [Kartsonakis]

Dino (Kartsonakis), who is considered one of the premier Christian pianists, has come a long way from Sixty-third Street in New York City. His twentieth album, *Rise Again,* on the Light Records label, was recently released, and features the Dove Award-nominated songs for 1978.

Dino is the son of John and Helen Kartsonakis. Born in Manhattan in 1942, he started playing the piano when he was three, began lessons when he was seven and studied all the way through high school and Kings College in Briarcliff Manor, New York, where he graduated with a bachelor's degree in Music Education, and a diploma in piano from The Juilliard School of Music in Manhattan. He has played throughout Europe and the United States and studied in France under the famed Arthur Rubinstein.

He recorded his first album when he was seventeen for Diadem Records. After service in the army, Dino moved to California, where he formed his own company and recorded five albums. He signed with Light Records in 1974 and has recorded thirteen more albums for that label.

In addition to his recording and concert career, Dino was the concert pianist for Kathryn Kuhlman for over three years and played for her nationally syndicated TV program *I Believe In Miracles.*

He received the Dove Award in 1978, and a Grammy in the same year as Best Instrumentalist for Sacred Music.

His wife, Debby, attended Oral Roberts University in Tulsa and sang with the World Action & Television Singers. She has appeared in numerous national TV commercials and has recorded a solo album, *Debby Sings Alleluia.* They now blend their talents in regular concert and television appearances and on records.

In addition to working on their next album, they are putting the final touches on their *Dino and Debby Show* for television.

DIXIE ECHOES

Dale Shelnut—Lead
Randy Shelnut—Baritone
Andrew Shelnut—Tenor
Randy Allred—Bass
Randy Harper—Piano
Jimmy Holmes—Drums

Organized in their home town of Pensacola, Florida in 1960, their sincere and dedicated approach to gospel music has propelled Dixie Echoes to fame. They are best known for their rendition of southern spirituals; however, they always include hymns, country gospel songs and heart-rending message songs in each performance. Many of the selections in their repertoire are written by members of the group.

Dale Shelnut, lead singer and manager of the Echoes, has been an outstanding personality in gospel music for many years. Dale has surrounded himself with

DIXIE ECHOES: *Sincere and dedicated approach*

THE DIXIE MELODY BOYS: *Singing their praises to God*

—F—

LL & FARRELL

...nd Jayne Farrell are a husband-...e team who have been traveling ...istering through their music for ... years. Before becoming true ...ns both were involved in secular ...—Bob played with several rock ...nd Jayne spent some time singing ...nightclub circuit.

...r accepting the Lord, each of them ...e involved in several individual ...ries before uniting as husband and ...For several years, in addition to her ...eling work with young women in ...reas of marriage and dating, Jayne ...a featured soloist in crusades. Bob ...his start in Jesus music in 1970 as ...under of the group Millennium. In ..., he joined one of the early pioneer ...stian bands, Dove, a group which ...ased an album on Myrrh in the early ...0s.

...s a music team, both Bob and Jayne ...re the vocalizing and lyric-writing re-...nsibilities, but Bob does most of the ...mposing. One of his most popular ...gs, "Lifesaver," became a big hit for ...pe of Glory, while another of his tunes, ...estored," was recorded by the Pat ...rry Group.

...The duo's first album for NewPax Rec-...rds, entitled Farrell & Farrell, highlights the pair's versatile songs ranging from soft country to light rock and easy ballads.

FIELD, FRED

Fred Field surrendered his life to the Lord Jesus Christ, and almost simultaneously three of his friends, all roommates and comrades in music, also received the blessing of a personal relationship with Jesus Christ. Together the four—Fred Field, Chuck Girard, Tom Coomes and Jay Truax—formed the group Love Song, pioneering a new kind of music. This exciting "new wave" in music, reflecting and embodying their musical and cultural roots, lyrically spoke of their new-found Meaning of Life.

In 1972, two years after coming into a personal relationship with the Lord, Fred traveled with a group called Noah to the Munich Olympics. For the ensuing two years Noah gave concerts across the expanse of the European continent and the Middle East, and recorded in Germany and Israel. Based in Amsterdam, but resident part of the time in Tel Aviv, the group did extensive work at United States military bases in Germany on behalf of military chaplains and their drug-prevention programs.

a group of five young men, including his two sons.

Dixie Echoes can be seen throughout the United States on the *The Gospel Singing Jubilee* TV show. Since 1960 they have made over twenty albums. They now record exclusively for Supreme Records.

THE DIXIE MELODY BOYS

Ed O'Neal—Bass
Henry Daniels—Baritone
David Kimbrell—Lead
Jamey Ragle—1st Tenor
Greg Simpkins—Piano
Allen O'Neal—Guitar
Reb Lancaster—Bass
Ron Well—Steel Guitar

The Dixie Melody Boys have been singing their praises to God since 1960 at fairs, churches and revivals. Made up of four singers and a four-piece band, The Dixie Melody Boys have also appeared as guests on many local and national TV programs. They record for QCA records in Cincinnati, and have had national hits from each of their albums. One of their latest and most notable releases was *Lord Don't Move That Mountain*.

DIXON, JESSY

"My singing was anointed, but I wasn't," says Jessy Dixon. Ever since his boyhood in San Antonio, Texas, Jessy had attended church. He is the first to admit, however, that as he grew older he attended for the music rather than the faith. Later he went to St. Mary's College as a music major. It was there that Jessy caught the ear of gospel vocalist James Cleveland.

Dixon relocated to Chicago as a vocalist, accompanist and composer for Cleveland's Gospel Chimes singers. His career moved ahead quickly. He organized his own group, The Jessy Dixon Singers, with a recording contract on the Savoy label. Success continued with twelve hit albums including Grammy nominee *He Ain't Heavy* and three singles—"Sit At His Feet and Be Blessed," "These Old Heavy Burdens," and "God Never Fails."

Jessy confesses it was frustrating working in the gospel world without really accepting Christ as his Lord and Savior. "I was making a living singing," he says. "It was all I knew how to do because it was all I had ever done."

Soon things happened that quickly changed his life. A close friend explained the difference that finding Jesus had made. Dixon attended a Bible study discussion on the book of Romans and a few days later heard a radio preacher teaching the same message. Dixon had found a new life.

Since his conversion in 1972, Dixon has appeared at numerous college concerts as well as such major music centers as Carnegie Hall, Madison Square Garden and Harlem's Apollo Theater.

Dixon's most recent album on Light Records, entitled *It's All Right Now,* as well as his work with co-producer Andrae Crouch, reflects his own joy in the Lord and his artistic maturation.

JESSY DIXON: *Reflects his own joy in the Lord*

DOGWOOD

Ron Elder
Steve Chapman

Dogwood is a team of two cheerful young men, friends from their teens who traveled many hard roads before committing themselves to a life in Jesus and sharing the truths they found through their music.

From similar backgrounds in West Virginia, Ron Elder and Steve Chapman are both sons of ministers. In addition to this common bond, they also shared the same interest in music—gospel and country.

Their paths parted when Steve joined the Navy and Ron went off to college. Separated from one another and their families for a short time, they temporarily fell away from the Lord. They met again, discovered that music was an important link between them and traveled together around the country. During their travels they renewed their commitment to Christ, entering into a positive musical ministry. They had found a direction and, in 1974, Dogwood was born.

After The Flood, Before The Fire was their first album and introduced them to the Jesus music audience. *Love Note* was the duo's second album and enhanced their growing reputation in contemporary Christian music. *Free Love* magazine called *Love Note* "a real progression for the group . . . an album that rises above the commonplace country gospel/ Jesus music genre to provide a real ministry." *Campus Life* described the album as "clean as spring water" featuring "crystal clear acoustics and vocals." Both The Imperials and The Boones have included Dogwood songs on their albums.

DOUGLAS, THE REVEREND ISAAC

The Reverend Isaac Douglas is a young man whose singing resounds with gruff, passionate vocal stylings. He knows how to drive any audience to its feet in

an outburst
ticipation. A
try and abr
lege audienc
halls.

Many feel t
long line of gr
that includes s
The Reverend
boy, Isaac hear
neers and he se
of the traditions
nal vocal inspirat
the most "progres
he never forgets hi

Born in Philade
New York in the n
his own all-male go
Douglas Singers. Th
lease, *Lord Have M
lish him as a young
found The New York
With this group, he
vocal background for
best-selling album *Tru
With his participation i
frequent appearances
Museum of Modern Ar
program *Soul,* Douglas b
gospel celebrity.

In the early seventies,
went a change of directi
the great James Clevelan
Los Angeles and joined
About this time, he also be
for Nashboro Records,
group, then with The New
munity Choir. To fortify
Nashboro, Douglas then mo
ville. Isaac has now recorded
from all over the country; re
The Johnson Ensemble, he re
plaintive "The Harvest Is Plenti

FARRE

Bob a
and-wif
and mi
several
Christia
music—
bands
on the
Aft
becam
minist
wife.
couns
the a
was
got
co-fo
197
Chr
rele
197
A
sha
spe
co
so
H
"p
T
o

Fred, back home in the States in 1975, recorded his first solo album, . . . *and Friends*, for Maranatha! Music, Costa Mesa, California. In addition to studio work, both on the performance and production side, Fred has appeared on TV and radio programs all over the United States, Europe, South America and Israel.

In the area of gospel music he has performed on numerous contemporary gospel albums, playing guitar, violin, mandolin and banjo. A gifted songwriter, Fred's compositions have been recorded by many top gospel musicians and groups such as, Love Song, Pat Boone, Brush Arbor, Ray Hildebrandt, Parable, and Gentle Faith, with songs on the widely accepted *Praise* series from Maranatha! Music.

FIREWORKS

Marty McCall—Vocals
Gary Pigg—Vocals
Cindy Lipford—Vocals
Lanny Avery—Bass
Chris Harris—Drums

Fireworks consists of Marty McCall, Gary Pigg, Cindy Lipford, Lanny Avery and Chris Harris. Based in Nashville, these five musicians were each very actively involved in Christian music well before they joined together as Fireworks.

Marty and Gary have been closely associated with the album productions of Chris Christian. As backup vocalists, they were featured on David Meece's album, *I Just Call On You,* and B. J.

Thomas' album, *Home Where I Belong.* They have also sung jingles for several commercials. Drummer Lanny Avery has worked as a studio engineer while bass player Chris Harris belonged to a Texas group called Brazos.

Fireworks was born when Marty and Gary met at a local church in Nashville and discovered their common interest in music. After a while, the duo was introduced to Chris Christian, who liked their smooth harmonies and invited them to work for his recording company as backup vocalists.

While they were singing for Chris, Marty began writing a lot of his own songs and it wasn't long before Chris heard and liked some of his material. He suggested that the two of them join together; thus, the seeds of Fireworks were planted. Later, Cindy entered the group and the trio was on its way.

At first, the three played mainly in local churches and fellowships around Nashville. Initially, the group's performance consisted of the three voices accompanied by a piano. This arrangement continued for several months until they decided to add a fuller sound with the drumming of Chris Harris and bass rhythms of Lanny Avery.

After playing together as a unit for a year, Fireworks released its debut album on Myrrh.

FISCHER, JOHN

"I have a commitment to deep truths without 'religious' terminology," explained John Fischer. "I also want to

JOHN FISCHER: *A commitment to deep truths*

cluded in two albums—*The Cold Cathedral* and *Have You Seen Jesus My Lord*—were an expression of John's deep devotion and love for the Lord.

Folk music was the style John chose to express his feelings, at a time when folk music was new to many churches. In 1970, he commented that "Christian music has been relegated to an ancient internal expression for long enough. I hope my music will appeal to and speak to young people that truly feel popular music as their expression."

After an extensive overseas tour, Fischer formed the Discovery Art Guild, with the aid of the Peninsula Bible Church. The Guild was an expression of John's desire to introduce Jesus through contemporary music. Yet another goal of the Guild was to help other artists get started and to foster their development.

John has released four albums for Light Records—*Still Life, The New Covenant, Naphtali* and *Johnny's Cafe.*

open eyes to people's needs. We must be sensitive to the world around us. I show how truth relates to a person's own experience in everyday life."

John Fischer was one of the first performers of Jesus music. As a child, he sang in the church choir where his father was music director; he also played the ukelele, piano, trumpet and guitar.

John's involvement and interest in music increased during his collegiate years at Wheaton College. By the time he was a sophomore he composed his own songs. The resulting compositions, in-

THE FLORIDA BOYS

Len Beasley—Lead, M.C.
Glen Allred—Baritone
Derrell Stewart—Pianist
Buddy Liles—Bass
Jerry Trammell—Tenor
Tommy Watwood—Musician

The Florida Boys have been recognized as one of the premier names in gospel music for over twenty years.

Pioneers in the field of television, The Florida Boys host the award-winning, na-

THE FLORIDA BOYS: *Premier names in gospel music*

tionally syndicated TV show *The Gospel Singing Jubilee.* Their twenty years of TV exposure has made their name a household word across the United States and in many foreign countries.

The Florida Boys record for Canaan Records and hold the distinction of being the first group signed by Canaan approximately ten years ago when Word Records started the company. The Florida Boys continue to be one of the label's leading sellers.

Les Beasley is the manager, emcee and lead singer for the group. Additionally, he is also active in composing and arranging. For over twelve years, Les has been the emcee and producer of *The Gospel Singing Jubilee.* He has served two terms as president of the Gospel Music Association, and is a lifetime trustee of the organization. He is also a trustee of the Gospel Music Hall of Fame.

Glen Allred is recognized by his peers as one of the strongest baritone singers in gospel music. He doubles as lead guitarist and has composed several gospel songs. Originally from Tennessee, this veteran performer has been with The Florida Boys for most of their existence.

Derrell Stewart, pianist for the group, is easily identified by his big, wide smile and famous trademark—flaming red socks. A star among stars, Derrell has received the *Singing News* Award for musician of the year.

Buddy Liles came to The Florida Boys with many years of experience as a bass singer. Many of The Florida Boys' most popular songs feature his booming bass voice. Recognized as one of the deepest basses in the business, Buddy is equally at home in a higher register performing a soul-stirring inspirational song. He has written many of the songs performed and recorded by the group.

Jerry Trammell has never wanted to do anything but sing tenor and travel with a sextet. This is evident when you listen and watch him perform. He is featured on chart songs such as "Scars in the Hands of Jesus" and "Here They Come" among other songs The Florida Boys made famous.

Tommy Watwood, musician and composer, is a valuable asset to The Florida Boys. He plays bass, trumpet, piano, guitar, drums, organ and practically any other instrument placed before him.

FONG, ODEN

"Music is just my tool to telegraph the messages God delivers to me. I'm just a messenger."

Oden Fong, a one-time lead vocalist and songwriter with the widely known and much loved Christian rock group Mustard Seed Faith, of *Sail On Sailor* fame, once said of their ministry: "We're like the Israelites going into Canaan proclaiming the Gospel in new territory."

That spirit of adventure and freedom, coupled with a dynamically positive faith in Jesus Christ, has caused this "soldier" to stand alone and hold his ground through many of life's storms.

This only son of a well-known actor spent his early childhood in the midst of the razzle-dazzle glitter of the Hollywood scene. Even his lengthy voyage through the maze of Eastern religions and psychic sciences did not yield the fulfillment and minister: "I don't see myself just as a professional musician because I'm not a Christian music entertainer."

The versatility of this musical messenger was evidenced in his debut solo album on the Maranatha! Music label entitled *Come For The Children*. The songs are excitingly vivid statements, addressed to both Christians and non-Christians and couched in a colorful range of musical styles.

Oden, who has recorded songs on a number of Maranatha! Music albums—including the classic *Sail On Sailor, Maranatha! Three, Maranatha! Four* and *Maranatha! Five*—loves to break new territory, and undoubtedly new terrain lies ahead.

ODEN FONG: *"I'm just a messenger"*

identity Oden was to find through his personal relationship with Jesus Christ.

The early "boot camp" training in one of the first Maranatha! Music Christian rock groups of the 1970s produced both a tough and a compassionate communicator. He has the gift of pinpointing man's deepest needs and problems. Both Oden's lyrics and music compound the range of man's emotions—compassionate and sensitive, yet tinged with the humor that points to the ultimate, positive salvation in Jesus Christ.

Although he communicates with sensitivity and humor, Oden is adamant about the fact that he sees himself first as a

FORD, DAVID

For years David Ford has impressed audiences and critics with his rich bass voice in performances throughout the United States, South America, the Soviet Union and Europe.

Born in Kansas City, Missouri, David grew up in Texas where he received most of his musical training. David earned a Bachelor of Music degree from Baylor University in Waco, Texas, where he also was a graduate student. Additional graduate study was pursued at the Southern Baptist Theological Seminary in, Louisville, Kentucky.

Ford has performed with, among others, the Cleveland, Dallas and Nashville Symphony Orchestras, as well as at many Southern Baptist Convention meetings. He has given concerts in churches and colleges across several states.

Because Ford feels that the Lord has especially blessed his ability to communicate the gospel through music, he has now decided to devote all of his musical efforts to a busy sacred concert schedule. This decision came after ten years of steady concerts while serving in a church as a minister of music. His return to the professional concert arena is enhanced by two gospel albums, *David Ford Sings . . . Words of Life* and *Peace Like A River* which are on Triangle Records.

FORD, TENNESSEE ERNIE

The man affectionately known as "Old Ern" was born Ernest Jennings Ford in Bristol, Tennessee, where he attended grade school and high school. Ernie's fascination with entertaining dates back to those early days in Bristol, when he used to hang around the local radio station, WOPI. He was eventually hired at age eighteen as staff announcer at ten dollars a week. From there he went to the Cincinnati Conservatory of Music to study voice, and in 1939 he returned to radio in Atlanta and Knoxville.

After the war, Ernie Ford returned to radio in California, where he met Cliff Stone and Merle Travis, both of whom have been instrumental in the development of Ernie's career. In fact, one of Ernie's biggest hits, "Sixteen Tons," was written by Travis. Since its release in October 1955, the song has sold over four million copies.

DAVID FORD: *Especially blessed to communicate the gospel through music*

Tennessee Ernie Ford has been known nationwide for over a quarter century. From 1950 through 1955, he had his own network radio program on CBS and ABC, and in September, 1956 he began a five-year stint as star of his own nighttime TV series. In 1961, Ernie took time out from his busy schedule, leaving behind his popular television show, to spend a year at his home in northern California so that he could devote more time to his family. He returned to television in 1962 with a weekly program, which remained on the air until 1965.

In the fall of 1974, Ford headlined a tour of the Soviet Union with the show "Country Music, USA" as part of the U.S./U.S.S.R. cultural exchange pro-

TENNESSEE ERNIE FORD: *Relaxing a little more than he used to*

gram. The group gave twenty-seven performances in five of the largest cities in the Soviet Union: Moscow, Leningrad, Baku, Tbilisi and Yerevan. They played to S.R.O. crowds at every concert, and on their return home they were warmly greeted by President Gerald Ford.

Lately Ernie has been relaxing a little more than he used to, but he still maintains an active schedule. He makes a few

FOUND FREE: *Unique Christian band*

select personal appearances each year, as well as an occasional television special and guest shots on friends' TV shows.

Ernie joined the Word family in 1977, with the release of his album *He Touched Me.* But that was only the beginning of a very happy relationship, for that release was so successful that Ford decided to do another one.

His second, entitled *Swing Wide Your Golden Gates,* was, like his first, a collection of some of gospel's favorite hymns, sung in the downhome, rich baritone that is Ernie's trademark.

FOUND FREE

Keith Lancaster—Vocals
David Michael Ed—Keyboard, Vocals
Catherine MacCallum—Vocals
Bish Alverson—Drums
Jack Faulkner—Bass
Wayne Farley—Guitar
Rebecca Ed—Vocals

A contemporary Christian band based in Philadelphia, Pennsylvania, Found Free is in its seventh year of full-time Christian entertaining. Stylistically, the music of Found Free varies from blues to jazz to light rock. Their performance schedule includes churches, colleges and community concerts. The members of the group are Keith Lancaster, vocals; David Michael Ed, keyboard and vocals; Catherine MacCallum, vocals; Bish Alverson, drums; Jack Faulkner, bass; Wayne Farley, guitar; and Rebecca Ed, vocals.

Found Free records on the Greentree label. Jim Van Hook, senior vice-president, Creative Division, for The Benson Company, is the group producer. He comments that "Found Free is one of the most unique Christian bands in the business."

FRANCISCO, DON

"I try to follow the leading of the Spirit in presenting the Word of God in contemporary language and song."

Don Francisco was born and raised on a seminary campus and attended church regularly during his childhood.

By the summer of 1974, fed up with Eastern philosophies, Don realized he had tried everything and had no idea of what to do next. It was at this point in his life in Decatur, Georgia, that he heard the Lord speak to him, saying, "I am Jesus, and I am alive in your heart. Read my word and do it."

After a period of intensive spiritual and physical healing, getting back together with his wife, and studying the Word, Don slowly began to compose songs for the Lord. The result of this early work was heard on his first New Pax album, *Brother Of The Sun.*

Don describes his music and ministry: "My format consists of my own songs, older hymns and a few songs of others, interspersed with personal testimony and teaching from the Word. My purpose is to bring those who do not know the Lord to a saving knowledge of Jesus Christ, and to help Christians to worship and draw closer to Jesus."

G

THE BILL GAITHER TRIO
Bill Gaither
Gloria Gaither
Gary McSpadden

In a little more than ten years The Bill Gaither Trio has progressed from concerts in small Indiana churches to major arenas and coliseums, appearing before a total of more than four million people. In constant demand, they are the only gospel group which consistently fills the major facilities.

Bill, his wife, Gloria, and Gary McSpadden make up the Trio. They have received two Grammy Awards, ten Dove Awards, recorded twenty-two albums, sold over three million records and written more than three hundred songs.

They average more than 500,000 in attendance for their seventy-five annual concerts.

Their first album for Word Records, *The Very Best of the Very Best,* featured songs which have played an important part in their rise to the top of the gospel field.

The album includes such Gaither compositions as "He Touched Me," "Because He Lives," "The King Is Coming," "God Gave The Song," "The Church Trium-

phant" and "There's Something About That Name."

Bill Gaither started singing and composing music as a hobby in the 1950s as a high school teacher in Alexandria, Indiana. By 1961, friends and members of his church were demanding his songs so often that he thought seriously about a musical career and formed Gaither Music Company to publish songs he had written.

He married fellow teacher Gloria Sickal and they performed in churches and high school auditoriums in the Midwest.

Along with Bill's brother, Danny, Bill and Gloria founded the Bill Gaither Trio. Their first album appeared in 1964.

In 1967 both Bill and Gloria left teaching to devote full-time to "communicating the resurrection principle in daily life through the message of the Christian song." Their popularity grew rapidly.

The 1970s have seen a continued growth in the Gaithers' ministry as well as some changes. Danny is now pursuing his own musical career and has been replaced by Gary McSpadden. And the familiar Gaither sound has been augmented by the addition of brass, rhythm and backup singers.

Remembering how he started as a song-

THE BILL GAITHER TRIO: *"First comes serving the Lord . . ."*

writer in local churches, Bill reflected on his present-day popularity.

"We graduated into bigger concerts and auditoriums out of necessity," he said. "I feel God has given the concerts as a bonus. In the early days we had never considered ourselves as serious performers and still had a habit of giving the songs we wrote to the first good singer we found."

At that point Gaither's record producer, Bob MacKenzie, suggested that they not give away every song before they could record them. The first recording of their own song was "I Am Loved," now a church standard.

From a small beginning with three people, the Gaithers have grown to over one hundred employees with four companies. Alexandria House is involved in selling, merchandising, advertising and distributing music by the Gaithers. They also own Springhouse Associates, a booking agency which promotes their concerts, and Gaither Music Company, which produces their musical material.

Their Pinewood Studio records the Gaithers, as well as other Christian artists, in their twenty-four-track studio and operates around the clock to meet demands.

Bill Gaither receives so many concert offers that the Trio could easily perform several times every night in the year.

They hold it to about seventy-five a year for two very specific reasons:

"If we do too many concerts there is a tendency to let quantity interfere with quality," Gaither says. "I believe we should spend as much time with creatives as possible. The biggest reason is that with Gloria and I away it is difficult to keep a home life going. We believe our basic responsibility must be to the family."

He has his priorities clearly fixed in his mind. "First comes serving the Lord and how that is involved with our family life," he says. "Second comes writing music because it can go places we can't and can be sung by others. Third is making records because they can also go where we can't. Our fourth priority is the Christian concerts."

Gaither found the transition from smaller auditoriums to major arenas required a whole new energy level.

"We had always been a low-key operation and you can do that in a smaller room. But when you hit a larger situation you just can't sit there quietly and think that everyone is going to jump in where you are. I think there has to be a higher energy level spent on the whole thing. You've got to think in terms of a bigger concept."

He is very conscious of productively using every second on stage. "You don't have that much time. You've got to know where you're going, what you're going to do, and think faster."

Gaither acknowledges that the concerts are a break-even proposition at best. They also take no salary from any of the companies, but receive personal income only from song-writing royalties.

Ten years ago, the Trio traveled with just a bass player who also served as bus driver. They now carry twenty-two people. Bill, Gloria and the female singers fly to concerts while Gary McSpadden commutes by air from his home in Fort Worth, where he pastors a church.

In addition to the Trio, they use five backup singers, four brass, keyboard, guitar, bass and percussion with Bill Gaither frequently on piano. Their road crew also includes a lighting technician and two sound men.

"I'm not defensive on whether people like our style of music or not. I'm more concerned about communicating to them what we feel very deeply. If I can get their attention at that level, I think our style is neither here nor there.

"I think some people have come in and been so defensive of their art that all of a sudden they are a casualty because they are just protecting their own art, and art comes and goes. Some stays, most of it comes and goes.

"Our actual 'sound' has been drawn from many different styles depending on what we are saying. Some is M.O.R. (middle-of-the-road), some contemporary, some country, some ballad or an easy-flowing style.

"We're all creating the sounds we have heard. And every individual in the audience assumes the sound he likes is the best and everyone else is either to the right or left of him. We all assume we're in the center and it's best."

The present and future success of The Bill Gaither Trio can best be summed up by their West Coast promoter, Polly Grimes.

"Although they continue to sell out the arenas year after year, each time they sell out farther in advance," she says. "Their performing art is unique. Each person sees himself in the songs and stories they tell.

"They simply don't peak in popularity like other artists," she continues. "They keep building because they consistently provide fresh ideas. They are unbelievable communicators. I feel the Gaithers are going to be around setting trends and spreading their love and joy for a long time to come."

GAITHER, DANNY

Danny Gaither has developed a voice and style which are unsurpassed partly because he began singing at a very early age.

At age three, Danny was singing before audiences around his hometown of Alexandria, Virginia. His mother "booked" him and also accompanied him on the piano. Very soon his brother, Bill, joined in. Before long, a favorite cousin was added. The trio was already traveling a great deal with Mom playing piano. By the time Mary Ann, Danny and Bill's sister, reached the ripe old age of eleven, she was ready to go on the road! So they traveled and sang for several years . . . until it was time to leave for college.

The trio came together again, except this time instead of Mary Ann (she had decided to be a housewife) Bill's wife, Gloria, sang with the group. In 1970, The Bill Gaither Trio began traveling full-time and Danny joined to sing lead. Active with the group for seven years, Danny became very popular for such moving solo performances as "I Walked Today Where Jesus Walked," "O Love That Wilt Not Let Me Go" and "It Is Well With My Soul."

In 1977, Danny made the decision to leave the Trio in order to have the freedom to pursue a solo career. The first few months after Danny left the group, he took care of business interests and made decisions about his future. However, still singing and getting a lot of requests, Danny began to feel, more and more, the need to pursue his singing on a full-time basis.

With two solo albums already re-

DANNY GAITHER: *Deep love for his fellow man*

corded, Danny began working with The Benson Company, of Nashville, and producer Joe Huffman on a new record. Then Danny talked with musicians and booking agents, got together a band and began traveling and singing. Danny's new album contains songs that will reach and touch all ages. With new songs featured like "Daybreak" and "You Needed Me," Danny is sure to appeal to the younger group.

A very sincere individual with a deep love for his fellow man, Danny's decision to continue ministering is genuine. His ability to be himself and reach out to people is very welcome in this era of cold-heartedness and unconcern.

GILBERT, JIM

Light Records artist Jim Gilbert travels both nationally and internationally as a

speaker, concert artist and contemporary missionary.

James M. (Jim) Gilbert was born August 2, 1950, the son of The Reverend and Mrs. Jack Gilbert, Baltimore, Maryland. His father pastored small churches in West Virginia until Jim was eight years old.

He attended Western Maryland College in Westminster, Maryland for his first semester on a music scholarship, majoring in vocal music, and transferred to Oral Roberts University for one semester.

Because of his outstanding music ability, he was asked by O.R.U. to help with the beginning of their weekend music ministry, which soon became the original Living Sound.

During his years with Living Sound, he has helped form three of the four teams now touring. He has also served at various times as vocalist, keyboardist, music director, arranger, composer, evangelist and group leader.

Since 1969, he has sung and played in almost two thousand Living Sound concerts in high schools, universities, clubs, military facilities, stadiums and hundreds of churches and cathedrals, traveling 500,000 miles on ground alone.

As a recording artist, he has been featured on numerous Living Sound albums. His first solo album, which he composed and arranged, was released on Light Records in November, 1978. The title song, "I Love You With The Love Of The Lord," has been recorded by many artists and is one of the most widely known in Christian music. It is currently

JIM GILBERT: *Outstanding music ability*

81

being sung in at least six foreign languages.

As Jim fills his engagements as speaker, concert artist and contemporary missionary, he remains closely associated with Living Sound.

He is planning a European solo tour in 1980 to include the United Kingdom, Western Europe and the Soviet Union, as well as a Spanish-language tour.

GIRARD, CHUCK

"When I was young my life was rock and roll music . . . but who'd ever thought I'd be a rock and roll preacher singin' my song so you could hear the Good News?" asks Chuck Girard.

Songwriter, leader, soloist and creative genius behind the successful group Love Song, Chuck is a man making history in Christian music. His music is strong, powerful and direct in communicating the gospel of Jesus Christ.

Although his singing career was a success, his life was one big search through contemporary ideas, cults and drugs. Finally, his search for an ultimate answer led him to Calvary Chapel in Costa Mesa, California, where he later found Jesus Christ to be all He claimed to be.

During early Calvary Chapel days, Girard was playing in a rock band called

CHUCK GIRARD: *"A rock and roll preacher"*

Love Song. While Girard was making his decision for Christ at Calvary Chapel, so, too, were other members of the band. They began singing some of their own songs there, and after that their full scale ministry began.

Love Song's music was by no means all rock. In fact, they were better known among Jesus music fans for their soft blend of beautiful harmony exemplified by their most popular composition, "Love Song."

THE HAPPY GOODMAN FAMILY

Howard Goodman
Rusty Goodman—Bass
Sam Goodman—Baritone
Vestal Goodman—Vocals
Tanya Goodman Price—Vocals
Johnny Cook—Tenor

The success of the famous Happy Goodman Family is the product of the life-long dream of four individuals— Howard, Rusty, Sam and Vestal Goodman. All four have been nominated and been recipients of many of the annual gospel music awards. In 1968 they received the Grammy Award for Best Gospel Album. Vestal was nominated, and several times won, the award for Best Female Gospel Vocalist. She also received the Gospel Music Association's award in 1969 for Best Female Vocalist of the Year. Brother Sam won the Favorite Baritone award in the fan awards of 1974 presented by *Singing News*. Younger brother Rusty, a prolific songwriter, has

won the Favorite Bass Singer and also Best Male Vocalist two years in a row.

The Happy Goodman Family were original members of *The Gospel Singing Jubilee* TV program pioneering gospel music to the television audience. They have appeared on numerous TV shows including Oral Roberts' *Weekend* program, *The Dinah Shore Show* and their own *Happy Goodman Family Hour*.

Having recorded over fifteen albums, in 1975 they celebrated sales of over one million albums. The Happy Goodmans record exclusively for Canaan Records, a division of Word, Inc.

Rusty Goodman has written many gospel songs that have become classics, such as "I Wouldn't Take Nothing For My Journey Now," "Had It Not Been," "Who Am I," "Until You've Known The Love of God" and "Wait'll You See My Brand New Home." Rusty produces all of The Happy Goodman Family's recordings.

In 1973, after nine years of working as a unit of four, the group was joined by Johnny Cook, one of America's greatest tenors. Johnny has won many of the coveted annual awards, including the Gospel Music Association's Dove Award for Top Male Vocalist of 1976.

GOSPEL SEED

Michael Moore
Gary Luttrell

Gospel Seed is a contemporary musical duo consisting of Michael Moore and Gary Luttrell. Initiated in 1974, the duo has traveled extensively during the past

THE HAPPY GOODMAN FAMILY: *A life-long dream*

four years. In addition to performing in coffee houses, schools and jails, Gospel Seed has also appeared on the *700 Club* and *PTL Club* TV programs.

The duo has a unique sound, blending their intricate harmonies with the mellow sounds of guitar and autoharp. The group also stresses the importance of participating in a ministry rather than being merely a means of entertainment.

"We feel that our music ministry is just that, a ministry. The songs we write and sing tell a message of what Jesus Christ can do in a life. Our message in song is geared to exhort and challenge Christians, as well as to show unbelievers their need for a Savior."

GRANDQUIST, NANCY

Singer, songwriter, recording artist, minister's wife, mother—Nancy Grandquist almost literally grew up in church. Although radio, television and rock music were not a part of her childhood, she recalls the music of Mahalia Jackson and other great black gospel singers of the fifties as having had an influence on her. She began taking piano lessons at age four and showed considerable talent as well as a desire to expand her musical horizons.

At the age of fourteen Nancy enrolled at the Christian Life Center in Stockton, California, a combination high school, Bible college and church. It was there that she met her husband, Richard.

Nancy currently records for the New-Pax label.

GRANT, AMY

"It has really surprised me to see how Jesus can be shared so freely through music."

A native of Nashville, eighteen-year-old Amy Grant began her musical career when just a small child by taking piano lessons in the third grade.

Realizing her musical talent was a gift from the Lord, Amy decided to devote herself to the Holy Spirit. Knowing she was no longer in control of her singing ability, she lost all fear and inhibitions when appearing before large audiences. The Lord blessed her faithfulness, and she soon found herself singing before local Youth For Christ meetings, women's clubs and school assemblies. "I just sing when I'm asked to," says Amy, "and the ministry just slips out without me even knowing it."

Amy's ministry is an example of how God uses people of all ages and sizes to carry out this work. "Sometimes," Amy confesses, "I wonder why I am so blessed to be given the chance to share my music with so many people. I can only say that I'm sure that it is a work that Jesus wants to do in me, and I must say it feels good to know Jesus can use even me to share His life."

Amy's first Myrrh recording was produced by Chris Christian and features the vocal talents of Fireworks' Gary Pigg, Gwen Moore and Marty McCall.

KEITH GREEN: *Without Jesus his was an empty life*

GREEN, KEITH

GREEN, LILLY

"I'll never play music again unless You give me the words to sing and You give me the places to play." That's the commitment Keith Green made to the Lord when he asked the Holy Spirit to take control of his life and his music.

Born into a musical family in Brooklyn, Keith Green started singing and playing the ukulele at age three, played piano at six, and by his eighth birthday was writing songs. At age eleven, he became the youngest member of ASCAP (American Society of Composers, Authors and Publishers) and began recording for Decca Records. From that time until he came to know the Lord, he completed several recording contracts and traveled extensively doing concerts.

Keith feels that without Jesus his was an empty life.

Since becoming a born-again Christian, Keith has been sharing at churches and fellowships in California and his ministry is warmly welcomed.

He has appeared on Barry McGuire's television show, *Anyone But Jesus,* and plays at many Christian clubs and coffee houses.

Keith and his wife, Melody, are staff writers for CBS/April Blackwood Music, writing for recording artists. Since becoming Christians, they write about their experiences and their relationship with the Lord.

His first album on Sparrow Records was called *For Him Who Has Ears To Hear,* followed by the album *No Compromise.*

Lilly Green was born Lilly Crozier in Renfrew, Ontario, Canada on September 13, 1951. She began singing as soon as she could talk and most of the singing in her younger years was with her sister in a gospel form of sister duo. She and her sister frequently performed at church and on local television.

At fifteen, Lilly learned to play the guitar, and could finally sing Christian music the way she felt it. Audiences responded enthusiastically by asking her to sing more and more.

Lilly moved to Michigan to continue her schooling, and toured Scandinavia with an organization called The Solid Rock Foundation. In 1972, she relocated in California and became an active member of the Jesus music movement. After marrying Kelly Green, she became an active member of the Shekinah Fellowship, where her husband is the Minister of Music.

Lilly has a very personal relationship with God, and she expresses it musically in a singular way. Whether she creates her music with the guitar or at the piano, the special Lilly Green personality is evident. She sings only her own material.

When asked about her style of music, Lilly labeled it "kind of soul contemporary." Lilly clarified this by adding, "I only write about things that are happening to me now. And I only write when I feel it. When I sit down to 'make myself' write a song, it doesn't come out right. But when a song comes to me, I sit down and write it in fifteen or twenty minutes

. . . because it's something there, really in me, coming from my deepest feelings."

Lilly indicates her favorite song is the latest one she's written . . . because it's the latest of her deepest feelings. But she also names "God, A Woman And A Man" (which she wrote for her husband, Kelly, and which was sung at their wedding), as one of her best-known songs.

GRINE, JANNY

Talking about her ministry of today, Janny Grine says, "All I know is what God has called me to do, that is to minister the Word to the extent that I know it. And to be uncompromising in standing on His Word, encouraging others to do the same . . . the medium I present it through is music."

This singer and songwriter, who hails from Arkansas, went the whole classic route from singing in bars and nightclubs to getting her life together through conversion to Jesus. With her husband, Bill, an award-winning photographer, Janny writes songs that give the listener a way out of life's problems—not just a statement of what's wrong.

Janny's album *He Made Me Worthy* appears on the Sparrow label.

JANNY GRINE:
"All I know is what God has called me to do"

H

HALE, ROBERT

Robert Hale's vocal talent has taken him to concert and opera stages in the United States and Europe. As leading baritone of the New York City Opera, he has performed major roles in *Faust, Lucia di Lammermoor, The Barber of Seville, Don Giovanni, The Marriage of Figaro, Rigoletto* and *Carmen*.

Born in Kerrville, Texas, Hale received his Bachelor of Arts degree at Bethany Nazarene College, and a Master of Arts at Oklahoma University at Norman. He also earned an Artist's Diploma from the New England Conservatory of Music in Boston.

Hale is comfortable with a variety of musical styles and his wide range of abilities has brought him many honors.

His classical training, combined with his deep Christian commitment, has opened a tremendously exciting opportunity for a sacred concert ministry. He has toured with well-known tenor Dean Wilder since 1966, performing in more than two thousand sacred concerts in cities around the world. During their association, they have recorded eighteen albums.

ROBERT HALE: *Comfortable with a variety of material*

HARRIS, LARNELLE

Larnelle lives in Louisville, Kentucky and graduated from Western Kentucky University with a degree in music education that concentrated on singing.

For several years he traveled with The Spurrlows, gaining invaluable experience that has aided him immensely. Larnelle knows audiences and individual people, as well, and has totally committed his life to letting the love of Christ shine through everything he attempts. He has recorded three albums for Word: *Tell It To Jesus, Larnelle . . . More,* and *Free.*

WALTER HAWKINS: *The patriarch of a most remarkable family*

HAWKINS, WALTER

Walter Hawkins—husband, father, composer, singer, minister—is the patriarch of a most remarkable family, including:

Tramaine, Walter's talented wife and lead singer; brother Edwin, who gained nationwide fame for his award-winning record of "Oh Happy Day"; sisters Carole, Freddie and Lynette, who are all gifted vocalists along with Walter's cousin, Shirley Miller; his brother, Daniel, organist, electric bass player and singer; plus Joe Smith, Walter's nephew and youngest member of the group, who is drummer, organist and bass player.

Shortly after Edwin's hit, "Oh Happy Day," Walter founded his Love Center church in 1975 as an ordained minister of the Church of God in Christ.

"God has given me a gift of both a ministry and a musical ministry and one has been a steppingstone for the other," he said.

Now, with three albums to his credit and standing at the top of the record charts, Walter recalls that his first album represented rather a humble beginning.

"I said impulsively to the church choir one night, 'Let's do an album,' " he said. Andrae Crouch contacted Bill Cole, Light Records vice president, who listened to a tape and Walter soon signed with Light.

Following *Love Alive,* his first album, he recorded *Jesus Christ Is The Way* and, most recently, *Love Alive II. Bookstore Journal* describes their sounds as "Soul gospel at its peak of perfection."

Just as Walter gives his gospel from

THE HEMPHILLS: *Something for everyone*

the pulpit—straight—that's the sound he wants on the albums.

His awards include top honors in *Cash Box* magazine's annual Gospel Awards with first place for Best Gospel Male Vocalist and Most Often On The Charts. He also received a 1979 Grammy Award nomination for Best Soul Gospel Performance, Contemporary, for *Love Alive II*.

THE HEMPHILLS

Joel Hemphill—Vocals
LaBreeska Hemphill—Vocals
Joel Hemphill, Jr.—Vocals
Trent Hemphill—Bass Player
Candy Hemphill—Vocals

Good, Deep South gospel music delivered in a downhome country style—

that's the sound of The Hemphills. This gospel music family (comprising Joel Hemphill, his wife, LaBreeska, sons Joel Jr. and Trent, and daughter Candy) has received Dove Award nominations time and again in such categories as Best Mixed Group, Songwriter of the Year and Best Album.

Joel Hemphill, who pastored a church in Bastrop, Louisiana, from 1961 to 1971, started The Hemphills' professional singing career in 1968. In 1972, Joel and LaBreeska moved to Nashville where eventually Joel Jr. and Candy joined them in their singing. Their younger son, Trent, is band director and bass player. Other members are Gary Smith, piano; Jerry Burnside, lead and rhythm guitar; Mike Allen, drums; and Glen Paul, steel guitar.

Joel has written such well-known songs as "I'll Soon Be Gone," "Sweetest Words He Ever Said (I Forgive)" and "I Came On Business For The King." The Hemphills record on the HeartWarming label. *Home Cookin'*, their latest release, is a full-course feast seasoned with the various styles of the family members. *Home Cookin'* features the traditional Hemphill sound that Joel has established, together with the light and happy sound that LaBreeska is known for, and the more contemporary styles of Joel Jr. and Candy. They are a musical family with a wide variety of styles and something for everyone!

HERNDON, JAMES

Herndon's career in gospel music covers a span of over twenty-five years. He and gospel singer Shirley Caesar grew up together in Durham, North Carolina, both graduating from Hillside High School. His relationship with Shirley continued when she asked him to join The Caravans as a singer/pianist. Thus, from 1959 to 1967, he traveled with Caesar and The Caravans.

Herndon himself also established a gospel group called The Wright Special in Detroit. He worked with Motown recording artist Kim Weston, serving as both pianist and group leader. He also worked with Aretha Franklin.

Steadily, Herndon has established his own reputation as a performer, and his eighth album, *Nobody But You,* was described as "joyous music even if it's not upbeat. It's traditional in essence but still contemporary enough to appeal to young and old."

HIBBARD, BRUCE

In a world of too many questions without answers and intense darkness broken by so few torchbearers, the music of Bruce Hibbard is shedding welcome rays of light and warmth.

As he grew musically and spiritually, Bruce learned some invaluable lessons in faith and trust which have indelibly shaped his music. Songs like "All That I Want To Be" and "Given Myself Over" speak eloquently about Bruce's spiritual growth.

Stints with Amplified Version, Sonlight and a period as a church choir director all brought Bruce further musical and spiritual refinement as a songwriter and performer. But he had a difficult time getting his smooth, mellow, contemporary sounds published and recorded. When Paul Clark "miraculously" showed up and signed Bruce to a contract with Seed Records, the necessary songs began to flow and finally all the right tracks were laid.

A Light Within and Bruce Hibbard promise to be a magnificent source of light and warmth for many years to come. For as Bruce says, "When you try to do it on your own it won't last . . . but the lasting things are those the Lord lays down."

THE HINSONS

Ronny Hinson
Kenny Hinson
Larry Hinson
Chris Hawkins

In a few short years of working as professionals, The Hinsons have soared to the top of the gospel music profession.

In this case, the word "top" means such achievements as:

1. Having four songs from one album in the national popularity charts.

THE HINSONS: *Greater international recognition for their work*

DALLAS HOLM: *Concern for the spiritual well-being of others reflected in his songwriting*

2. Having at least one record in the national Top 20 continuously during the past three years.

3. Winning both the *Singing News* Award and the Dove Award for the same song in a single year ("The Lighthouse").

4. Being one of the five final nominees for the 1975 Dove Award classification, Best Mixed Group.

For the past two years The Hinsons have been regular members of The Florida Boys' fabulously popular television series *The Gospel Singing Jubilee,* which has helped attract even greater international recognition for their work.

They first began working together in 1969. Three Hinson brothers—Ronny, Kenny and Larry—and sister Yvonne started the troupe in Salinas, California.

About two years ago, Yvonne left the group and was replaced by nineteen-year-old Chris Hawkins.

HOLM, DALLAS

Dallas Holm takes his life seriously. His deep concern for the spiritual well-being of others is reflected in his songwriting.

In November,1978 he became the first person other than Bill Gaither to be named Songwriter of the Year in the ten-year history of the Gospel Music Association's Dove Awards. Dallas also captured top honors as Male Gospel Vocalist, while he and his band, Praise, were tabbed the leading Mixed Gospel Group. He is also part of the David Wilkerson Crusade Team. Performing for nine years now in this outreach situation has done much to mold Dallas' songwriting.

With his first Greentree release, *Just Right,* Dallas Holm established himself as a songwriter, singer and incredible musician. The follow-up albums, *Dallas Holm and Praise* and *Tell 'Em Again,* and the phenomenal success of his song "Rise Again," have put Dallas at the top in the gospel music industry.

HONEYTREE [Nancy Henigbaum]

Music has always been a part of Honeytree's life. Her parents were both musicians—her father a violinist and orchestral conductor, her mother a violist.

As a teenager, Honeytree performed in coffeehouses and during these years she managed to meet a small circle of friends who made her feel that they really cared about her. These friends discovered that her last name, Henigbaum, was German for Honeytree; because of their friendship, the name came to signify love and acceptance for her. She's been using the name ever since. Her first name is Nancy, but to thousands of fans she's just Honeytree.

Her conversion came about during her senior year in high school while visiting her sister in Fort Wayne, Indiana. One of the main topics of conversation concerned some former friends who had become "religious fanatics." Honeytree waited eagerly to meet them but when she finally did, however, they turned out to be the friendliest "fanatics" she had ever encountered. They invited her to church, and through them she met a man named John Lloyd, whose testimony changed her life. She accepted Jesus Christ as her personal Savior.

Honeytree returned home filled with her new convictions, but then wondered if this new faith was strong enough. Returning to Fort Wayne to find the answer, she discovered that Lloyd and some of his friends had established a coffeehouse called the Adam's Apple. Soon she was singing there regularly and giving her testimony, and the undertaking developed into a full-time pursuit.

Honeytree's time is now absorbed by her mission. She works full-time for the Adam's Apple, performs musical programs on weekends and appears at festivals all over the country during the summer. This young woman's talent, faith and energy have brought her to the pinnacle of her profession and made her the "First Lady of Jesus music."

Honeytree's musical career has blossomed on the several albums she has recorded for Myrrh Records. Her set entitled *The Melodies in Me* exhibits the sounds and thoughts of Honeytree in her most talented offering to date. And, one senses, the best is yet to be.

freshness and pure musicianship found in few performances," says Tedd Smith.

And according to *Christianity Today* Tom is "one of California's top Jesus music musicians."

When you listen to Tom's music, you hear a whole new sound. It's a kind of quiet rock, definitely great technique and all Jesus music.

After studying with brilliant twentieth-century composer Paul Fetler, Howard graduated from the University of Minnesota with a B.A. degree in Music Theory.

He then moved onto the secular paths of sessions man and arranger in Minneapolis studios, playing piano for dance and ballet classes at the Guild of Performing Arts and playing piano with the Metropolitan Jazz Ensemble.

But things weren't right for Tom and he knew it. So he gave up his blossoming secular career and dedicated his talents as composer, arranger, singer and writer to the furtherance of God's Kingdom.

Since then, Tom's been active in every form of Jesus music. He's played at coffeehouses and Christian festivals throughout the nation, particularly on the West Coast. He's a frequent guest at colleges and churches and at Young Life and Campus Life retreats and conferences.

HOWARD, TOM

"Tom Howard's music reflects craftsmanship at every level of performance. His unique singing style, combined with first-rate guitar work and exceptional piano playing, produces a combination of

HUFFAM, TEDDY & THE GEMS

Teddy Huffam
Bill Anderson
Burton Lewis
Leon Brown—Bass Guitar
James Branch—Drums
Gary Shelton—Tenor

TEDDY HUFFAM & THE GEMS: *A long life of prayer*

The success of Teddy Huffam is the product of a long life of prayer. He was born in poverty in a ghetto of Richmond, Virginia, the son of a struggling waitress who, though she had practically nothing, encouraged him to study piano for years.

From a vision in the late 1960s, Teddy sought the Lord once again for help to complete his ministry. Through this experience came the birth of The Gems. Today The Gems and Teddy are fast becoming the most exciting and enjoyable group in gospel music.

The years have brought about many changes in personnel. Bill Anderson and Burton Lewis, who Teddy often refers to as "old war veterans," stayed in spite of many crossroads and obstacles. Today, Teddy, Bill and Burton have been nominated for, and received, many gospel music awards. In 1978 they became the first black gospel group ever to be nominated for a Dove Award in the Male Group of the Year category. In both 1977 and 1978 The Gems were finalists in the contest for the Dove Award's Gospel Soul Album of the Year.

Bill and Burton are the original members of the group, and are joined by Leon Brown, bass guitarist, and James Branch, drummer and Gary Shelton, tenor.

J. G. Whitfield has presented them among the stars in his annual *Singing News* Fan Festival, held in Nashville and Birmingham.

Teddy Huffam & The Gems record exclusively for Canaan Records, a division of Word, Inc. In 1976, Canaan provided the soil for this God-given seed of gospel music to take root and, today, what Marvin Norcross, president of Canaan, refers to as "Gray" gospel is taking hold.

When Teddy & The Gems appear before capacity crowds, healing takes place outside and behind the stage as he stops to pray for the sick and needy. This is a ministry that shows what "real" gospel music is all about. In fact, these very words were spoken by Hovie Lister from the stage at the National Quartet convention in Nashville as Teddy & The Gems broke up the auditorium with a quick sermonette and a praise song that left people standing, weeping and praising the Lord. Without microphones he and the Gems walked through the audience and began to touch and minister to the people. "Now that's what God wants, a service, not a show," says Teddy.

Another important ingredient in Teddy Huffam's success lies in his ability to compose a gospel song. His writings include such great tunes as "Jesus said, 'Lean on Me,' " "So Many Years," "Take Another Chance On Me" and "You Can't Take These Things With You." In his own unique way, he can take what's known as a white gospel song, add a touch of "soul" and make it a winner every time.

— I —

THE IMPERIALS

Armond Morales—Bass
Jim Murray—Tenor
Dave Will—Lead
Russell Taff—Baritone
John Lutz—Trumpet
Mike Kinard—Drums
James Hollihan—Bass Guitar
Bill George—Piano

The Imperials—a group which is changing the face of gospel music! They aren't just gospel singers; they're innovative musicians. By no means do The Imperials neglect their traditional roots in gospel music, but they're also busy exploring new directions, combining musical styles in unique ways.

As The Imperials' music has changed over the years, so have their personnel. Today there are eight Imperials: Armond Morales, who sings bass and manages the group; Jim Murray, tenor; Dave Will, lead singer; Russell Taff, baritone. John Lutz joins the singers on trumpet and guitar along with Mike Kinard, drums; James Hollihan, bass guitar; and Bill George, keyboards.

The group has grown from a traditional gospel quartet to a group with sophisticated and diverse musical experience. And The Imperials put this diversity to work, bridging gaps between such seemingly incompatible types of music as southern gospel and contemporary, al-ways looking for new ways of spreading the Lord's good news. Their innovative skill has even helped them win a Grammy Award in the Best Contemporary Gospel Album category for their album *Sail On* released by Word's DaySpring Records.

In the past dozen years, The Imperials have recorded over twenty albums. They have toured all over the world from West Berlin to Las Vegas and Pittsburgh. They have sung with Elvis Presley, Jimmy Dean, Pat Boone and Carol Channing. Their television appearances include the Mike Douglas, David Frost, Merv Griffin and Joey Bishop shows. And in Europe they've displayed their talents via specials in Holland and Germany.

INGLES, DAVID

David Ingles is a popular singer, songwriter and evangelist who's making a favorable impact in gospel music.

His cut of "There's A Whole Lot of People Going Home" recently hit sales and air-play charts.

His first album for The Benson Company, *I Want To Stroll Over Heaven With You*, achieved phenomenal sales during its first month on the market.

Stylistically, David is known for his smooth, mellow interpretations. His material, firmly rooted in scripture, features

THE IMPERIALS: *Looking for new ways of spreading the Lord's Good News*

songs of healing and praise and the confidence that comes from walking through life with Christ at your side.

David Ingles travels throughout the country ministering in evangelist crusades. His home is in Tulsa, where he lives with his wife, Sharon, and their three children.

INSTITUTIONAL RADIO CHOIR

The Institutional Radio Choir has been one of the nation's top gospel choirs for more than twenty-five years. Founded in the summer of 1954, the choir has been acclaimed for its superb performances by critics and gospel personalities who have fondly nicknamed it "The Hitmakers"— and rightly so. This famous group's accomplishments include the National Association of Television and Radio Announcers (NATRA) Golden Mike Award, symbolizing the nation's top recording choir of 1968; a gold record for its recording of "Stretch Out" in 1967; and winning the Joe Bostic Award for the best gospel recording of 1972 for "One More Day."

The Institutional Radio Choir has recorded more than fifteen albums and its original compositions have been sung by every gospel choir in the country. Among their more famous hit tunes are "Stretch Out," "Little More Grace," "Keys To The Kingdom," "Heavens Belong To You," "It's God, It's God," "Satisfied," "Well Done," "This Is The Right Time," "When He Comes Back In A Cloud," "Let's Go Back To The Top Of The Mountain," "I

DAVID INGLES: *Firmly rooted in scripture*

Surrender All," "It's Mighty Nice To Be A Witness," "He Is Standing By," "Say Something For The Lord" and "Love Brought Me Back."

The choir members have appeared in the most prestigious concert halls and theaters throughout America and abroad. The Choir has appeared on national television and telecasts in Europe and the Far East. For the past twenty-five years, the Choir has broadcast over Radio Station WWRL in New York City. The Institutional Radio Choir is based at the Institutional Church of God in Christ,

101

where Bishop C. E. Williams Sr. is the founding pastor. The Choir's musical staff is headed by Elder J. C. White, composer, director, minister, singer and leader of the famed J. C. White Singers; Carl E. Williams Jr.; Brother I. (Butch) Heyward, organist, writer, composer, arranger; and Alfred White, keyboard genius and older brother of J. C.

The Choir is also blessed with some of the top lead singers in the nation, among whom are evangelists Gloria White, J. C. White, Maxine Jones, Joyce Taylor, Carolyn White, Janet Napper, Deborah Britt, Delores Phillips, Doris White, Eddie Rollins, Tyrita White, Betty Campbell, Beverly Graham, Betty Cooper and Carl Williams Jr.

—◄ J ►—

JACKSON, MAHALIA

No serious discussion of gospel music would be complete without including the late Mahalia Jackson. Perhaps the greatest name in twentieth-century gospel music, Mahalia Jackson has influenced countless performers with her vibrant style and inspired artistry.

Born in New Orleans on October 16, 1911, Jackson was brought up in a strict religious atmosphere involving disapproval of all kinds of secular music. As one of six children of a longshoreman and barber who preached on Sundays at

a local church, she was forced to confine her own musical activities to singing in his choir and listening, without his knowledge, to recordings of Bessie Smith and Ida Cox. At age sixteen, she went to Chicago and joined the Greater Salem Baptist Church Choir. Her amazing contralto voice led to her selection as a soloist. She was popular in storefront churches but was not accepted for some time by formal black congregations because of the strong rhythms in her songs. However, her fame grew, and in 1934 her first recording, "God Gonna Separate The Wheat From The Tares," became very popular. Her first big hit was "Move On Up A Little Higher" in 1945. Eight of Mahalia's records sold more than a million copies each. Among her other famous songs were "I Believe," "He's Got The Whole World In His Hands," "Just Over The Hill," "Just A Little While To Stay Here," "I Can Put My Trust In Jesus," and "When I Wake Up In Glory." These were songs drawn from biblical themes and influenced by the intensity of the blues. Even though she possessed one of the greatest potential blues voices, she never sang anything but religious songs.

Mahalia was revered in America and throughout the world—filling Carnegie Hall and singing at the Newport Jazz Festival in a program devoted entirely to gospel music, as well as having best-selling records abroad. She also sang at the inauguration of President John F. Kennedy in 1961. In her later years she was closely associated with the civil rights movement, even though her ill health placed a burden on her demanding schedule.

It could be ventured that the present-day status of gospel, as well as of such individual performers as Andrae Crouch, Jessy Dixon, Walter Hawkins and the late Reverend Clevant Derricks, owes a deep debt to this great singer. Mahalia Jackson died in Illinois on January 27, 1972, but her spirit, her music and her accomplishments will live forever.

JEREMIAH PEOPLE

The nine members of Jeremiah People, a presentation of Continental Ministries, are the only full-time Christian group performing in music, comedy and drama.

JEREMIAH PEOPLE: *Confronting Christians everywhere with biblical truths*

Set in a fast-paced format, their ninety-minute program combines comedy sketches, original music, pantomimes and monologues.

Formed in 1972, the purpose of Jeremiah People is both to entertain and communicate the gospel. They confront Christians everywhere with the Biblical truths of commitment and discipleship.

Over the past seven years the group has recorded five albums for Light Records, their latest being *Reflections and Images*.

In addition to their national television engagements, they appeared in the movie *Say It With Music*.

103

JERRY AND THE SINGING GOFFS: *Vivacious dignity and excitement*

JERRY AND THE SINGING GOFFS

Jerry Goff—Trumpet
Wally Goff—Baritone, Piano
Roger Horne—Tenor
Becky Horne—Vocals

Jerry and The Singing Goffs is one of the most exciting aggregations in gospel music. These versatile successes evince vivacious dignity and excitement; a spiritual depth that is rare and delightful. They play music geared for today using the piano, organ, trumpet, bass and guitar.

Jerry Goff, "Mr. Gospel Trumpet," is a Dove Award-winner, Gold-record winner, nominated as top musician and lead singer in gospel music; a charter member of the Board of Directors of the Gospel Music Association, and songwriter of the first degree. He has produced more gospel TV programs than any other person: *Gospel Singing Caravan, Gospel Roundup, LeFevre Family Show, Jake Hess Show, Prophets in Concert* and *America Sings.* He holds several degrees and is listed in *Who's Who in America.*

Wally Goff is an organist, pianist, arranger and baritone. As general manager of Goff Publishing Company, involved in publishing, producing and promoting gospel music, he has a behind-the-scenes knowledge of the field. As a performer, his keyboard agility is captivating, rich and warm.

Roger Horne, long considered to be one of the finest tenors in the gospel music industry, has traveled and sung with some of America's top groups. He is sought after for his abilities in the areas of vocal teaching and arranging as well as record producing. He is a successful songwriter, and many of his compositions have been recorded by major recording artists.

Becky Horne's voice generates excitement wherever she sings. An unusually versatile singer, she projects a genuine warmth and sincerity.

JOHNSON, MIKE

Mike Johnson's ambition in life was to become one of the world's greatest jazz/rock guitarists. As a member of the Mike Bloomfield Blues Band, which recorded for Columbia Records, he was well on his way to realizing his dream. But he wasn't happy with his "synthetic success and happiness" so he began to search for the true meaning of life.

With his new faith he naturally turned to his music in witness for Christ. "My music had to relate my life in Christ without using the old clichés. I wanted to define the gospel in my music and my raps."

From this self-analysis and determination, Mike started the Excursions, one of the first Christian jazz/rock bands. He toured the East, appearing before thousands on the beaches of Ft. Lauderdale, Florida, with the Inter-Varsity Christian Fellowship, in a coffeehouse with the Billy Graham Crusade in New York City, on college campuses and in the ghettoes of Pittsburgh with Young Life.

In the fall of 1970, Mike felt the Lord calling him to New England for a different ministry. By the spring of 1971 he was performing as a solo artist as well as a speaker. Continuing this ministry, he and his wife moved to Virginia to work with the Christian Broadcasting Network. There he started a youth concert series and was house guitarist for The 700 Club.

Mike Johnson has worked with numerous Christian organizations and has had a working relationship with some of the most respected Christian artists and ministries in America. He has recorded several albums on various labels, including his first NewPax recording, *The Artist/The Riddle*. In addition to his extensive solo work, Mike also released an album with Randy Matthews and Danny Taylor.

Stressing the concept that what a Christian artist does is more than just a form of entertainment, the album *More Than Just An Act* featured several of Mike's best songs yet—"Love Will Last," "The Lord Is My Shepherd" and "I Have Not Forgotten."

JOHNSON, PHIL

Producer, writer, singer and recording artist are a few of the ways to describe versatile Phil Johnson. Phil is vice president of Artists and Repertoire at The Benson Company and produces such well-known artists as Dallas Holm & Praise, The Lanny Wolfe Trio, Reba, The Rambos, Andrus, Blackwood & Company, Jimmy Swaggart, and Henry and Hazel Slaughter. He began producing gospel records on a part-time basis in 1973 when he came to The Benson Company as a song-plugger. Gradually he acquired more and more artists and soon it

became a full-time job. Today, Phil is perhaps the best known gospel producer in the business.

Phil's success as a composer has been evident in the popularity of such songs as "Give Them All," "More (Than You'll Ever Know)" and "When I Say Jesus." His genuine Christian experience is reflected in his songs as he shares things that are personally important to him. He is very sensitive to the needs of others and the problems in the world. And his songs express the love and joy and peace found in Jesus.

On his first album, *Somebody Like You,* he wrote eight of the ten tunes. The other two he co-authored with Reba and Lanny Wolfe. Among the most popular are "The Day He Wore My Crown" (recorded by Doug Oldham), "Don't Take Your Love Away" and the title song "Somebody Like You."

Most of his time is spent writing and producing. Lately Phil has been doing a great deal of backup singing in the studio. He has appeared on such albums as *Songtailor* by Tim Sheppard, *The Prodigal* by Reba and *Following You* by Andrus, Blackwood & Co.

GLENN JONES AND THE MODULATIONS

Out of the Deep South came seven talented Jacksonville, Florida singers and musicians. The Modulations have a soulful sound that's hard to beat.

Leader of the group, and brother of Glenn Jones, is Lewis Jones. Lewis has been the group's guardian since its origin

PHIL JOHNSON:
*Sharing things that
are personally
important to him*

and first recording contract with Venture Recording Company in Philadelphia, which later led to a forty-five release on Savoy Records. Glenn Jones, a veteran in every sense of the word, has been traveling professionally since he was eight years old with the famous Bivens Specials, also of Jacksonville.

Glenn Jones and The Modulations have been compared favorably with the choreography of The Temptations, the soulful sound of Stevie Wonder, the harmonies of The Spinners, the vocal control of the late Donny Hathaway and the groovy and soulful delivery of Billy Preston. They are gospel and it's no secret: "The Gospel is our life and Jesus is our Saviour."

Ninety per cent of the group's music is composed or arranged by Glenn Jones and The Modulations.

THE JORDANAIRES

Neal Matthews
Gordon Stoker
Hoyt Hawkins
Ray Walker

The Jordanaires include Neal Matthews, Gordon Stoker, Hoyt Hawkins and Ray Walker. Former members of the group, which was organized in 1949, are Hugh Jarrett and Culle Holt. The Jordanaires recorded albums that include *Land of Jordan, Gloryland, Heavenly Spirit* and *A Friend We Have,* with Tennessee Ernie Ford, and *To God Be The Glory.* Former backup singers with Elvis Presley, they primarily work studio sessions in Nashville.

—K—

KEAGGY, PHIL

Before Phil Keaggy met Jesus, music was the center of his life. Like many of today's musicians, the desire to become the world's greatest guitar player was the sole driving force in his life. "Music was all I cared about," he says. "My whole world was guitars, amps, records—anything related to music."

After accepting Christ, Phil's life changed. He didn't leave the group Glass Harp right away, but it wasn't long before he realized his association with the group was stifling his relationship with the Lord. So, in 1972, he left the band to continue singing solely for Jesus Christ.

Since then, Phil has been involved in various aspects of the music ministry. After Glass Harp, he traveled with Peter York for a few years, then later played and toured with both Love Song and Paul Clark. He's also performed on numerous Christian recordings by the Second Chapter of Acts and Honeytree.

Phil's first musical expression of his life in Christ was his *What A Day* album which has become standard fare with Jesus music fans. His second album, *Love Broke Thru*, established Phil as one of the most popular Christian artists any-

PHIL KEAGGY: *His association with the group was stifling his relationship with the Lord*

where with top songs like "Love Broke Thru," "Take Me Closer" and "Abraham."

Phil's third album, *Emerging,* marked a new beginning in his musical career because it features the talents of his recently formed band that includes Dan Cunningham (bass), Lynn Nichols (guitar), Terry Anderson (drums) and Phil Madeira (keyboards).

THE KINGSMEN

Eldridge Fox—Baritone
Ernie Phillips—Tenor
Jim Hamill—Lead
Ray Dean Reese—Bass
Mark Trammell—Bass Guitar
Gary Dillard—Steel Guitar
Greg Fox—Drums
Anthony Burger—Piano

In 22 years, The Kingsmen Quartet of Asheville, North Carolina has come a long way—from a group of young men singing for fun to the top of the professional gospel singing world. People sing gospel in many and varied ways: The Kingsmen have a style of excitement that has grown to be a gospel music legend.

The group has skyrocketed to prominence among its peers in just eight years since going full time. They have sold over 250,000 records and eight-track tapes under 41 titles, grossing $20 million in sales. The group's first live album, *Big And Live,* won the Gospel Music Industry's Dove Award in 1974, and their second live album, *Chattanooga Live,* sold

over 65,000 copies in the first six months and won the Dove Award in 1978.

The Kingsmen is the only gospel group to be among the Top Five finalists the past five years for both the Dove Award and the Singing News Award at the same time. In addition, each member of the group has been nominated regularly for individual Dove and Fan honors. The quartet has won four Fan Awards in the past, two for Favorite Lead, one for Favorite First Tenor, and one for the Men of Music. For two years, the singers had their own syndicated television show, *Music City Special,* which was viewed in 66 markets; now they are regulars on the *Archie Campbell & The Kingsmen* TV program.

Named Official Goodwill Ambassadors for North Carolina in 1975, The Kingsmen involve many of their fans in working vacations each year to Hawaii and Nassau.

None of the original 1957 Kingsmen are still with the group. Eldridge Fox, owner of the quartet and baritone singer, joined the group about a year after it began, and has been with it through thick and thin, acquiring full control in 1971.

Ray Dean Reese, the bass singer, is second oldest in the quartet in point of service. Ray has been with The Kingsmen since 1970, and prior to that, in the early 1960s, he sang with The Kingsmen for a year and a half.

Jim Hamill, the lead, joined the group in 1971 and has been a driving force in the quartet's move to the top.

Tenor Ernie Phillips came with The Kingsmen in 1977.

From beginning to end and everywhere in between, The Kingsmen are an unforgettable experience.

KLAUDT INDIAN FAMILY: *Close, family-type vocal harmony*

THE KLAUDT INDIAN FAMILY

Vernon Klaudt
Ken Klaudt
Ray Klaudt
Melvin Klaudt
Lillian Klaudt
Ralph Seibel

The Klaudts are four brothers and their mother, Lillian, all of whom live in Norcross, Georgia. The father, Ronald H. Klaudt, sang with the group years ago but now travels with them as manager.

The Klaudt Indian Family are Arikara Indians, originally from Fort Berthold Indian Reservation in North Dakota. Their pianist, Ralph Seibel, is a non-Indian from Kansas. The Klaudts have been gospel musicians, traveling and doing concerts, TV and radio appearances for nearly fifty years. They do a close, family-style vocal harmony, along with solos. They also play tenor and baritone saxophones and slide trombone, along with bass, guitar and piano. The Klaudt Indian Family still give their shows a distinctive touch by wearing authentic costumes for their appearances.

THE KINGSMEN: *Down-to-earth, fun-loving men with a true inspirational message*

L

LAFFERTY, KAREN

Probably the most important ingredient in Karen Lafferty's ministry of music —beyond musical talent and training, beyond her caring for the people she can reach with her music—is experience, particularly her experience as a professional entertainer. Not so much the poise and polish gained in her days as a nightclub singer, but rather the understanding that there is nothing at all wrong with entertainment per se, as long as the entertainer is right with God.

KAREN LAFFERTY: *Straightforward statements of her loving relationship with God*

Her songs are straightforward statements of her loving relationship with God, simple and direct in lyric and melody. Not all are as uncomplicated as "Seek Ye First," one of her earliest compositions and a classic among contemporary worship songs. Yet as her songs have developed in two Maranatha! Music albums and hundreds of performances, the message of God's love has remained pure and crystal clear.

Sweet Communion, her most recent album, shows remarkable growth over her first album, the well-received *Bird In A Golden Sky.*

Karen's in-person performances are as direct as her songs. Her warmth and desire to serve God have made her a popular addition to many programs in the United States as well as overseas.

She lives the life of a twentieth-century gospel troubadour, driving from place to place in her small camper truck or jetting longer distances. One of the finest things to her in the role God has awarded her is meeting other believers and discovering how the Lord is using them.

Born and raised in Alamogordo, New Mexico, Karen was "born again" at the age of ten. Yet it wasn't until she had finished college (Bachelor of Arts in Music Education, at Eastern New Mexico University), and was performing regularly in New Orleans saloons and clubs, that her friends challenged her relationship with Christ. "It was then that I learned of the power of the Holy Spirit and the importance of studying God's Word," she recalls.

Eventually, her cousins introduced her to Calvary Chapel of Costa Mesa, which was then in the early stages of its tremendous growth. She was a part of the

DOUG LAWRENCE: *Sought after by some of the world's most prestigious concert centers*

Maranatha! Music Family from its beginnings as a performer on early Maranatha! albums as a singer and oboist.

LAWRENCE, DOUG

Douglas Lawrence, a native Californian who is establishing himself as one of the principal baritone oratorio and recital singers, has been sought after by some of the world's most prestigious concert centers since the late impresario Sol Hurok added Mr. Lawrence's name to his illustrious roster. His career has included over forty performances in Los Angeles, both at the Hollywood Bowl and the Dorothy Chandler Pavilion. His recording of Bloch's *Sacred Service* on Angel Records was released in the summer of 1977.

Lawrence recorded the album *Doug Lawrence* for Light Records with the Ralph Carmichael Orchestra and Chorus. He has also been a featured soloist on other Light albums, including *Specially for Shepherds, Festival of Praise I* and *Easter Celebration.*

LEE, J.J.

J.J. Lee, whose debut album *J.J.* was released on NewPax Records, grew up in a faith-filled home. Her early life centered around the usual church music involvement—both choir singing and piano lessons began at age seven.

At thirteen, J.J. began formal voice training and later used her talent to direct choirs in the Baptist churches her father pastored. At about the age of eighteen, J.J. decided she needed to make her own way rather than to lean on the background of her family. Thus began her eight-year search to find the best way to display her talent.

The year 1968 brought J.J. an introduction into The Spurrlows as a soprano soloist. This positive step ended prematurely when J.J. broke her leg, cutting short another promising vehicle for her talent.

After eight years of experiencing the fickle ups and downs of a musical career, J.J. finally came face to face with the reality of the emptiness in her life. Coming to grips with the realization that she had been running from the Christ who could fill the emptiness she had known for so long, she decided to turn her life in His direction.

Her renewed relationship with Christ brought an ease to songwriting that she'd never before experienced. Thus, J.J. penned "Peace," a slow melody about the inner security that comes with forgiveness. As J.J. says, "It is the first song I ever had both published and recorded. 'Peace' gave me a purpose and reason for being here."

Written while she was a writer for Canaanland Music, "Peace" has since been recorded by several Christian artists.

THE LeFEVRES

(See Rex Nelon Singers.)

One of the most outstanding names in gospel music, the LeFevre family has spread their message since the early 1920s. Traveling throughout America for personal appearances, as well as through such radio and television shows as the *Gospel Singing Caravan* and the *New Gospel Singing Caravan,* the LeFevres have provided joy and inspiration to all who have heard them.

Just a few of the many songs they are known for are "Just A Closer Walk With Thee," "All Aboard," "Shake the Master's Hand" and "Without Him."

THE LEWIS FAMILY

Roy (Pop) Lewis Sr.—Vocals
Roy Lewis Jr.—Banjo
Wallace Lewis—Lead, Guitar
Miggie Lewis—Vocals
Polly Lewis—Vocals, Piano
Janis Lewis Phillips—Vocals
Travis Lewis—Bass, Mandolin
Lewis Phillips—Vocals, Banjo

The undisputed "First Family of Bluegrass Gospel Music," The Lewis Family's success over the past decade rests on the solid foundation of their powerful and uplifting music.

The patriarch and guiding force ever since the family troupe had its beginnings in the early 1950s is Roy (Pop) Lewis Sr. The first "singings" by Pop Lewis and "my children" in small rural churches throughout Northeast Georgia and Western South Carolina led to a live, regular Sunday show on WJBF Television in Augusta, Georgia. Started in 1954, the telecast continues to this day, although it is now videotaped and widely syndicated throughout the South and the Eastern Seaboard.

The group's stage and television appearances showcase the fine lead singing and rhythm guitar work of Wallace Lewis, who writes many of their songs. The featured instrument is the driving five-string banjo of Roy Lewis Jr., called "Little Roy" since beginning his career as a child prodigy. For many fans the favorite part of any Lewis Family concert is the gospel trio harmony singing of "the girls," Miggie, Polly and Janis. They routinely vary their vocal arrangements and often the listener is treated, as a change of pace, to the solo voice of one of the girls. Polly is regarded as one of the finest piano players in gospel.

Three generations are now represented in the still all-family cast. Wallace's son, Travis Lewis, began to play bass and mandolin in the group even before finishing high school. More recently, "Little Lewis" Phillips began to sing and play the five-string banjo. Lewis is the son of Earl and Janis (Lewis) Phillips.

The Lewis Family displays poise and professionalism derived from live performances numbering literally in the thousands and from recording more than 30 albums, the first on the Starday label. Since 1969 they have recorded for Canaan Records. The impact of these releases is evidenced by the growing use of their songs by other groups.

LIMPIC & RAYBURN

Gerry Limpic
Mark Rayburn
Dave Pollard

Five years ago Limpic & Rayburn was a relatively unknown duo which performed mainly before small local church audiences. Like many Christian groups, the duo started playing in small fellowships and churches, but it didn't take long for their popularity to grow beyond the boundaries of their hometown of San Diego.

Drawing audiences ranging from young teens to middle-aged adults, Limpic & Rayburn have traveled throughout most of the country, ministering with their soft folk sounds in concerts, cru-

115

THE LEWIS FAMILY: *First Family of Bluegrass Gospel Music*

sades and festivals. Perhaps their largest audience was thirty thousand people, at a San Diego Billy Graham Crusade.

A native of San Diego, Gerry Limpic is single and attends San Diego State University, where he is pursuing studies in youth counseling. Gerry has been active in both the Campus Life and Youth for Christ programs in San Diego. As a musician, he was formerly a member of the recording group Random Sample.

Mark Rayburn is from Los Alamos, New Mexico, and is also single. His musical activities include his work with Up With People and Logos as well as his partnership with Gerry Limpic.

Three years ago, Limpic & Rayburn in-

vited Dave Pollard to join them and he's been their bass player ever since. Because Limpic & Rayburn had been together for over a year before he joined them, the name has remained the same.

The group's debut album, entitled *Limpic & Rayburn,* was released on the Myrrh label in early 1977, and featured such popular songs as "Sunshine In My Soul" and "Come To The River."

Building on the success of their first release, their next album, *Caught In The Crossfire,* features a much fuller sound that enhances their popular folk-rock style. Two of the most promising new songs on the album were "Domino" and the title track, "Caught In The Crossfire."

M

MANN, JOHNNY

Johnny Mann has become a household personality through nearly three years with his television show *Stand Up And Cheer* plus thirty-four albums, two Grammy Awards and five nominations.

His entire family sang in the choir in old St. Paul's in Baltimore, the oldest church in America. His first real break came when he became choral director under Al Goodman on the old *NBC Comedy Hour*. He later backed top names like Frank Sinatra.

He orchestrated seven motion pictures for Warner Brothers, Twentieth Century-Fox and Columbia Studios.

Mann's second major break came when he organized The Johnny Mann Singers to cut a demonstration record for Liberty Records which led to a long association and many albums.

On February 9, 1971 a new show, *Stand Up And Cheer,* was premiered on television, ran for nearly three years and made Johnny Mann a household word internationally.

Following the close of the show, his career took a drastic change.

In 1975, with the guidance of his wife, Lynn, composer-arranger Paul Johnson and others, Mann accepted Christ and

JOHNNY MANN: *A household word internationally*

started a whole new career in Christian music.

Johnny and Lynn Mann first presented

117

two-person concerts in churches, which quickly grew to working with entire church choirs and orchestras, with Johnny conducting and Lynn featured as soloist.

"This is the thing I love to do the most in my life," he said. "I feel this is my calling now. We're involved in the church and its people."

He has received awards from the Freedom's Foundation, Valley Forge, top awards from the National Disabled Veterans, the Medal of Honor from the National DAR, the Silver Helmets award from the American VETS, the National Honor Medal from the Veterans of Foreign Wars and numerous citations from the American Legion.

LYNN MANN: *Now joins Johnny on an active concert tour*

MANN, LYNN

Lynn Mann, the former Lynn Bolin, came from a well-known West Coast musical family, was a member of the Doodletown Pipers and later The Johnny Mann Singers, and has numerous television credits. She has also written and recorded her first album for Light Records, *God's Quiet Love*.

She became a member of The Johnny Mann Singers in July 1970 for a tour of his new show, *Stand Up And Cheer,* which first toured the country live and then stayed on television for nearly three years.

Christian performers such as arranger Paul Johnson and singer Sharalee Lucas and Mike Redman were a great influence on Lynn's life and led her to Christ in

1974. Johnny Mann followed with his decision for Christ in 1975.

Sharalee featured Lynn's song "Oh God, I Hurt Inside" on her album and encouraged the start of Lynn's career as a songwriter.

Lynn Mann now joins Johnny on an active concert tour of churches and auditoriums where she is featured vocalist.

McGUIRE, BARRY

"I sing to people because I love 'em and because I care about what's happenin' to 'em," says Barry McGuire, who has spent a lot of years before audiences around the world. He got his professional start in music playing in a bar for twenty dollars a night. Then, in 1961, his friends Art Podell, Nick Woods and Randy Sparks formed The New Christy Minstrels and asked Barry to join them. Barry wrote many of their songs, including two of his million-selling compositions, "Green Green."

BARRY McGUIRE: *A vibrant, living relationship with Jesus*

After many years of singing the same songs Barry left The New Christy Minstrels and, with Phil Sloan, recorded the best-seller "The Eve Of Destruction." From the spectacular reaction to that hit, Barry went on to play the male lead in *Hair!*, but after that entered a period of disillusionment.

In 1971 he became a Christian and committed his life and music to Jesus Christ. Barry says:

> I came into a vibrant, living relationship with Jesus. At first, I didn't know what to do, so I got myself an owner's manual (a New Testament) and spent most of the next six months just finding out more about who Jesus is and what kind of person He wanted me to be. I didn't know if I was ever going to sing again and I really didn't care. . . . I started receiving new songs of life and love that dealt with all the old questions I'd raised in "The Eve of Destruction."

In 1973 Barry released his first "born-again" album, *Seeds*. It was followed in 1974 by *Lighten Up;* then came an in-concert album titled *To The Bride*.

Barry signed with Sparrow Records in 1976. He is now settled in Texas with his wife, Marie, and his two children.

THE McKEITHENS

Tim McKeithen
Dixie McKeithen
Robert McKeithen
Angelina Ruth McKeithen

Although the McKeithen Family is new as a group to the gospel music field, Tim and Dixie McKeithen have been in

THE McKEITHENS: *A tightly knit family group*

gospel music for twelve years. For seven and a half years they were associated with Tim's family, The Singing Hemphills.

A tightly knit family group, The Mc-Keithens are led by Tim, who sings lead and plays the guitar. Tim's wife, Dixie, plays piano, sings alto, and for the past two years has written most of their material. Also joining them is Tim's cousin,

120

Robert, who plays bass and sings baritone. Highlighting their shows is the singing of their four-year-old daughter, Angelina Ruth.

McSPADDEN, GARY

"Once I thought I had to sing. It has been a long, hard process, but I am learning that my singing is not so important. The *Song* is what must be heard," confesses Gary McSpadden, the son of a preacher, who grew up singing.

His first public appearance was at four; at ten he decided he wanted to be a quartet singer. He spent most of his free time preparing for his goal and listening to all the records he could find. At nineteen he sang with The Statesmen Quartet, then joined The Oak Ridge Quartet for two years before becoming a member of The Imperials. Because the time spent on the road was hurting his marriage, Gary left The Imperials and began teaching a singing class in Waxahachie, Texas.

His old friend Bill Gaither dropped in to see Gary and asked him to join his group, but it wasn't until ten years later that Gary actually came to The Bill Gaither Trio.

Now a permanent member and lead singer of The Bill Gaither Trio, Gary spends his time in the concert arena yet never misses preaching every Sunday morning. He feels he is someone blessed with the opportunity to function in the two realms he loves. "Back home, no one asks for my autograph or treats me like a celebrity," he says, "they ask me to pray with them and counsel them."

McVAY, LEWIS

Less than a year after his salvation, Lewis McVay became drummer for the influential group Mustard Seed Faith. Mustard Seed, as the group came to be known, toured all over the nation and in Europe, bringing contemporary gospel music to young people. Their sole Maranatha! Music album, with its distinctive Rick Griffin cover painting, continues to place high on charts of contemporary gospel music after four years in release.

Sail On Sailor, the album's title song, is a McVay composition, and reflects his love of sailing and the sea. Lewis and his wife, Dianne, live not far from the sea in Costa Mesa, California and they spend most of their free time on the water.

McVay's musical growth is evident in his album. By the time he left Mustard Seed he was writing a good portion of the group's material, playing guitar with the band and moving into keyboards.

"I'm sure people will seek all kinds of meanings that aren't there," comments Lewis. "All I'm doing, though, is sharing the love of Jesus Christ as creatively as I know how."

MEECE, DAVID

David Meece began his astonishing musical career at age fourteen, when he made his conducting debut by appearing with the Houston Chamber Orchestra. At fifteen he toured Europe as featured pianist with Youth for Christ Interna-

THE MERCY RIVER BOYS (The Singing Christians): *Professional ability dedicated to God*

tional. Back in Houston at sixteen, he made a guest appearance with André Previn and the Houston Symphony. He's been winning prestigious musical awards ever since.

Meece attended the renowned Peabody Conservatory of Music in Baltimore, where he had a four-year scholarship.

And all this classical training and experience has prepared David for what he feels is his true ministry: writing and performing Jesus music. His mastery of the piano has given him his ability in contemporary music, which has provided the opportunity to present his own music in a style that's exciting and unforgettable.

Someone once wrote the following description: "When listening to David Meece perform his music, it often sounds as if he were playing and singing on top of a mountain, the open sky his canopy, with an audience of thousands as company. And yet, at other times it is almost as if we were overhearing a private dialogue between David and his Creator."

Though David Meece may still be considered a newcomer to Jesus music, his one album has several songs that will tickle the memory: "I'll Sing This Song For You," "Come Home," "America" and "Imagine What It'd Be Like."

THE MERCY RIVER BOYS

(The Singing Christians)

Texas' Singing Christians, The Mercy River Boys, have shared their unique style of music ministry with people across the United States and Canada for over a decade. Few other teams have achieved the versatility with which these young men are able to entertain both young and old.

The Mercy River Boys may be accurately described as "an outstanding collection of musical talent and professional ability dedicated to God."

THE MIGHTY CLOUDS OF JOY

Joe Ligon—Lead
Johnny Martin—Lead
Richard Wallace—Bass
Elmeo Franklin—Baritone

For twenty years, The Mighty Clouds of Joy have been leaders in the world of gospel, playing over two hundred concerts a year. Since they first began recording for Peacock Records in Houston twenty years ago, The Clouds have recorded twenty albums. Their approach to gospel is an example of a very special musical hybrid, a blending of music that transcends categories. With equal grace and ease, they mix contemporary sounds with traditionalism. To them, modern music is the proper vehicle to spread the true gospel. In twenty years, The Mighty Clouds of Joy have mastered every nuance of popular gospel, cutting through the separating barriers of religious and temporal worlds in every song they sing. They are as at home with country as they are with traditional church music.

The Clouds started in Los Angeles, the brainchild of Joe Ligon, born in Troy, Alabama. All four met in high school, though only Johnny Martin was born in California. Richard Wallace is from rural

THE MIGHTY CLOUDS OF JOY: *A very special musical hybrid*

Georgia, while Elmeo Franklin was born in Florida. The group's most recent addition is the well-known Paul Beasley, formerly of The Gospel Keytones.

The Mighty Clouds of Joy are undeniably one of the best examples of gospel's true calling. They bring a spiritual message to everyday life, making belief in God and enjoyment of temporal pleasures one and the same. And their principal virtue is that neither is diminished in importance.

N

THE REX NELON SINGERS
(See The LeFevres.)

Rex Nelon—Bass
Kelly Nelon—Alto
Janet Paschal—Soprano
Rodney Swain—Lead
Rex Foster—Piano
Greg Cothran—Guitar
Robbie Willis—Drums

The Rex Nelon Singers, formerly known as The LeFevres, are a rare new breed of singers.

Named after its widely acclaimed bass singer Rex Nelon, the entire range of gospel music is spanned by this active group: quartet style, gospel spirituals, Andrae Crouch music, Nancy Harmon songs and old-fashioned hymns.

This Atlanta group of polished musicians records on the Canaan label and is in great demand for television. They are regular guests on such leading syndicated shows as *The PTL Club* and *The Gospel Singing Jubilee.*

Rex Nelon, the group's leader, is one of the most experienced bass singers in gospel music today, having traveled a quarter of a century on the concert circuit, first with the original Homeland Harmony Quartet, then with the LeFevres.

Also owner of the Rex Nelon Music Company and on the board of the Gospel Music Association and Gospel Music Hall of Fame, Rex is one of the most respected singers in the country. As one of the pillars of gospel music, Rex's stability keeps the group in an easy mood as they perform almost 250 concerts each year.

Kelly Nelon, one of the youngest altos in gospel music, is in her teens and gaining popularity with her many talents as a singer and writer. She is one of the brightest faces on the horizon of gospel singing.

Janet Paschal, relatively new to gospel, has rapidly become one of the most popular sopranos. She has the power and ability to move and spellbind audiences.

Rodney Swain, lead singer, came to the group in early 1976, bringing over a decade of experience in gospel music with The Jacobs Brothers and Rozie Rozel and The Searchers. He was at one time youth pastor at Huffman Assembly of God in Birmingham.

"I know the man I sing about," he says. "During every concert I feel the presence of God. In some way, I relate everything the group does to Christ, so the people know what we stand for."

Rex Foster, piano, Greg Cothran, guitar, and Robbie Willis, drums, round out the group.

THE REX NELON SINGERS: *"The people know what we stand for"*

NELSON, ERICK

Erick Nelson is twenty-seven and lives in Huntington Beach, California. In September of 1968, he was challenged to initiate a personal, living relationship with Jesus Christ, and subsequently accepted Him as his Master, Savior and Teacher. Since then "all things have become new," life has taken on a very specific meaning, and the dreams and hopes of a lifetime are being fulfilled in a day-to-day setting.

The music he once played took on a new form: it spoke of this very relationship, and of the joy and seriousness such a commitment entails. He has toured with the groups Selah and Good News, and, as a solo, to thirty states and Canada. He has been recorded on the albums *Maranatha! Two, Three, Four* and *Five, Praise One* and *Two,* and the *Joy Album,* as well as his own group's album *Good News.* His solo album *Flow River Flow* has also been released on the Maranatha! label.

NETHERTON, TOM

A year before his debut on *The Lawrence Welk Show,* Tom was a student at a conservative Bible college in Minnesota, no better known than the next guy. During the summer of 1973, while he was singing in the Madora Festival in North Dakota, Tom met Harold and Shilah Schaffer, the owners of *The Lawrence Welk Show.* One day when Harold and Shilah were playing golf with Lawrence Welk, they asked him to give Tom an audition. It resulted in Tom's being invited to appear with Welk's traveling company based in St. Paul. The response to his performance was so overwhelming that he was flown to Hollywood to tape

TOM NETHERTON: *In the armed forces when he first accepted Christ*

127

a number for the TV program; soon afterward he became a regular member of the television cast.

Tom was in the armed forces in Panama when he first accepted Christ. He had been asked to be a counselor for the Billy Graham film *The Restless Ones* and he realized that he couldn't do the job without knowing Christ. Thus, he stepped forward in a Baptist church in Panama and surrendered his life.

Tom's first two Word albums, *What A Friend . . . We Have In Jesus,* and *Just As I Am,* established him, in the minds of many observers, as one of the new leading male gospel artists.

NIELSON AND YOUNG

Stephen Nielson
Ovid Young (See page 188.)

Stephen Nielson brings to gospel music an impressive background on the classical stage. His masterful keyboard expertise and Christian dedication have placed him in the front rank of today's performing artists.

A Phi Beta Kappa graduate of Indiana University School of Music who lives in Dallas, Nielson has gained an international reputation as a concert artist and

NIELSON AND YOUNG:
Christian dedication

orchestral soloist. His tours have taken him to leading cities of the United States, Central America and Europe.

Aside from his solo work, Nielson joins Ovid Young, well-known pianist, organist, conductor and arranger, for two-piano concerts across the country, performing over one hundred concerts a year. They are gaining much recognition in the Christian concert field. Drawing from a repertoire which includes the great piano and sacred classics, hymns and gospel songs, their rare musical gift is the ability to combine their extraordinary talents with their Christian faith to make their music speak.

Nielson and Young record for Paragon Records.

THE NORMAN BROTHERS

Ervin Norman Jr.
Larry Norman
Roosevelt Norman
Terry Norman
Douglas Ellison
Randy Banks
Ronnie Hester

Good gospel music endures through generations of gospel singers. Under the leadership of his father, The Reverend Ervin Norman, Ervin Norman Jr. began singing at an early age with The Gospel Bells of Elberton, Georgia. Norman later lead The Silverton Gospel Singers, now known as The Norman Brothers.

Besides Ervin, the group comprises Larry Norman, Roosevelt Norman, Terry Norman, Douglas Ellison, Randy Banks and Ronnie Hester.

Their first three albums were *Get Right With God, What A Friend We Have In Jesus* and *All Of My Hard Times.*

NORMAN, LARRY

Larry Norman says: "The only important and lasting thing in the whole world is Jesus. That's all my music is hanging on. Outside of Jesus it has no value."

Larry has been called "the poet laureate of Jesus music" by *Time* magazine. *The New York Times* labeled him "Christian rock music's most intelligent writer and greatest asset." He was one of the first, perhaps *the* first, singer-songwriter to take a stand boldly for Jesus Christ in the midst of a rock and roll career.

Larry began singing at two, playing the piano at four and composing at nine. By the time he was out of high school, he'd already written over five hundred songs. Unlike many other contemporary Christian performers whose conversions to Christianity have come after years of secular music, Larry's faith in Jesus existed early. He wrote his first Bible-oriented song, "Moses," at fifteen.

"When I started singing the rock songs about Jesus," says Larry, "I called it Jesus rock because Jesus is the rock. If we build our lives upon Him, they will be steady." He adds, "I'm trying to find every available outlet to tell others that Jesus is their answer, whether or not they know it."

And he *is* telling people about Jesus . . . in his own particular way. In choosing art over propaganda, individuality over conformity, poetry over clichés, and the evocative over the literal, Larry has become a center of controversy and conjecture. But for him it's the only way. As he puts it, "God calls each of us to be a servant and to serve our brothers and sisters, and He doesn't call us to be leaders. If He puts you in a position of leadership, then that's being a servant, too."

Norman's tremendous talents of singing and composing as his way of serving God have made his music the original base for the Jesus music movement. Some of his more memorable songs include: "I Am A Servant," "UFO," "666," "I Wish We'd All Been Ready," "Sweet, Sweet Song of Salvation," "One Way," "Why Don't You Look Into Jesus" and "I Love You."

In addition to writing songs, acting, producing albums and touring the nation, Larry devotes much of his time to opening doors for other Christian performing artists through his Street Level Artists Agency and Solid Rock Records.

NUTSHELL

Paul Field—Guitar, Piano, Vocals
Pam Thiele—Vocals, Piano, Autoharp
Heather Barlow—Vocals, Guitar

"Our songs are reactions to everyday experiences, people we meet, and situations we're in. In writing a song you express feelings which are important to you; and so for us it is natural that our Chris-

tian beliefs are reflected in our music," says Paul Field, the writer of Nutshell's material.

The British group Nutshell has done a lot of work for church organizations, but they don't like to consider themselves "just a Christian group." Their music has been enjoyed in folk clubs as well as universities and concert halls. They do not view themselves as preachers, or their music as merely a vehicle for evangelism.

Nutshell has been together since 1972, but it wasn't until 1976 that the trio began a full-time singing ministry. Since then, they have traveled over twenty thousand miles, performing throughout Great Britain, Holland, Germany and Scandinavia. In addition, they have made several appearances on British television and have been featured on numerous radio programs there.

Nutshell consists of Paul Field, Pam Thiele and Heather Barlow. Paul plays guitar, piano and sings. In addition to his work with Nutshell, he has appeared on Dutch television as a solo artist. He's also had several songs recorded by other musicians, including Barry McGuire. Pam Thiele sings and plays the autoharp and piano. Heather Barlow also sings and plays guitar.

Nutshell made their American debut with *Flyaway*. Spotlighting their superb harmonies, *Flyaway* features some of the same personnel who performed on the Malcolm & Alwyn albums. *Buzz* magazine, a British Christian publication, hails *Flyaway* as "the finest British release for a long time. Through it, Paul Field has established himself among the truly inspired writers of intelligent gospel music."

—O—

THE OAK RIDGE BOYS

Bill Golden—Baritone
Duane Allen—Lead
Richard Sterban—Bass
Joe Bonsall—Tenor

The Oak Ridge Boys sang gospel music for well over ten years, and are the recipients of many awards. In the fall of 1978, the Country Music Association named the four singers Vocal Group of the Year and The Oak Ridge Boys' four-

THE OAK RIDGE BOYS: *Good friends as well as business associates*

DOUG OLDHAM: *A minister of music*

piece band Instrumental Group of the Year. *Billboard* magazine chose them as their Number One Country Music Group of the Year, *Record World* cited them as Number One Vocal Group of the Year. *Cashbox* and *Radio & Records* declared them Country Vocal Group of the Year. Following their receipt of four Grammy Awards and fifteen Dove Awards, they signed with ABC Records.

Originally called The Country Cut-Ups, The Oak Ridge Boys were formed during World War II in Knoxville. Often appearing on weekends at the atomic energy plant in Oak Ridge, the group was soon dubbed The Oak Ridge Quartet. Because of the general feeling of pessimism during the war, their most popular selections proved to be gospel songs. They disbanded after the war, but re-formed in the mid-1950s as The Oak Ridge Boys.

The group is now composed of Bill Golden, Duane Allen, Richard Sterban and Joe Bonsall—and they're good friends as well as business associates. They own two publishing companies and a recording studio in the Nashville suburb of Hendersonville. The musicians who play with The Oak Ridge Boys are Skip Mitchell, lead guitar; Mark Ellerbee, drums; Don Breland, bass guitar; and Garland, keyboard.

OLDHAM, DOUG

Before coming full-time into the concert ministry, Doug Oldham served as a minister of music and performed as featured soloist at the Thomas Road Baptist Church in Lynchburg, Virginia—one of the best-known churches in America. Doug continues to be in great demand for concerts throughout the country. From large halls to private concert groups, Oldham has always gone with the purpose of sharing a true and living Christ with all those around him.

Voted Best Gospel Male Vocalist of the Year (1974) by The Evangelical Film Foundation; host of his own television show, *Hi, Doug!,* broadcast to over one hundred cities in the Christian Broadcasting Network; host of his own syndicated radio program, *Hi, Doug!,* and artist of *Alleluia,* the very first gospel album to turn gold—Oldham spreads the good news of Christ through personal testimony and song.

A master of song interpretation, whose ability to dramatize the joy of triumph in a song has become his trademark, Doug performs in churches, auditoriums and on college campuses. His pianist, Steve Adams, is a well-known talent in his own right. He's written such songs as "All In The Name Of Jesus," "Ever Gentle, Ever Sweet" and "Where The Spirit Of The Lord Is." Doug also travels with a bass guitarist and sometimes uses soundtracked accompaniment.

Doug and his wife, Laura Lee, recently moved their whole family to Nashville. There, he is close to his producer, Joe Huffman, and The Benson Company. Impact Books, a division of The Benson Company, has published his autobiography, *I Don't Live There Anymore.* It relates the story of his life as a talented Christian, his salvation experience and the evidence and blessings of his life thereafter.

Doug's latest recording on Impact is

Special Delivery. He has recorded seventeen albums with The Benson Company. Some of his most popular tunes include "The King Is Coming," "Because He Lives," "I Just Feel Like Something Good Is About To Happen" and "He Touched Me."

OMARTIAN, MICHAEL

Michael Omartian's apprenticeship in music began with his membership in a jazz quartet. But when he arrived in Hollywood he quickly found a place for himself in the West Coast establishment —in two directions.

Omartian became a highly sought-after keyboard-session man. His name appeared on top albums with such artists as The Four Tops, Gladys Knight and The Pips, Vikki Carr, Billy Joel, Neil Diamond, Art Garfunkel, Johnny Rivers, Austin Roberts, Seals and Crofts, Albert Hammond and David Cassidy.

His production and arranging abilities are evident on recordings by such artists as Helen Reddy, Steely Dan and Glen Campbell.

But Michael is perhaps best known for his production of the million-seller "Theme From S.W.A.T."

Meanwhile, he was involved with Christian music. He worked as a Campus Crusade staffer, and he played prominent parts in a number of recording projects including work with Jimmy Owens. He also accomplished some outstanding arrangement work with Barry McGuire and the Second Chapter of Acts recordings.

Michael's first solo album turned out to be a classic that adds a progressive flair to contemporary Christian music. It's a personal statement about his faith, and it's co-written with his wife, Stormie.

Some Omartian songs that will be long remembered are "White Horse," "Jeremiah" and "Silver Fish."

ONE TRUTH

Randy Butler
Terry Butler
Ron Butler
Floyd Butler
Bill Dragoo
Andy Osbrink
Smitty Price

The secret of the solid gospel-rock sound created by One Truth lies within the conviction and talent of the young men comprising this California-based group. They're a group of versatile and hardworking young men whose goal is ministering to the needs of others.

Randy, Terry, Ron and Floyd Butler write the material performed by the group, while Smitty Price arranges and co-produces One Truth recordings. During performances they sing and play instruments as well. Additional group members are Bill Dragoo, drummer and percussionist, and Andy Osbrink, who plays bass and performs background vocals.

One Truth records on the Greentree label. Their latest album is *Gospel Truth.*

ONE TRUTH: *Ministering to the needs of others*

OWENS-COLLINS, JAMIE

After cautiously emerging from "singing in my room where I thought no one could hear me," Jamie Owens-Collins has become one of the top female vocalists in gospel music.

When she was fifteen, her father and mother, composers Jimmy and Carol Owens, encouraged her into the public spotlight as lead singer in Jimmy Owens' Christian musical *Show Me!*

JAMIE OWENS-COLLINS:
*Recognizing God's love in a
new dimension*

In 1973 she recorded her first Light Records album, *Laughter in Your Soul,* which became the best-selling contemporary Christian album in Great Britain in 1975. *Growing Pains,* which established her as a songwriter, followed in 1976.

Since her marriage that year to Dan Collins, who produced her latest album, *Love Eyes,* she now speaks of "recognizing God's love in a new dimension as a wife and mother."

Her musical ministry focuses on two points: "I want to thank God for all He's given me, and to share with people my learning relationship with Jesus . . . that the Lord loves them as much as He loves me."

P

PANTANO/SALSBURY

Back when Ron Salsbury started JC Power Outlet in 1971 with his good friend John Pantano, they were part of one of the rare Christian rock bands then in existence. They were uncompromising in their desire to bring the sounds of their generation into the field of gospel music.

Although at first the group lacked experience, it wasn't long before JC Power Outlet developed into a polished band of professionals with many admirers. One of these, Larry Norman, asked the band to play a couple of songs in the studio with him. Though never released officially, the songs appeared on Norman's early underground album, *Bootleg.*

JC Power Outlet soon recorded their first album for Word Records on the newly formed Myrrh label. The album contained several Ron Salsbury classics. Their second, *Forgiven,* featured such popular Jesus music tunes as "I Choose To Follow You" and "Don't Let Jesus Pass You By." The group then decided to take their music to the people. They bought a van and began traveling all over the United States to schools, night spots and coffee houses.

In 1975, JC Power Outlet left the Myrrh label and Ron and John disbanded the group. Although they stopped touring and dropped the name, the duo still continued to write songs. During all the years the band had been together, Ron and John had remained in contact with Larry Norman. When Larry formed his own record label, he asked if they wanted to join him. They agreed, and Pantano/Salsbury became a part of solid rock. Their premier recording, entitled *Hit The Switch,* was produced by Larry Norman.

PANTRY, JOHN

John Pantry, a soft-spoken Englishman who is a producer-singer-songwriter, began his long, hard climb up the ladder to success as a studio engineer in London's famed West End.

The reputation he earned was largely due to his work on the production of albums by The Bee Gees, The Who and The New Seekers. But his quest for achievement caused John to leave the confines of the studio in order to search for wider musical horizons.

His involvement in the production of a Christian record, *Light Up The Fire,* was the first spark in a life that was soon to burn for Jesus Christ. The single placed high on the BBC's popularity charts, but after making that testimony and observing the lives of the Christian artists he

JOHN PANTRY: *"I found the thing I'd searched for all along"*

worked with, he began to feel the void at the center of his life.

Then, from the world of secular music, he moved to a vital, personal relationship with Jesus Christ. "When I read the words from You, somehow love just cut right through, and I found the thing I'd searched for all along."

Presently John, his wife, Jackie, and their children, Joanne and Benjie, are based in the United States and he is at Maranatha! Music. There he produced two albums for European release, co-produced and engineered the Ernie and Debby album, *Changin',* and produced Lewis McVay's exciting album *Spirit Of St. Lewis.*

PATILLO, LEON

"I see the emphasis of my ministry as giving freedom to believers through better communication with the Lord," says Leon Patillo. "I think my ministry is to all races, but especially to black people, who I believe are getting a lot of preaching but not much teaching."

There are those Christian musicians who are concerned about "crossing over" from acceptance by the Body of Christ to popularity on *Billboard*'s Hot 100 charts. Then there are those who have "crossed over" in the opposite direction—from the best the world can offer to a place where they are using their music to help Christians walk more closely with God.

Leon Patillo, formerly lead vocalist and keyboard player with the group Santana, is of the latter persuasion. Much of his time since leaving "the music business" has been spent studying the Word, praying and writing songs based on the scriptures.

Patillo's ministry began with the recording of his first solo album for Maranatha! Music, *Dance Children Dance,* which he produced and on which he plays most of the instruments. The album is a celebration of Leon's life in Jesus Christ, and is aimed both at the believer who already knows Him and the unbeliever who doesn't.

When not traveling or recording, Leon and his wife, Jackie, enjoy being at home in the mountains above the northern California coastal city of Santa Cruz.

PAXTON, GARY S.

LEON PATILLO: *Giving freedom to believers through better communication with the Lord*

Gary S. Paxton has been described as astonishing, outrageous, amazing, incredible and unbelievable. Artist, songwriter and the head of nine publishing, two production and nine record companies, and part owner of a studio, he has also won a Dove Award for co-producing *No Shortage* by The Imperials, and a Grammy for his own album.

Currently referred to as a "Mini-Empire," he has not always been on top. In 1970 he lost almost everything he had; then in 1971 everything turned around

for him and he was "saved." Since that time, he has directed his personal life toward Jesus. As a result he is not only a reformed and spiritually level person, but also a man who is once again tremendously successful.

Involved with his own television show, *The Gary S. Paxton Christian Grit Revue,* he also has plans for the production of

139

Christian animated cartoons to be used in churches as teaching tools for young people.

Along with all this, Paxton keeps up with a full touring schedule of concerts.

POPE, DAVE

"It's amazing how people want to put a label on what I do. They ask me whether I am an evangelist or a singer! I would like to think that I am both, because God has given me something to say and someone to share, and I would like to think that my music complements my message," says Midlands, England-born Dave Pope.

Dave organizes his ministry as an evangelistic and gospel singer. He prefers to hide the fact that he has an honors degree in Behavioral Science so that people can accept him for what he is—a down-to-earth guy with a genuine love and concern for people.

Pope's progress as a singer extends from his work with the Alethians, a folk group based in the Midlands, and also from his evangelistic ministry with the Movement for World Evangelization. He spends much of his time speaking and strumming in colleges, schools, coffee bars and churches.

He certainly has wide experience in communicating the gospel and has been involved in a variety of situations: TV programs for Ulster Television, Tyne Tees, Southern and Dutch TV, radio shows, two albums with the Alethians and two solo sets, with a third on the way. He has frequently appeared with Cliff Richard on the TEAR Fund Concerts, and has also begun to produce records for other gospel groups. His ministry has taken him to Eastern Europe, Western Europe, the United States, Scandinavia and South Africa, and his album *Writing On The Wall* is one of the best-selling, British-produced albums. But Dave prefers to brush such achievements to one side, and concentrate on his ministry.

POWELL, SARA JORDAN

Sara Jordan Powell, a native of Houston, is the daughter of the late Reverend Samuel A. Jordan and Mrs. Mabel Ruth Jordan. The wise religious teachings of God-fearing parents gave Sara a solid foundation that has motivated her Christian life.

She began singing during her early childhood. With her precocious talent and dedication, she traveled extensively with her evangelist father and family from coast to coast.

After resigning from a career of teaching, Sara became totally involved in witnessing through her singing ministry. She has received numerous citations and awards for ministries on radio, television, in concerts, churches and auditoriums, outdoor rallies and conventions and is also an outstanding recording artist.

Not only concerned with the land of the eternal day beyond the sunset, but also with "touching somebody's life" here and now, Sara expresses this dedication in song and testimony on university campuses, in hospitals, prison camps or wherever the need arises.

She has an irrevocable determination to communicate to all mankind the story of God's glorious salvation.

PRESLEY, ELVIS

Elvis Presley's undeniable influence on all aspects of modern music guarantees him a niche in the archives of gospel music. Born in East Tupelo, Mississippi on January 8, 1935, Elvis' spectacular rise to international stardom is now a legend. One of twin boys (the other died during birth), Elvis grew up in Mississippi and Tennessee, singing at home, for friends, at camp meetings. While working as a truck driver for $35 a week, he decided to change his luck, went to the offices of Sun Records in Memphis and was recorded by Sam Phillips. Contrary to the myth, he was not an overnight success, but when Colonel Parker stepped into his life, all of that changed. Elvis quickly moved to radio, television and movies. Parker went on to promote him to top worldwide success, adding to the Presley mystique by keeping the singer's private life totally under wraps.

Presley received 47 gold records. He recorded many gospel albums, including *His Hand In Mine, How Great Thou Art* and *He Touched Me*. It can be said that Elvis was truly a musical personality, with an influence transcending any single genre of our time. His original approach to music will not be soon forgotten. The Presley career ended with his death on August 16, 1977, but the legend and the unique legacy of recordings he left behind continue to intrigue his legions of admirers.

PRESTON, BILLY

Mention Billy Preston to just about anybody aware of the contemporary music scene and they will recognize the name. They'll recall his solo albums, his hit singles like "Will It Go Round In Circles" and "Nothing From Nothing," his association with The Beatles and appearance at the Concert for Bangladesh.

What most people don't realize is that Preston is also a long-established gospel performer. In fact, he has been playing gospel music since he was three years old, when he sat on the piano bench beside his mother and picked out tunes he had heard. By the age of seven, he was directing a hundred-voice choir at Victory Baptist Church in Los Angeles. At ten he was playing in church with James Cleveland and appearing with Mahalia Jackson. As a teenager he played and recorded along with Andrae Crouch in a gospel group called the Cogics.

In spite of his wide exposure to the wild world of secular rock, Billy Preston remains the humble servant of God through music. On each of his secular albums he includes at least one gospel song. He now has an opportunity to record albums which are exclusively gospel music.

The first of these, entitled *Behold*, on Word Records' Myrrh label, is not only Billy's first all-gospel collection, but also his strongest statement of his faith to date. As usual with his albums, Preston handles most of the songwriting duties himself. The result is one of his best lyrical efforts. Combined with his distinctive and unequaled keyboard work, the

BILLY PRESTON: *Playing gospel music since he was three years old*

Her first album for Light Records, *Back Home,* appeared in 1973.

Her five musicals for Light Records and Lexicon Music include *Our House, I Like the Sound of Music, And That's the Truth, The Best You Can Be* and her most recent, *Christmas 2001.*

Flo is active performing gospel music in concerts, at church meetings and in conferences, frequently appearing as a featured vocalist on radio network and television gospel programs, as well as composing new songs, many especially for children.

album promises a long and happy future for this very believing man of gospel music.

PRICE, FLO

As an actress, writer, composer and performer, Flo Price has specialized in writing children's musicals for the last five years.

She recorded her first album, *Let Not Your Heart Be Troubled,* for Word Records in 1959. Other Word releases include *Bright New World, Flo Price Sings* (with the Ralph Carmichael Orchestra), *Gonna Wake Up Singin'* and a children's album, *You Don't Have to be Very Big at All.*

FLO PRICE: *Specializing in writing children's musicals*

Hostess of the syndicated television series *Tree House Club,* she also has appeared on *Days of Our Lives* and has been featured in five movies, including *Beloved Enemy, The Haunted Church Bell, My Favorite Phony, God Owns My Business* and *Bringing In The Peach.*

She has authored three books for Word Books, including *Coffeetime Desserts* and her latest, *Super Salads,* featuring recipes of celebrities.

The National Evangelical Film Foundation chose Flo Price Best Female Vocalist in 1962 and 1970.

R

THE RAMBOS

Buck Rambo
Dottie Rambo
Pattie Carpenter

One of the best-known families in gospel music, Buck and Dottie Rambo have blended their down-home warmth with their uptown country sound to establish themselves as one of the most versatile and exciting groups on today's gospel music scene. A concert by The Rambos is highlighted by the favorites that have always thrilled their fans, such as "He Looked Beyond My Faults." Then there are the newer songs like "I've Never Been This Homesick," or "He Was The Talk Of The Town." For their efforts, they have received the coveted Grammy Award and various nominations for Dove Awards as well as being recipients of many gospel music fan awards throughout the years.

A large church in Indiana . . . a municipal auditorium in Georgia . . . a Jesus festival in Pennsylvania with forty thousand people . . . a small country church in Kentucky . . . a hospital in Vietnam . . . wherever The Rambos appear in concert, audiences agree that they remain Number One in gospel music.

Married over twenty-five years, Buck and Dottie have had almost fifty successful long-play albums, but their success has not changed them. With humility, they give all the credit to the Lord. The Rambo sound is never a duplication of anyone else's efforts.

The Rambos' rise to the top in gospel music is due largely to the unique and distinctive sound they create. This uniqueness is characterized by Dottie's famed

THE RAMBOS: *Never a duplication of anyone else's efforts*

songwriting. The Rambos perform only songs written by Dottie. She has written over seven hundred, each with a unique story behind it. Songwriting comes naturally to her. Her most recent work is a children's musical called *Down By The Creekbank*. She is currently working on an adult musical, as yet untitled.

Although many people believe that The Rambos are strictly country singers, they are mistaken. The harmonic blends of Buck's country-style singing and Dottie's mountain-style, black soul music combine to make the distinctive Rambo sound. It is impossible to classify The Rambos. They're just The Rambos, singing many different styles with their own brand of down-to-earthness.

The Rambos record on the Heart-Warming label. Their latest release is *Queen of Paradise*.

RAMBO, DOTTIE

The First Lady among gospel songwriters, Dottie Rambo has composed over seven hundred songs. Having written her first song at nine, she learned to play the guitar by the time she was eleven. Together with her husband, Buck, and Pattie Carpenter, Dottie travels as part of The Rambos.

Dottie is a fine vocalist offering vocal styles that range from down-home southern gospel to metropolitan country with a sprinkling of soul. Many of her songs have been recorded by major gospel figures. And as part of Country Music Week, she was honored in Nashville by BMI Records for her fine work in gospel

music. Her song called "Holy Spirit, Thou Art Welcome" was nominated for Best Song Award by the Gospel Music Association.

REBA

"Reba is definitely one of the best singers I've ever heard," says John Styll in *Contemporary Christian Music*. And that's just one of the favorable comments that Reba has been drawing from nationwide music critics. Reba has definitely come a long way from country gospel to contemporary gospel, while creating some of the finest music ever made.

Born in Kentucky, to Buck and Dottie Rambo, Reba traveled during her first six years with her singing parents, The Rambos. When she was thirteen, her parents sought a replacement for a singer who had married and left the group. Although she had never sung with her parents before, Reba had memorized all the lyrics and music of the songs they performed. They had difficulty finding someone with the right range to complement their sound, so Reba offered to rehearse with them. Stunning and delighting her parents with her ability to sing and harmonize, she became a member of The Rambos, and traveled the next six years with them, continuing her studies through correspondence. This resulted in her first song, "Keep on Marching Home," which was recorded on her first solo album, *Folk Side of Gospel*.

When Reba was nineteen, the Rambos took a year off and Reba headed for Cal-

DOTTIE RAMBO: *First lady among gospel songwriters*

ifornia. For nine months she sang with Andrae Crouch and The Disciples. This was a time of great musical expansion and spiritual growth for her. Crouch's influence on her life and his fresh, different way of expressing his love for God gave a new dimension to her relationship with Him. Fear of a distant, faraway God was replaced by a newfound, personal love relationship. After their year's hiatus, The Rambos resumed travel, rejoined by Reba until 1977—when she decided to launch a solo career.

Evidently Reba made the right de-

REBA: *"God on more of a human basis"*

cision. With two very successful new albums, *Lady* and *Lady Is A Child*, to her credit, she reaped the praises of both music-makers and listeners in Christian as well as secular fields. She has repeatedly been nominee and recipient of top musical awards. *Lady* received a Dove Award in 1977 for Best Contemporary Album. Appearing solo or with a seven-piece backup band effectively complementing her dynamism, her music and performances set a new standard in the inspirational market.

Reba is very serious about her ministry and has a deep desire to spread the gospel through music. Commenting on the songs of her two recent albums, Reba says: "I think they talk about God on more of a human basis. I've heard so much about God being far away, and I want to bring Him more to the people's level, to more of a father-relationship . . . a friend."

ERNIE AND DEBBIE RETTINO:
"Continuing our lives just growing together with the Lord"

THE REBELS QUARTET

Organized in 1949, The Rebels Quartet members have included John Matthews, Jimmy Taylor, Horace Parrish and London Parrish. Their most notable albums are *Sacred Gems, My Greatest Moment* and *Peace In The Valley,* while some of their most outstanding songs include "I'm Bound For That City," "What A Day That Will Be," "The Highest Hill" and "I'll Meet You By The River."

RETTINO, ERNIE AND DEBBIE

Ernie and Debbie Rettino, veterans of the Christian music ministry, are a multi-talented couple from a distinctive Judeo-Christian background (Debbie Kerner, daughter of a Jewish movie producer and a former Broadway chorus girl, and Ernest William Rettino, born into an Italian Jewish-Catholic family). They are articulate and enthusiastic about the changes in their lives produced by their personal relationship with Jesus Christ.

God has welded two dedicated and committed people into a devoted ministry. In their relationship they reflect the peace and power that can only be found in a strong personal relationship with Jesus Christ—a far cry from the insecurities of the jet-set Hollywood scene Debbie experienced as she grew up and that Ernie later knew in his varied show business career.

Debbie's life began changing from the day she knelt by her bed and asked Jesus to come into her life. Ernie entered a personal relationship with Christ after experiencing the tough world of professional entertainment and the heartache of family hardship and suffering. They both found new and exciting alterations in their lives as they grew in their individual relationships with God.

For Ernie, one of the stimulating changes was brought about by his meeting and friendship with Debbie Kerner, at Calvary Chapel, in Costa Mesa, California. From this grew a ministry as they shared in song together.

Debbie, who had already recorded a title on the very first Maranatha! Music album and released her first solo album, *Come Walk With Me,* confides—"I was very much in love with him, but we remained 'just friends.'" That is, until February 7, 1976, when, after five years of ministering the Word of Life together, they sealed a lifelong partnership in a Judeo-Christian ceremony at Calvary Chapel.

Changin', their album on Maranatha! Music, plus their three other albums—*Friends, Joy In The Morning, More Than Friends*—and their children's musical, *Joseph,* demonstrate the range and scope of their personal vision.

Ernie says it this way—"We're continuing our lives just growing together with the Lord as the center of our marriage and family." It's an infectious faith that is displayed in their lives which they share, openly and honestly, on their concert ministry tours and in their television and radio interviews.

149

JEANNIE C. RILEY: *Faith in the One who set her free*

THE REVELATOR QUARTET

Organized in 1957, the quartet members have included Scranton Ark Hall, Dale Baker, Kenneth R. Biggs, Jack K. Bryson, Jerry Evans, Bobby Burks, Sanford Williams, and Bobby Ball.

Their best known recordings are *Climbing Higher And Higher, What A Happy Day, Where No One Stands Alone, I'll Never Be Lonely* and *I've Heard About A City*.

RILEY, JEANNIE C.

Jeannie C. Riley, a country girl from Anson, Texas, came to Nashville to work on Music Row as a secretary with dreams of succeeding in the country music industry. This dream came true with the release of the multi-million-selling single which swept the nation in 1968—"Harper Valley PTA." In a short period, the life of Jeannie C. Riley went through a revolutionary change.

In 1972, she experienced a complete turnaround when she accepted Jesus Christ as her Savior. Since that time she has begun writing songs about her new experience with Christ. Jeannie established herself with the country market and then moved into the gospel field. Musically, she clings to her first love—down-home country pickin'. Lyrically she's singing a new song—of her faith in the One who set her free.

This change in her image was difficult to make, but because of her genuineness it is becoming a reality. Although Jeannie stopped working in clubs several years ago, fairs, concerts and television appearances have been constant. She has also turned up as a frequent guest on such Christian programs as *PTL* and *The 700 Club*.

Jeannie released a new album on the Cross-Country Label of Great Circle Records, a division of The Benson Company, entitled *Wings to Fly*. It contains her own songs and those of such other prominent gospel songwriters as John Stallings and Dottie Rambo.

Jeannie lives in Franklin, Tennessee, with her daughter, Kim.

ROBINSON, BISHOP

Born in New Rochelle, New York, Bishop Robinson is now a resident of the Bronx. At age eleven, he began playing the piano, while at fourteen, he founded his first gospel group, The Calvary Joy Gospel Singers, and went on to form The Holy Light Singers, The Gospel Light Singers, The Imperial Harmonettes, The Gospel Majors, The Joy Singers and The Jerusalem Specials.

The first professional groups he sang in were The Robert Paterson Singers and The Anna Tuell Holy Hour Singers. In 1972 he directed the Eastern New York Mass Choir (three hundred voices) of the International Churches of God in Christ. Bishop Robinson has written such songs as "Where There Is Life, There Is

151

Hope," "Thankful I'll Ever Be," "My Faith" and "Somewhere Over In Glory."

He records with the Garden of Prayer Cathedral Choir.

ROGERS, ROY AND DALE EVANS

Two of the greatest entertainers in show business history, Roy Rogers and Dale Evans, continue their mass popularity wherever they appear, either individually or together.

Roy and Dale have signed the 155-year-old American Bible Society's Christmas letter for the past several years and the number circulated has risen from 13,-369,030 copies in 1952 to 134,933,653 in 1975, proving their ever-increasing popularity with the public, as well as the phenomenal growth of the Society. Roy and Dale became Honorary Life Members of the Society in 1970. They are the only stars from the entertainment industry to be so honored.

Roy was selected by the Round Table International as Honorary Knight for Life and Dale as a Lady of Camelot. The citation, bestowed only eighteen times previously in thirty years and never before to show business personalities, recognized them for "distinguished service to humanity and to their country in the fields of clean entertainment, of unselfish and effective leadership in service of homeless and orphaned children, and to the mentally retarded, and as volunteer entertainers to the armed forces."

The Rogers family is well known for the adoption of orphans and more than five thousand charitable appearances. They are the only show-business couple to receive a national citation from the American Legion. Other awards include one to Dale as Woman of the World from International Orphans, Inc., and Church Woman of the Year from Religious Heritage of America.

Roy Rogers starred in innumerable feature films, thirty-five of them with Dale as his co-star. He was rated the number one box-office star of Westerns for twelve consecutive years. His movies are still playing in theaters throughout the world and all have been syndicated for domestic and foreign television. The couple's radio and television shows have achieved high ratings on three different networks.

Their activities include a multitude of individual or joint projects. Dale's albums *Get To Know The Lord, It's Real, Faith, Hope And Charity, Heart Of The Country* and *In The Sweet Bye And Bye,* are all released by Word Records.

Roy and Dale were married December 31, 1947. They have a family of nine children and sixteen grandchildren.

Throughout their careers, Roy Rogers and Dale Evans have maintained a magnificent image through their clean, wholesome entertainment. The Rogers represent complete, all-round, all-time, all-American, family entertainment. Their love of God and country is evident wherever they appear.

—S—

SANDQUIST, TED

Ted Sandquist has been an integral part of the Love Inn Community in Freeville, New York, since 1970. As Scott Ross' assistant, Ted has been responsible for activities ranging from administration to discipling. Ted was raised in a strong Christian environment. His father was the pastor of an Evangelical Covenant Church, and young Ted accepted the Lord when he was eleven years old. He is now involved in full-time ministry at the Love Inn Community and is well known as a musician for his songwriting abilities. He has written numerous praise and worship songs, and has been an integral part of coffee house and concert ministries. Many of his choruses are popular among church and youth groups, although most of the people singing the songs are not aware that Ted wrote them. Ted's first album, *Courts Of The King,* featured his sensitive songwriting talents, as well as those of Phil Keaggy, Nedra Ross and other members of the Love Inn Company.

THE SCENICLAND BOYS

Fay Sims—Bass
Stan Shuman—Baritone
Jerry Hester—Lead
Whitey Cantrell—Tenor
Jim Davis—Steel Guitar
Terry Weeks—Piano
Dennis Cagle—Bass
Randy Davis—Drums

The Scenicland Boys have been busy both entertaining and inspiring audiences for the past twenty years. They play music geared for today, modern, alive music using the piano, steel guitar, bass and drums. Singing and performing with excitement, quality and dignity, The Scenicland Boys have worked some of the largest concerts in gospel music, such as the National Quartet Convention, Blackwoods' Homecoming, Goodmans' Homecoming and the Silverdome in Pontiac, Michigan. They also make numerous television appearances on the *Gospel Singing Jubilee* and the *Warren Roberts Program,* as well as having their own television show.

SCENICLAND BOYS: *Music geared for today*

The Scenicland Boys have recorded over thirty albums and now own their own label, SRP. The smooth voices of the quartet blended with the sound of their four-piece band produce the southern gospel style for which the Scenicland Boys are most noted.

THE 2ND CHAPTER OF ACTS

Annie Herring
Nelly Greisen
Matthew Ward

"Growing in the Lord and being taught are no small part of our lives. We are learning who we are in Jesus and you do have to know yourself to minister effectively," says Buck Herring, manager and producer of The 2nd Chapter of Acts.

One of the first groups to pioneer the seventies sound known as Jesus music or gospel rock, this ensemble has a message about Jesus Christ. They emphasize that they should be described as a ministry, a family ministry. Annie Herring, Nelly Greisen and Matthew Ward

THE 2ND CHAPTER OF ACTS: *"Learning who we are in Jesus"*

SEGO BROTHERS & NAOMI: *Quality in its fullest*

are the family that comprises The 2nd Chapter of Acts.

They have performed from coast to coast and throughout Europe; they've shared ministries with Barry McGuire and Phil Keaggy and Annie was honored as Top New Female Vocalist of 1977 in the special gospel issue of *Record World* magazine. Their fifth album, recorded for Sparrow Records, was entitled *Mansion Builder*.

THE SEGO BROTHERS AND NAOMI

James Sego
W. R. Sego
Mike Sego
Ronnie Sego
Danny Clark
Eddie Boland
Gene Tucker
Naomi Sego

A rare combination of humility and sincerity coupled with their down-to-earth singing places The Sego Brothers and Naomi at the top of the list of favorites in the hearts of gospel fans throughout America.

Polished professionals who take their work seriously, The Segos boast a gospel record for having sold a million records of the hit song "Sorry I Never Knew You."

Talented, witty and sincere, The Segos have the unusual capacity for captivating an audience from the moment they walk on stage until they return for the last encore.

James Sego, who handles well the chore of master of ceremonies, possesses a seldom-found trait in the music business. Under James' guidance, the family group, who hail originally from Macon, Georgia, recorded and made famous the song "Sorry I Never Knew You," as well as the equally famous recording "Is My Lord Satisfied With Me."

The Segos make their home in White House, Tennessee, a suburb of Nashville.

The sound of The Sego Brothers and Naomi hinges on a country-gospel sound complemented with the rousing, touching soul-of-the-old-camp-meeting style.

Perhaps The Segos are best loved throughout America for the warmth and genuine feelings they project from the stage.

Quality in its fullest meaning denotes the warmth and love of God projected by The Segos.

THE SENSATIONAL FRIENDLY FOUR

Russell H. Hardy—Lead
Robert Fuller—Lead
George Bolden—Bass
Henry Fails—Baritone
Percy Tripp—Tenor

Since 1960, when The Sensational Friendly Four was organized in Selma, Alabama under the direction of Ernest Dillard, the group has grown both in members and stature to become known as one of the leading gospel aggregations as its members deliver God's message in their songs of praise.

The Sensational Friendly Four cut their first album, entitled *Home Going,* in 1975 and their second album, *This Little Light Of Mine,* was released a year later. Their third and fourth albums, *Back Home* and *Live So God Can Use You,* were released on the HSE label.

The group consists of Russell H. Hardy (lead); Robert Fuller (lead); George Bolden (bass); Henry Fails (baritone); and Percy Tripp (tenor); along with musicians Wayne Dillard, Henry Craig, Ronald Craig and Jim Hardy Jr.

THE SENSATIONAL GOSPELAIRES

The Rev. Walter Ellis
George Bowen
Clarence Ellis
Bernard Milliner
Larry Ellis
Bernard Ellis
Dryal Ellis
David Dickerson

The Sensational Gospelaires bring an exciting sound and rhythm to the gospel singing field. Organized in 1959 by J. T. Ziegler and David Dickerson, the group has traveled throughout the South and Midwest rendering spiritual inspiration.

The group consists of The Reverend Walter Ellis, George Bowen, Clarence Ellis, Bernard Milliner, Larry Ellis, Bernard Ellis, Dryal Ellis and David Dickerson.

THE SENSATIONAL HARMONIZERS

Still one of the hottest and freshest groups playing and singing today, The Sensational Harmonizers were founded over seventeen years ago by Billy George, with R. C. Williams, who named the group, Jerry Sillemon, Eldridge Taylor, Willie Sillemon and Sammie Hoof, lead singer.

Harmony is their specialty, as evidenced by their two lead singers—Jesse Williams and Richard Miles. Some of their most notable songs include "God Is Real," "Where Could I Go," "I Can't Make The Journey Alone" and "Back To The Dust."

SHARALEE

Sharalee Lucas, singer, composer, musician and actress, is truly something special. This vibrant new talent enchants all who come in contact with her and her work.

Sharalee has toured the world, giving concerts in Asia, Israel and Canada, in addition to the numerous colleges, universities and concert halls she has played in the United States. Perhaps her greatest honor was her invitation to perform before Congress and at the White House.

Married to Jerry Lucas, former New York Knicks basketball star, and mother of two, Sharalee makes her home in California. She has appeared on *The Tonight Show, Stand Up and Cheer, Your Hit*

Parade, Good Morning, America, Dan August, The Dating Game, Ed Sullivan, The Emmys and *The 700 Club*. She has done many network television commercials, sang the title song for the movie *Love Minus One,* and has three albums to her credit. In 1978 she hosted the Dove Awards. Sharalee has also performed at many conventions ranging from Miami to San Francisco, and in 1978 her first book, *Always Becoming,* was published.

Sharalee's first album on the Greentree label was *Daughter of Music.*

THE SHARRETTS

Fred Sharrett
Ed Sharrett
Bob Sharrett

Not since The Lettermen and The Beach Boys has there been such "pleasure-on-the-ears" harmony as The Sharretts' spirit-filled pure praise for the Lord.

Fred and Ed Sharrett are twins and Bob is two years younger. Together, the brothers form a trio that brings an exciting new sound to contemporary Christian music—hum-along melodies with musical excellence, orchestral perfection and a variety of sounds extending from easy listening to up-tempo, smooth, contemporary pop.

As active members of their local church during their youth, the trio started singing gospel music at an early age. Each brother began individual voice lessons at age five. The work, practice, prayer and discipline have paid off, for the Sharretts present musical enjoyment that can only be produced by a closely-knit, family-loving group.

The boys started singing publicly in churches first, but soon their performances took them to county fairs and other forms of competition. In addition to their singing abilities, Fred played trombone and Ed played trumpet in the high school band. At the same time, Bob was studying classical guitar.

By the time they attended Southeastern Bible College, the Sharretts had become well known as a very popular singing group. Almost every weekend was filled with traveling somewhere to sing the Lord's praises.

SHARALEE: *"Always Becoming"*

The Sharretts have recorded two albums for Word, Inc., and their latest release, *You Turn Me Around,* on the DaySpring label, features an all-star cast of musicians and promises to take them onto a whole new musical plateau.

SHEA, GEORGE BEVERLY

Often called "America's Most Beloved Gospel Singer," George Beverly Shea cannot be claimed by only one country. Born in Canada and now residing in the United States (in Western Springs, Ill.), he is a favorite in many nations. He was the best-known vocalist of Billy Graham's Crusades and has been singing gospel around the globe for more than thirty years.

Born in Winchester, Ontario, the son of a Methodist minister, his first public appearance was in the choir of his father's church.

Since 1944 he has been heard regularly on network radio. In more recent years, his bass-baritone voice has also been transmitted on weekly, worldwide short-wave programs.

Every hymn he sings is a testimony to the saving power of Jesus Christ and to Shea's faith in Him. He is also a composer, and the songs he has written incorporate the same message. One of his best-known solos is "I'd Rather Have Jesus." Others include "The Wonder Of It All," "Sing Me A Song Of Sharon's Rose" and "I Love Thy Presence, Lord."

His network radio singing started on *Club Time,* a program carried for over eight years on ABC and the Armed Forces networks. Billy Graham recalled

hearing Shea's radio singing and enlisted him to help with his broadcast—the beginning of their long association. The fledgling evangelistic team worked together in several Graham Crusades.

Known and loved by millions, Shea is noted for the simplicity of his faith and testimony. All his life and work is aimed at telling "of the Christ who died for me."

In 1978, The Gospel Music Association bestowed its highest honor on Shea by electing him to the Gospel Music Hall of Fame.

SHEPPARD, TIM

Tim Sheppard, composer, lyricist and pianist, says that God has equipped him to share Jesus with his generation: "In obedience to God's call on my life, I wish to share His life and love with everyone I meet."

Being a "preacher's kid," Tim was raised in a healthy Christian environment. At age sixteen, he met Jesus Christ and began focusing his songwriting on his daily Christian experiences. He started singing in churches and coffeehouses, strongly emphasizing that musical ability alone would not satisfy a person's heart.

Tim's abilities were recognized internationally in 1975 when he won the Amateur Gospel Award of the American Song Festival based in Hollywood. His song "Sweet Lovin' Grace" was chosen over fifty thousand others in this international songwriting competition.

That same year, with the help of recording artist and composer Dallas Holm, Tim submitted some of his songs to The

GEORGE BEVERLY SHEA: *"America's Most Beloved Gospel Singer"*

Imperials, who recorded "Would You Believe In Me?" They have since recorded more of Tim's songs as have other groups such as Truth, Andrus, Blackwood & Co., The Sharrett Brothers and Gary McSpadden.

In 1976, Holm introduced Sheppard to Phil Johnson, house producer for The Benson Company in Nashville. Johnson signed Tim to a recording contract with Greentree Records, Benson's contemporary Christian label. Since then he's re-leased two albums, *Diary* and *Inside My Room,* both of which feature his original compositions. His third album on Greentree Records, *Songtailor,* includes songs such as "Hey There Stranger," "Fiddler," "Till I Met You" and "Come Back Home," plus seven more.

Since 1976, Tim has been traveling full-time in the United States and Canada, continuing his concert ministry in churches, coffeehouses, colleges and concert halls. He has appeared in concert with such artists as Andrae Crouch, Chuck Girard, The Rambos, The Archers, Reba and Dallas Holm.

Tim uses a personal and honest approach in his concert ministry. "Just as a person would write entries in a diary, I have written entries with my music," explains Tim. "I want to open my musical diary and share it with others."

SLAUGHTER, HENRY AND HAZEL

Henry and Hazel Slaughter are a gifted husband-and-wife team. They combine their strong faith with an excellent musical presentation to create a warm, spiritual atmosphere at all of their concerts.

The Slaughters have released fifteen albums on the HeartWarming label, including four instrumental albums by Henry. He was honored with the Gospel Music Association's Dove Award as Best Gospel Instrumentalist for five consecutive years, and has written such songs as "The Answer Came," "What A Precious Friend Is He," "I've Never Loved Him Better Than Today," "The Sweetest Hal-

TIM SHEPPARD: *"I want to open my musical diary and share it with others"*

HENRY AND HAZEL SLAUGHTER: *Motivated by the love the Lord has given them*

lelujah" and "If The Lord Wasn't Walking By My Side."

They appear regularly as guests on three national telecasts and present approximately 150 concerts each year. Henry writes and publishes successful gospel piano and organ instruction courses, and also produces various gospel recording artists in his recording studio in Nashville.

The Slaughters' latest album is entitled *Just The Way We Are.*

Henry and Hazel share a part of their lives with audiences as they travel across the country, motivated by the love the Lord has given them.

163

SMITH, CONNIE

"I feel God wants me workin' for whatever purpose and I'm not happy unless I do what I feel He wants me to do," said Connie Smith in an interview in *Nashville Gospel* magazine.

Songwriter and singer Connie Smith didn't always have that relationship with God. Born in Indiana and raised in West Virginia and Ohio, her childhood was filled with heartaches and deprivation. Then, in 1964, she became an almost overnight sensation with her version of Bill Anderson's "Once A Day." She had several other songs at the top of the charts and for a while was called "the Cinderella girl of country music." Voted the most promising country singer of 1964 by *Billboard* and Most Outstanding Female Country Vocalist in 1966 by *Cashbox,* Connie Smith went on to earn numerous other awards. Her records have been bestsellers since she began her career. In 1965 she became a regular on Grand Ole Opry and also starred in a number of country movies including *Las Vegas Hillbillies* and *Second Fiddle to a Steel Guitar.*

Yet, up to the time that Connie Smith discovered her own personal faith, her life was not particularly happy. Her conversion came when she was singing on a gospel TV show and the talk turned to God. "I started crying just like I did in church," she told *Nashville Gospel* magazine. "When I found God through Jesus and found out that He loved me . . . that's what really saved my life."

Her life has changed drastically since that time. With a family that includes two children from her previous marriages and three with her present husband, Marshall, she reported to *Nashville Gospel* that "a whole other area of my life has opened up. A married life in the Lord. . . . I've always had a lot of inhibitions about my singing. . . . But with the Lord, I say, well, I really like this song and I'd like to sing it. . . . So I'm a lot freer in my singing. . . . God chose me to make music. . . . I'm still waitin' on the Lord. I thought probably He'd have my husband be a great preacher and let me be his singer. And I'm just waitin' on that."

SNELL, ADRIAN

At the ripe old age of six, when most children are learning to read and write, Adrian Snell composed his first piece of piano music.

Though it was far less ambitious than the symphony Mozart wrote at that age, it was the beginning of a life of music which was to take this bishop's son into one of the most effective contemporary music ministries in the United Kingdom.

Over the years the multi-talented composer-singer has extended his instrumental expertise to the organ, synthesizer, acoustic and electric guitars, double bass, cello, percussion and harmonica.

So far Snell's career has produced three albums, including *Listen To The Peace* which was voted Top British Gospel Album of 1978.

Both secular and Christian critics have recognized the unique style of Snell's music, blending jazz, rock and the classics.

THE SOUL STIRRERS

James Davis—Lead
Dillard Crume—Lead
Rufus Crume—Baritone, Bass Guitar
Arthur Crume—Tenor, Guitar

The Soul Stirrers have long been recognized as one of the nation's top gospel groups. For over a quarter century, they have been synonymous with the most intense inspirational and highly perfected group singing in the entire gospel world. With various changes in personnel, The Soul Stirrers have toured the nation almost constantly since their founding in 1934. Considering the fact that they have been singing for many years, the two recently acquired lead singers, James Davis and Dillard Crume, give the group a fresh new sound.

The background blending, however, has remained unchanged through the years and therein lies a reason. Rufus Crume, baritone singer who plays the bass guitar, and Arthur Crume, tenor singer who plays lead guitar, are the oldest members of the group in terms of service. These gentlemen have worked very hard to maintain the consistently smooth and blending harmonies that cushion and enhance the lead singers.

Some of the great lead singers who have worked as members of the group: Jimmy Outlaw, Paul Foster, Sam Cooke, Johnnie Taylor and R. H. Harris.

THE SPEER FAMILY

Brock Speer
Ben Speer
Faye Speer
Brian Speer
Harold Lane—Arranger, Songwriter
Diane Mays—Lead, Piano
John Mays—Bass
Steve Williams—Guitar

A unique talent, a great performance and strong communication are all facets of America's First Family of gospel music, The Speers.

A Speers concert is inspirational entertainment in its highest form, the concept which guided Dad Speer's career from its earliest beginnings in 1921.

Third-generation Speers continue to share their music with all ages. Their repertoire includes old favorites as well as contemporary songs and arrangements that have introduced younger audiences to the Speer sound.

Mom and Dad Speer, who originally envisioned this special ministry, developed the group and then left it under the capable leadership of Ben and Brock Speer. They are joined by Brock's wife, Faye, and son, Brian. "Adopted Speers" are: Harold Lane, arranger and songwriter; Diane Mays, lead singer and pianist, husband John playing bass; and Steve Williams on guitar. Their style ranges from old-time southern gospel to bright new progressive gospel.

Their distinguished contributions to the industry have earned the Speers the following honors:

The Gospel Music Association's Dove Award, presented to them seven times for Mixed Gospel Group of the year.

The Gospel Music Association's Dove Award, for best Traditional Gospel Album of the year.

THE SPEER FAMILY: *America's First Family of Gospel Music*

Grammy nomination for the album *Cornerstone* from the National Association of Recording Arts and Sciences.

Dad, Mom and Brock Speer were inducted into the prestigious Gospel Music Association Hall of Fame in Nashville.

THE STATESMEN

Hovie Lister—Piano, M.C.
Tommy Thompson—Bass
Ed Hill—Baritone
R. D. Rozell—Tenor
Budd Burton—Lead

From 1948, when the idea of The Statesmen was born to the mind of Hovie Lister, until now, it has been years of hard work and many hundreds of thousands of miles traveled to reach the plateau of Number One. In sound, style and presentation, they have been the pacesetters in every phase of gospel music.

But, The Statesmen have known bad and good times. From a meager beginning with a local radio show and their own custom record label, they traveled thousands of miles at a very nominal remuneration, crowded into an automobile, missing many meals to meet a demanding schedule. The Statesmen, who found that humility, sincerity, friendliness, hard work and dedication paid off handsomely for them, made a name for themselves that is synonymous with gospel music.

For many years The Statesmen were among the top sellers of RCA, grew to the stature of appearances on syndicated television and radio shows seen and heard

HOVIE LISTER: *The idea of The Statesmen was born to his mind*

via the NBC, CBS and ABC networks on Garroway's Wide Wide World, and the Jimmy Dean Show, plus many others; were selected to record the theme from two major film productions. . . . "God Is My Partner" and "A Man Called Peter."

Hovie Lister and The Statesmen, with God-given talent and desire to give of themselves to others, have worked diligently and sincerely to enhance and perfect every phase of their life by devoting this talent and their every waking hour to gospel music. They have attained a place unrivaled in the hearts of millions of dedicated Christian men, women and children, as well as in the whole entertainment industry.

THE STATESMEN: *God-given talent and desire to give of themselves*

STONEHILL, RANDY

Randy Stonehill is tall and lean, with an open, friendly face. He started singing at four, played the guitar at ten and started his first rock and roll band at fifteen.

Randy's friendship with Larry Norman led him to his spiritual ministry; he found Christ at the age of eighteen.

After that Randy began writing down his spiritual feelings in the medium that came most naturally to him—his music. His songs have been described as "brilliant excursions into the regions of the heart, of hope and faith and doubt."

In 1970, Randy recorded "Born Twice" and sang the lead role in Jimmy Owen's first musical, *Show Me.* He's acted in three movies, but is probably better known for singing "Gone Away" and his own song, "I Love You," in the Billy Graham film *Time To Run.* "I Love You" and "Christmas Song For All Year Round" are other notable Stonehill contributions to the field of Jesus music.

Though still a prolific songwriter, Randy devotes most of his time to a demanding concert schedule that spans both the United States and England.

STOOKEY, NOEL PAUL

Known to many as Paul, of Peter, Paul & Mary, Noel Paul Stookey has totally changed his life and now lives quietly in Blue Hill, Maine, with his wife, Betty, and his three children.

His conversion to Christ created the change: "My old life was discarded—I woke up the next morning and I was new—and the Spirit made me different. The old Noel was replaced with the new."

Today he is at home in Maine, running his Neworld Productions, a recording/animation studio complex, as an alternative for musicians who wish to create, free of city distractions. His albums, *Real to Reel,* a live concert recorded in Australia, and *Something New and Fresh,* are on Neworld and distributed by Sparrow Records.

Although he achieved fame and fortune in the 1960s, he believes he did not find himself until he gave himself to Jesus Christ. "I'm happy now only in my relationship with Christ," he says. "That means total commitment."

NOEL PAUL STOOKEY: *"The old Noel was replaced with the new"*

J. D. SUMNER AND THE STAMPS

"Gospel music is more than standing on a stage somewhere singing or a way to earn a living. It's more than that to me, much more. Gospel music is my life." Those words from J. D. Sumner tell just what he and The Stamps stand for—belief in gospel music and belief in love. His life has been spent in the effort to bring recognition to gospel music.

Sumner first gained recognition as the bass singer for The Blackwood Brothers Quartet. He was given the job in 1954 after the tragic plane crash that took the lives of R. W. Blackwood Sr. and Bill Lyles Sr. The marriage of Sumner and The Stamps came through a quirk of fate in 1963. James Blackwood was looking for a publishing company to purchase and bought the music company owned by Frank Stamps. In purchasing the Stamps Publishing Company, J. D. and James also inherited The Stamps Quartet, which was at that time a convention group. J. D. developed them into a professional quartet that ranks as one of gospel's all-time best.

As a singer J. D. has been called the world's lowest bass voice. As a writer he has held the record for having more songs recorded than any other gospel music composer. Among his credits are: "The Old Country Church," "Crossing Chilly Jordan," "He Means All The World To Me," "Inside The Gate" and "Lord, Teach Me How To Pray."

People often try to label a gospel group, using words like "pure gospel" or "contemporary gospel." The Stamps defy labeling. They are simply singers who sing the good news. Without a doubt, J. D. Sumner and The Stamps have been one of the most influential forces in gospel music. With moral and financial support from J. D. and the Blackwood organization, the National Quartet Convention was brought to life, an event that brings together entertainers and fans from all over the world.

J. D. and The Stamps have helped open new doors for gospel music, singing in churches, concert halls and touring with the late Elvis Presley. As J. D. has stated in his book *Gospel Music Is My Life* and in many interviews, "Gospel music was designed by Christian people as a means of reaching the lost. I believe that so deeply that I wouldn't be on the road as much as I am, staying away from my family, if it were not so. If we can inspire people to live better lives, we've performed a ministry."

SUTTER, LYNN

Lynn Sutter combines her delicate vocal artistry with a personal sensitivity that she brings to audiences throughout America.

She was born in Oklahoma but now lives in Athens, Georgia. A young woman, Lynn has committed her life to

J. D. SUMNER AND THE STAMPS: *"Gospel music is my life"*

the Lord. With His leadership, her life has become exciting and fulfilling, highlighted by an equal amount of struggles and victories. Lynn's singing performance communicates the joy, vitality and constant commitment of her faith in Christ. Through her singing, she focuses attention on relationships with people and the Lord. Her vocal selections range from lovely, soft ballads to up-tempo traditional favorites. Each is warm, tender and sincere and flows directly from the heart, with words and music revealing her hopes, aspirations, misgivings, apprehensions, insights and observations.

Lynn's debut album, *Everlasting Kind Of Love,* is on the DaySpring label. The album is highlighted by a special duet number sung by Lynn and Chris Christian, entitled "Heed The Call." Other songs include "More of You" and "It's A New Day."

SWAGGART, JIMMY

Jimmy Swaggart is one of the best-known evangelists in the world today. A native of Ferriday, Louisiana, Jimmy surrendered to the ministry in the early 1950s, and in 1958 entered full-time evangelistic work. A major part of his ministry is his music. He began playing and singing before he preached, and, from the beginning, his audiences loved his music. Today Jimmy Swaggart has recorded thirty-eight albums and sold over six million copies, an achievement that places his sales among the largest in the gospel-record industry.

The ministry of Jimmy Swaggart is having a very real impact on the world. His love for the Lord and his genuine concern for people is demonstrated every time he appears.

Jimmy Swaggart has become one of the most recognizable people in gospel music. He preaches daily on *The Camp-Meeting Hour,* a fifteen-minute radio broadcast aired on over 540 stations. There is ample evidence to support the claim that he is "the most powerful radio preacher in the world." His weekly thirty-minute television program is offered on some two hundred stations in the United States and Canada.

Jimmy records for The Benson Company on the Jim Records label. His most recent albums are *Somewhere Listenin',* *The Jimmy Swaggart Christmas Spirit* and *Looking For A City.*

THE SWEET COMFORT BAND

Kevin Thompson—Guitar
Bryan Duncan—Keyboard
Rick Thompson—Drums
Randy Thomas—Guitar

"We let people know there is hope and it's simple," says Kevin Thompson, leader of The Sweet Comfort Band.

A Light Records recording group, The

JIMMY SWAGGART: *Having a very real impact on the world today*

173

Sweet Comfort Band is unique among Christian groups. They are among the hardest-working bands on the scene today, and have been especially successful in breaking into secular concerts and airplay.

Their initial album was released in 1976 on Maranatha! Music, and was successful enough to get the band booked for college concerts in California.

Kevin Thompson recalls, "Most of us did some secular work when we were younger and saw the futility of that because music alone doesn't satisfy. Our completion and satisfaction is in Jesus Christ."

In the summer of 1978 The Sweet Comfort Band signed with Light Records and production began on their new album, *Breakin' The Ice*. The music is progressive, and the message is enhanced by it.

The Band has appeared on the same program with Andrae Crouch, B. J. Thomas and Paul Stookey.

Based in Riverside, California, The Sweet Comfort Band now tours nationally, frequently adding a horn section to present a big, full sound.

The ministry of The Sweet Comfort Band is skillfully directed to the nonbeliever. Kevin Thompson sums up the band members' feelings, saying, "We have got to be recognized by the quality of our music to catch the non-Christian listener."

SWEET COMFORT BAND: *"We let people know there is hope"*

T

TAYLOR, DANNY

Whenever Danny Taylor is asked to describe the purpose of his music, his answer is always the same—"to bring healing." In our complex society, Danny tries to offer music that brings mental and spiritual healing to his listening audience.

Danny was born in Bremerton, Washington, and began playing guitar at the age of six. From that time on, music played a vital role in his life. In the fifth grade, he became interested in the drums and joined the school band. By the time he was fourteen, he was playing drums professionally.

In the spring of 1969, Danny began to devote his full time to a music ministry. He recorded his first album, *Taylor Made,* which includes ten of his earliest songs. In 1971, Danny did two songs: "You Can Go Your Way" and "If Jesus Came Today" on Metromedia Records.

In 1972 he sang at the first "Jesus Joy Concert" at Carnegie Hall in New York City. Combining Danny's ministry with audience response, Tempo Records released *Danny Taylor Live at Carnegie Hall.* Later in the same year, Danny appeared at Madison Square Garden, Carnegie Hall and Jesus '73, a teaching and music festival.

In the fall of 1977, Danny signed with New Pax Records and recorded a live album in Kansas City called *I'm Not A One Man Show.* He now makes Nashville his home, where he hopes to write more and become a team member of the Paragon/ New Pax family.

It is one of Danny's greatest desires to see men and women experience a newness in their life that only Christ can bring.

THE TELESTIALS

Beth Glass—Alto
Bethany Glass Brown—Alto
Betty Holmes—Alto
Roger Holmes—M.C.
Jerry Brown—Bass
Terry Darnell—Drums
Rodney LaShum—Piano
Michael Jan Lancaster—Lead

Eleven years of hard lessons, struggle, laughter, tears and prayer have thrust The Telestials into the seventies with their songs high on the list of gospel music's favorites. "Here They Come,"

THE TELESTIALS: *Versatility and spirituality*

written by group members and a Dove Award finalist in 1976, was selected as one of the top ten songs of the year by the Gospel Music Association. In 1977, "One Way Flight," another gospel hit written by group members, was also a Dove Award finalist and voted most popular song of the year by SESAC, as "Here They Come" had been the previous year.

The Telestials, who were also nominated for Best Mixed Group in 1977, make numerous television appearances. Among them are Nashville's *Grand Ole Gospel,* Jimmy Snow's *Ole Time Gospel Hour, 700 Club, PTL Club,* and *The Gospel Singing Jubilee.* They have nine albums to their credit. One of their most recent, *Experience The Telestials Live!,* was a combination of versatility and spirituality, reflecting the writing abilities of the group.

THOMAS, B. J.

"Ya know, sometimes you really have to be down flat on your back before you can tell which way is up," says B. J. Thomas. Those may be unusual words for the man who sang "Play Another Somebody Done Somebody Wrong Song," "Raindrops Keep Falling On My Head," "Hooked On A Feeling," "Mighty Clouds of Joy" and "I Just Can't Help Believing."

But despite his successful singing career, B. J. was miserable. "I was into everything from pills to cocaine," he said. "I was a pretty bad person." It seemed as if he was about as far gone as anyone could be.

Success did nothing to help B. J. straighten out his personal life. Deep inside, he says, he knew not only that he had a problem, but also what the solution was. He honestly wanted to find God, but he just didn't know how to go about it.

B. J.'s first active participation in music took place in school and church choirs. When he was fifteen his love for popular music motivated him to join a local Houston rock band, The Triumphs. They began to fare well in the Houston area, and then in 1965 they scored a national hit with Hank Williams' song "I'm So Lonesome I Could Cry." The record landed the group a contract with Scepter Records and "I'm So Lonesome" became a million-seller.

After that, B. J. toured with many top-name performers as a solo. "That was really the best time of my life," he says. "I really enjoyed it." And his joy was reflected in his "Hooked On A Feeling," which sold two million copies for starters. When he collaborated with Hal David and Burt Bacharach, one of the smash hits of the season was born—"Raindrops Keep Falling On My Head." "Everybody's Out Of Town" was yet another hit song for B. J. and the David-Bacharach team. But it was 1975 before he scored with another number-one song, even though several of his earlier records had sold in excess of one million copies. The new hit was "Play Another Somebody Done Somebody Wrong Song."

In 1976 Thomas was bankrupt. This was a sign of a new beginning for him. As he explained it, "In the death of every vision there is the birth of another vision." In January, 1976 he yielded totally to Jesus and said goodbye to his drug bondage.

177

B. J. THOMAS: *Testimony and gospel in each program*

His life has not been the same since then. He's now back with Gloria, his wife, and is completely drug-free. He hasn't given up his entertainment career, but he now includes his testimony and gospel songs in each program. He feels that's the best way he can reach those who have not yet come to Christ.

His first album on Myrrh was *Home Where I Belong*. It thrilled Christians all across the nation as well as the critics.

The album brought him a Grammy Award, Dove Award and *Record World*'s Gospel Album of the Year Award. His second Myrrh album was *Happy Man*.

Now, when B. J. Thomas ends his performances, he stops everything and gives his testimony. Then he closes with what has become his new theme song: "Doctor God." "The testimony I give at the end of my show opens up many ways of meeting people."

THE THRASHER BROTHERS

Jim Thrasher—Tenor
John Gresham—Bass
Joe Thrasher—Lead
Buddy Thrasher—Baritone
Roger Hallmark—Banjo
Tommy Watwood—Bass Guitar
Goldie Ashton—Drums
Danny Frabel—Sax
Steve Payne—Piano

Excitingly alive, exceptionally vivacious, these are the adjectives applied to The Thrasher Brothers. They were the first gospel group to appear on network television (*The Ted Mack Show,* 1953) and now have extended to their own exciting television show, *America Sings.*

Performing to over 2,130,000 each week via TV, they move skillfully through songs of patriotism and inspiration. Blending with harmony and unprecedented rhythm, they grace both stage and television with their singing and instrumentation. They adeptly apply electric guitar, drum, three trumpets and piano in a unique style that enraptures an audience.

The Thrasher Brothers have been nominated for and ended up in the Top Five in the NARS (Grammy awards) for four years in a row. In 1975 they introduced the song "One Day At A Time" which won the Dove Award at the Gospel Music Association Convention in Nashville.

All are musicians par excellence, playing several instruments each.

THE THRASHER BROTHERS: *Songs of patriotism and inspiration*

TORNQUIST, EVIE

Since her high school days, Evie Tornquist has been traveling between continents, spreading her message of the Christian lifestyle with enthusiasm and grace. She now tours almost all the time, touching down in cities like Detroit, London, Seattle, Sydney, New York, Los Angeles and Waco, Texas.

Evie's career began almost by accident when she was fourteen and visiting Norway with her parents, who are native Norwegians. The leader of a camp she was attending asked her if she would sing some gospel music at a camp meeting. A member of the audience was a director of a national television program, and after her performance he asked her to appear on his talk show. Evie sang three songs on the program and chatted casually with the other guests, which was a breath of fresh air compared to the typically stiff formality of Scandinavian television. So impressive was her appearance that she was deluged with offers to come and sing; she accepted eighty of them.

Evie Tornquist's fame spread from Europe to Canada and from there to the United States as well as Australia. In the eight years since she started performing publicly, Evie has established an impressive set of credentials. She has appeared in Carnegie Hall before the King of Norway and has sung for the President of the United States. She has been voted top female gospel artist in America by *Record World,* and has been nominated for a Grammy award.

But throughout her remarkable career, Evie has refused to compromise her principles and her commitment for the sake of success. She has turned down offers from record companies that wanted her to include some secular songs in her repertoire, and has declined to appear on talk shows in the United States if allowed to sing only pop songs.

Three of her popular works are the chart-topping *Mirror,* her Christmas album, *Come On Ring Those Bells,* and *A Little Song of Joy for My Little Friends.* This latter album is a departure for Evie in that it is devoted to songs, both old and new, for children. It's the fruit of an idea which Evie, always popular with the children, has had for years.

Evie records for Word Records.

TURNER, NORRIS

Turner was born in Troy, South Carolina, and started singing with a group called The Spiritualaires while in high school. He then moved to Brooklyn, where he sang with The Selahs.

Returning home after studying music at the American Guild of Variety Artists, he joined The Golden Stars of Greenwood, South Carolina. Some of their biggest recordings were "Searching For Jesus " and "Family Prayer." His first album on HSE Records, *Stop And Get Religion,* was highly praised because of Turner's ability to communicate his loving message through his songs. His second album, *I Want To Be Ready,* contained such outstanding songs as "Waiting And Watching," "They Call Me Crazy" and "Give God A Chance."

EVIE TORNQUIST: *Refuses to compromise her principles*

V

THE VOICES OF NASHVILLE

The Voices Of Nashville were organized in the late 1960s by Dr. Morgan Babb of radio station WVOL in Nashville. They are well known because of their two lead singers, Willie Love and Thomas Huggins Jr. Love was formerly lead singer for The Fairfield Four and Huggins was the baritone singer for the group. Their songs include such great favorites as "Tell God," "Just A Little More Time" and "Jesus I'll Never Forget."

W

WALKER, ALBERTINA

Albertina Walker, a native Chicagoan, is a gospel artist with a radiant spiritual glow that reflects her religious convictions. An institution as a gospel soloist of exceptional ability, she evokes a definite spiritual emotion in the souls of her listeners.

Albertina was one of one hundred women across the nation to receive an award on April 12, 1975 at Family Affair (sponsored by Operation PUSH) for outstanding service in the field of religion.

A lifetime member of West Point Baptist Church, she is featured in Volume I of the three-volume *Contemporary Black Americans,* put out by Johnson Publishing Company. Miss Walker is a member of the executive Board of PUSH, the National Council of Negro Women, the Chicago Urban League, the board of directors of Mau-Glo Day Care Center for Mentally Retarded Children and the American Federation of Television and Radio Artists.

She possesses two gold records.

THE ALWYN WALL BAND

Alwyn Wall—Guitar
Norman Barrat—Lead Guitar
Tony Hudson—Bass
Nick Brotherwood—Drums
Phil Holmes—Keyboard

Alwyn Wall is no stranger to America. He toured the United States some six times with Malcolm Wild, before they separated in 1976 to pursue individual ministries. Alwyn, born in 1949, was brought up on rock and roll. He was four years old when the first rock and roll record hit the American charts. Alwyn picked up a guitar when he was twelve, and formed his first group, The Night Riders, two years later. At fifteen, he joined The Zodiacs where he began his long friendship with Malcolm Wild.

The group's debut release, *The Prize,* spotlighted Alwyn's personal style of song writing. Included are songs about places where he has lived, the trials and joys of life on the road and his relationship with the Lord. Because they are a direct result

of things Alwyn has experienced, his songs are eminently human and generate immediate empathy from his audience.

The rest of the band includes lead guitarist Norman Barrat whose fame traces back to his days with the English rock group, Gravytrain. After he became a Christian, Norman played with the Christian group The Mighty Flyers. Bassist Tony Hudson and drummer Nick Brotherwood were also members of The Mighty Flyers. Performing on keyboard is Phil Holmes, whose musical experience goes back to his days with his own group, Apple Crumble.

THE WALL BROS. BAND

Kraig Wall—Vocals, Keyboards
Greg Wall—Vocals, Bass, Guitar
Randy Nelson—Vocals, Bass, Guitar
Bill Catron—Drums

Believing music to be one of the most effective communicators around, The Wall Bros. Band mixes theirs with the all-important message of the fulfilling and exciting life that can be lived by Christians.

Each member of the group is well qualified, and emerged from a solid musical background. Kraig Wall serves as vocalist and keyboard player for the band while brother Greg is a talented guitarist, bass player and vocalist. In 1977, bass player, guitarist and vocalist Randy Nelson joined forces with the Walls, and with the recent addition of drummer Bill Catron, the picture of The Wall Bros. Band is complete.

183

THE WALL BROS. BAND: *A strong Christian testimony*

Aside from their tremendous capabilities as musicians, the group also composes much of their own material. Additional compositions are penned by Lance DeMers, former drummer for the band.

In concert, The Wall Brothers exert a strong Christian testimony and a very unusual accessibility both onstage and off.

Their latest album, *Start All Over Again,* was recorded on the Greentree label and includes such songs as "I Am," "Walking On The Water" and "Clouds Of Joy."

The Wall Brothers perform at colleges and concert halls as well as churches throughout the country. They are rapidly becoming one of the most popular Christian bands within the gospel music industry.

WARD, CLARA

Born in Philadelphia, on April 21, 1924, the late Clara Ward, a dedicated Christian and one of the greatest gospel singers, composed over two hundred gospel songs. Among the favorites is "How I Got Over," which was a stellar vehicle for the late Mahalia Jackson. Other Ward compositions include "Packing Up," "Come In The Prayer Room" and "Prince Of Peace," each having attained gold-record status.

The youngest of three children born to George and Gertrude Ward, she received an early education in Christian training. At the age of five she joined the Ebenezer Baptist Church and, later, the Faith Tabernacle Mutchmore Memorial Baptist Church, and the Miracle Temple of Faith For All People, of which her mother was pastor. Clara was a very dedicated Christian, devoting her life to the singing of the gospel all over the world. Clara, her mother and her sister, Willa, sang together as a trio for eleven years, traveling extensively throughout the United States. After Willa's marriage, Mrs. Ward added Henrietta Waddy and Marion Williams, and the trio became The Original Famous Ward Singers.

Devoted to her mother, Clara did all she could to make her happy, fulfilling her mother's dream of thirty-five years by giving one tenth of her earnings to God's work.

Clara Ward died January 16, 1973. In the summer of 1977, she was saluted in a special display honoring women in music at the Songwriters Hall of Fame in New York City.

DEAN WILDER: *Has achieved much in the sacred concert field*

WILDER, DEAN

Dean Wilder is not only a well-known concert artist, but also an outstanding voice teacher. He is currently teacher of vocal studies at William Jewell College in Liberty, Missouri. Wilder's active performance career includes over a hundred concerts annually. He has performed as leading tenor with the New York City Opera and as soloist under such conductors as Leonard Bernstein and Robert Shaw.

In addition to his many solo performances and credits, Wilder has achieved much in the sacred concert field as the tenor of the prominent duo of Hale and Wilder. Dean Wilder joined Robert Hale in 1966, and since that time this vibrant duo has performed in more than two thousand concerts in churches around the world.

WILKIN, MARIJOHN

When Marijohn Wilkin found herself as a top professional songwriter and businesswoman, she relates, "Something was still missing in my life and, as death took my business partner and my mother, I felt stronger than ever the need to return to my religious heritage. It was reaching into myself and seeing myself as I truly was, needs and all, that I realized I *was* just a woman—a human being reaching for help—and that source of help was Jesus."

Marijohn became one of Nashville's top women songwriters with songs like "One Day At A Time," which, she explains, means to live every day as if you might meet your Maker tomorrow.

Highly successful in many facets of the music industry, she is a songwriter of note—a member of the Nashville Songwriters Association's Hall of Fame, Gospel Music Association Dove Awardee, music publisher, backup singer and teacher and solo performer with her touring group, Marijohn Wilkin on Tour.

Born in Kemp, Texas, Marijohn calls her father "the most God-like man I ever knew." He played the fiddle for hoedowns all over Texas, but after he became a born-again Christian her own musical inclinations leaned toward the inspirational. As early as five years old, she appeared in various churches and Baptist encampments. Later, she took jobs teaching music, then wrote her first song, "Take This Heart," which was soon followed by her hit, "Waterloo." She went on to write over three hundred much-recorded songs, earning eight BMI awards. She then formed The Marijohn Singers, whose background vocalizing for hundreds of hit records won wide recognition, and went on to establish her own publishing company, Buckhorn Music.

Marijohn lives in Hillsboro, near Nashville.

WILLARD, KELLY

Kelly Willard says of her ministry: "I want to tell of the freedom that realizing God's love for me has brought. We all have insecurities and fears and the Lord has laid it on my heart to openly share about these and point people to Jesus as the solution."

At twenty-two, Florida-born Kelly Willard, a convert at the tender age of ten, was already a veteran of the Christian music ministry as a singer, pianist, songwriter and arranger. Kelly's songs are for both Christians and non-Christians.

Through the combination of the fresh simplicity of her lyrics with her mellow contemporary style, Kelly has an inroad to the ears and hearts of young and old alike.

Kelly's husband, Dan, handles her booking and sound system and still finds time to engineer at Maranatha! Music Studios. Her first solo album on the Maranatha! Music label is entitled *Blame It On The One I Love.*

KELLY WILLARD: *"Pointing people to Jesus as the solution"*

THE LANNY WOLFE TRIO

Lanny Wolfe—Vocals
Marietta Wolfe—Vocals
Dave Peterson—Keyboard

The Lanny Wolfe Trio is composed of three people who say they are excited

THE LANNY WOLFE TRIO: *Excited about Christ and the things He's making possible*

about Christ and the things He is making possible for them.

Lanny and Marietta Wolfe, along with Dave Peterson, are the vocalists forming the trio—Lanny accompanies on keyboard. Their beautiful voices blend to produce the Trio's unforgettable music and message. Lanny is a dramatically gifted young songwriter who has written such beloved standards as "Greater Is He," "Come On, Let's Praise Him," "A Brand New Touch" and "God's Wonderful People." He also has many other songs and songwriting awards to his credit.

The group performs in concert all across the country. Their latest album is entitled, *Rejoice With Exceeding Great Joy.*

YOUNG, OVID

Ovid Young's exceptional talent as pianist, arranger and conductor has given him a multi-faceted and extremely busy career.

As an arranger, he has had several collections of hymn tunes published, including "The Choral Sounds of Ovid Young" (Broadman Press), "Praise Ye" (Benson) and "Now Sing We Joyfully Unto God" (Paragon). The last two are two-part hymn arrangements as sung by the duo of Robert Hale and Dean Wilder, with whom Young spends part of his time touring the United States.

Not only is he pianist for the duo, but has also arranged and conducted most of their music as well. He has performed on fourteen albums with Hale and Wilder and has recorded several solo sets as well, including *Praise Song* and *A Celebration of Praise.*

Aside from his solo work and his touring, Ovid joins well-known classical pianist Stephen Nielson for over one hundred sacred two-piano concerts each year.

Young, his wife, Laura, and their two sons reside in Bourbonnaise, Illinois.

Z

ZIMMER, NORMA

In addition to her weekly appearance on *The Lawrence Welk Show,* viewed by an estimated forty million people, Norma Zimmer is soloist in the Billy Graham Crusades and appears on *The Hour of Power* program with Dr. Robert Schuller from Garden Grove Community Church.

Norma has been associated with Welk

NORMA ZIMMER:
An expression of her profound personal faith

for seventeen years. He says, "Without a doubt, Norma is the most gracious and charming lady on television," and her host of fans echoes his sentiments.

Often referred to as "First Lady of Song," Miss Zimmer's background qualifies her activity in the field of sacred music. She grew up in Seattle and during her early years was given spiritual guidance by the director of her church choir, Carl A. Pitzer, who encouraged her sacred music activities. This all provided a foundation that has remained to this day an important adjunct to her professional career. Her singing is an expression of her profound personal faith.

She has appeared as soloist in the Hollywood Bowl, and performed with Carmen Dragon on concert tours throughout the continental United States and Hawaii. She has made her twelfth guest appearance at the Birmingham, Alabama Sacred Festival of Music.

Norma has recorded ten albums. In addition to her busy television and recording schedule, she accepts a limited number of sacred concerts each year, and was chosen Top Female Sacred Vocalist in 1973 by *Gospel West*.

Norma's autobiography, *Norma,* is published by Tyndale House.

Dove Award Winners

1969–1978

MALE GOSPEL GROUP

1969—Imperials
1970—Oak Ridge Boys
1972—Oak Ridge Boys
1973—Blackwood Brothers
1974—Blackwood Brothers
1975—Imperials
1976—Imperials
1977—Cathedral Quartet
1978—Imperials

MIXED GOSPEL GROUP

1969—Speer Family
1970—Speer Family
1972—Speer Family
1973—Speer Family
1974—Speer Family
1975—Gaither Trio
1976—Speer Family
1977—Speer Family
1978—Dallas Holm and Praise

MALE GOSPEL VOCALIST

1969—James Blackwood
1970—James Blackwood
1972—James Blackwood
1973—James Blackwood
1974—James Blackwood
1975—James Blackwood
1976—Johnny Cook
1977—James Blackwood
1978—Dallas Holm

FEMALE GOSPEL VOCALIST

1969—Vestal Goodman
1970—Ann Downing
1972—Sue Chenault
1973—Sue Chenault
1974—Sue Chenault Dodge
1975—Jeanne Johnson
1976—Joy McGuire
1977—Evie Tornquist
1978—Evie Tornquist

GOSPEL SONG OF THE YEAR
(*Title/Composer/Publishing Co./Performance rights affiliation*)

1969—Jesus Is Coming Soon
R. E. Winsett (R. E. Winsett Music Co.) SESAC
1970—The Night Before Easter
Don Sumner-Dwayne Friend (Gospel Quartet Music Co.) SESAC
1972—The Lighthouse
Ron Hinson (Journey Music Co.) BMI
1973—Why Me, Lord?
Kris Kristofferson (Resaca Music) BMI
1974—Because He Lives
Bill Gaither (Gaither Music Co.) ASCAP
1975—One Day At A Time
Marijohn Wilkin–Kris Kristofferson (Buckhorn Music) BMI
1976—Statue Of Liberty
Neil Enloe (Enloe Music) BMI
1977—Learning To Lean
John Stallings (HeartWarming Music) BMI
1978—Rise Again
Dallas Holm (Dimension)

GOSPEL SONGWRITER OF THE YEAR

1969—Bill Gaither
1970—Bill Gaither
1972—Bill Gaither

(*Songwriter cont.*)
1973—Bill Gaither
1974—Bill Gaither
1975—Bill Gaither
1976—Bill Gaither
1977—Bill Gaither
1978—Dallas Holm

GOSPEL INSTRUMENTALIST

1969—Dwayne Friend
1970—Dwayne Friend
1972—Tony Brown
1973—Henry Slaughter
1974—Henry Slaughter
1975—Henry Slaughter
1976—Henry Slaughter
1977—Henry Slaughter
1978—Dino Kartsonakis

GOSPEL DISC JOCKEY OF THE YEAR

1969—J.G. Whitfield
1970—J.G. Whitfield
1972—J.G. Whitfield
1973—Sid Hughes
1974—Jim Black
1975—Jim Black
1976—Sid Hughes
1977—Sid Hughes
1978—Sid Hughes

GOSPEL TELEVISION PROGRAM

1969—Gospel Jubilee/Florida Boys, Host
1970—Gospel Jubilee/Florida Boys, Host
1972—Gospel Jubilee/Florida Boys, Host

1973—Gospel Jubilee/Florida Boys, Host
1974—Gospel Jubilee/Florida Boys, Host
1975—Gospel Jubilee/Florida Boys, Host
1976—Gospel Jubilee/Florida Boys, Host
1977—PTL Club/Jim Bakker, Host
1978—Gospel Jubilee/Florida Boys, Host

BACKLINER NOTES OF A GOSPEL RECORD ALBUM
(*Annotator/Album Title/Artist*)

1969—No Award Given
1970—Mrs. Jake Hess
　　　Ain't That Beautiful Singing
　　　(*Jake Hess*)
1972—Johnny Cash
　　　Light (*Oak Ridge Boys*)
1973—Eddie Miller
　　　Release Me (*Blackwood Brothers*)
1974—Don Butler
　　　On Stage (*Blackwood Brothers*)
1975—Wendy Bagwell
　　　Bust Out Laffin' (*Wendy Bagwell & the Sunliters*)
1976—Sylvia Mays
　　　Just A Little Talk With Jesus
　　　(*Cleavant Derricks Family*)
1977—Joe Huffman
　　　Cornerstone (*Speer Family*)
1978—Joe and Nancy Cruse

GRAPHIC LAYOUT AND DESIGN OF A GOSPEL RECORD ALBUM
(*Graphic Artist/Album Title/Artist*)

1969—No Award Given

1970—Jerry Goff
  *Thasher Brothers at Fantastic
  Caverns (Thrasher Brothers)*
1972—Act Lehman
  *L-O-V-E Love (Blackwood
  Brothers)*
1973—Bob McConnell
  Street Gospel (Oak Ridge Boys)
1974—Charles Hooper
  On Stage (Blackwood Brothers)
1975—Bob McConnell
  *Praise Him . . . Live
  (Downings)*
1976—Bob McConnell
  No (Imperials)
1977—Dennis Hill
  *Shortage Then . . . & Now
  (Cathedral Quartet)*
1978—Bob McConnell

GOSPEL RECORD ALBUM COVER PHOTO OR COVER ART
(Photographer/Album Title/Artist)

1969—No Award Given
1970—Bill Grine
  This Is My Valley (Rambos)
1972—Bill Grine
  Light (Oak Ridge Boys)
1973—Bill Grine
  Street Gospel (Oak Ridge Boys)
1974—Hope Powell
  On Stage (Blackwood Brothers)
1975—Spears Photo
  *There He Goes (Blackwood
  Brothers)*
1976—Bill Barnes
  *Old Fashioned, Down Home,
  Hand Clappin', Foot Stomping,
  Southern Style, Gospel Quartet
  Music (Oak Ridge Boys)*

1977—Roy Tremble
  *Then . . . & Now (Cathedral
  Quartet)*
1978—Robert August
  *Live In London (Andrae Crouch
  and The Disciples)*

GOSPEL RECORD ALBUM OF THE YEAR
(Title/Artist/Label/Producer)

1969—It's Happening
  *Oak Ridge Boys
  (HeartWarming)
  Bob MacKenzie*
1970—Fill My Cup Lord
  *Blackwood Brothers (RCA
  Victor) Darol Rice*
1972—Light
  *Oak Ridge Boys
  (HeartWarming)
  Bob MacKenzie*
1973—Street Gospel
  *Oak Ridge Boys
  (HeartWarming)
  Bob MacKenzie*
1974—Big And Live
  *Kingsmen Quartet (Canaan)
  Marvin Norcross*
1975—I Just Feel Like Something Good
  Is About To Happen
  *Speer Family-Doug Oldham
  (HeartWarming)
  Bob MacKenzie*
1976—*Traditional*
  Between The Cross and Heaven
  *Speer Family (HeartWarming)
  Joe Huffman
  Contemporary*
  No Shortage
  *Imperials (Impact) Bob Mac-
  Kenzie-Gary Paxton
  Inspirational*

(*Record album cont.*)

Jesus We Just Want To Thank
You
*Bill Gaither Trip (HeartWarm-
ing) Bob MacKenzie*
By A Non-Gospel Artist
Sunday Morning With Charley
Pride
*Charley Pride / Charley Pride
(RCA) Jerry Bradley*
1977—*Traditional*
Then . . . & Now
*Cathedral Quartet (Canaan)
Ken Harding*
Contemporary
Reba-Lady
*Reba Rambo Gardner (Green-
tree) Phil Johnson*
Inspirational
Ovation
Couriers (Tempo) Jesse Peterson
By A Non-Gospel Artist
Home Where I Belong
B. J. Thomas (Myrrh)
Soul

This Is Another Day
*Andrae Crouch and The Disciples
(Light) Andrae Crouch
and Bill Maxwell*

ASSOCIATE MEMBERSHIP AWARD

1975—Blackwood Brothers
1976—Statue Of Liberty
*Neil Enloe / Neil Enloe Music /
BMI*
1977—Blackwood Brothers
1978—Blackwood Brothers
1978—*Traditional*
Live In Chattanooga
The Kingsmen
Contemporary
Transformation
The Cruse Family
Inspirational
Pilgrim's Progress
Bill Gaither Trio
Soul
Live In London
Andrae Crouch and The Disciples

Members of Gospel Music Hall of Fame

LEE ROY ABERNATHY (1973)

He has achieved a posture in several facets of gospel music that would be acknowledged as being great. Possessing a creative ability unsurpassed in this business, he can be credited with several firsts. He has taught thousands to play the piano by mail. He was the first to publish gospel music shaped notes in sheet music. When selecting the top few making the greatest contribution to gospel music as a writer, teacher, performer, producer or promoter to just an influential personality that inspires everyone around him to do greater things, very few would equal Abernathy. He sang and played piano with The Rangers, Homeland Harmony, Miracle Men, and The Happy Two with Shorty Bradford. He wrote "Everybody's Going To Have A Wonderful Time Up There" and "He's A Personal Savior."

JAMES BLACKWOOD, SR. (1974)

He has been singing gospel music for 43 years. He helped engineer the quartet motor travel by custom bus and helped guide the National Quartet Convention to become one of the biggest productions of gospel music. He and The Blackwood Brothers recorded and sold more gospel albums than any other group. James has won the Dove Award for "Best Gospel Male Vocalist" for six years. Jointly responsible for the Stamps-Blackwood School of Music, he has served as chairman of the Board of Directors of the Gospel Music Association and as President of the Gospel Music Hall of Fame (1971). He has appeared on numerous television shows with The Blackwood Brothers.

EVA MAE LeFEVRE (1977)

In 1934, at the age of seventeen, Eva Mae Whittington married Urias LeFevre and began a long career in gospel music. She is still playing and singing with as much dedication today as when she began. Mother of two girls, three boys and boasting eleven grandchildren, Eva Mae is equally loved by fans and fellow artists. She is the daughter of a country evangelist and traveled with him until she and Urias married. Eva Mae was named Miss Gospel Singer in 1953 and Queen of Gospel Music in the 1974 Singing News Fan Awards. The LeFevres were chosen to represent gospel music at the final program of the Grand Ole Opry in Nashville and asked to appear at the first program from Opryland Grand Ole Gospel. Eva Mae, playing the piano since age four, still promotes gospel music at every opportunity. She has dedicated her life, talents and lovely alto voice to her work for the Savior.

MOSIE LISTER (1976)

He was born in Cochran, Georgia and after elementary and secondary education attended Middle Georgia College, majoring in English and minoring in Harmony and Counterpoint and arranging for piano and organ. He began writing seriously for gospel groups in Atlanta in the late 1940's and became employed by The Statesmen in 1948. He founded Mosie Lister Publications in 1953 and merged with Lillenas Publishing Co. in 1969. Mosie was honored as "Layman of the Year" by the Tampa Baptist Laymen in 1971. He has composed such songs as "How Long Has It Been?," "Then I Met The Master," "Til The Storm Passes By."

GEORGE BEVERLY SHEA
(See Pictorial Encyclopedia)

JACK BROCK SPEER (1975)

He is the oldest child of Tom and Lena Speer. He has been a member of The Singing Speer Family ever since he was old enough to stand up. Since the death of Dad and Mom Speer, he and his brother, Ben, have been the leaders of the family singing group. A most congenial and concerned man, Brock has served gospel music in many capacities including chairman of the board of directors of the Gospel Music Association and past president. As a record producer for Skylite, he directed most of the major groups in their recordings. He is an ordained Elder in the Church of the Nazarene. He graduated from Trevecca College and Vanderbilt Divinity School. He is married to the former Faye Ihrig and they have three children, Susan, Marc and Bryan.

Deceased Members

E. M. BARTLETT
(1884–1941)

E. M. Bartlett was born in Waynesville, Missouri and became a gospel singer, composer, teacher, editor and publisher. He married Joan Tatum in 1916 and they had two sons, E. M. Bartlett Jr. and Charles Scott Bartlett. He was head of the Hartford Music Company from 1918 to 1935. Bartlett graduated from the Hall-Moody Institute in Martin, Tennessee with degrees in Arts, Science, Music and Oratory. His best known composition is "Victory In Jesus."

J. R. BAXTER JR.
(1887–1960)

J. R. Baxter, one of the foremost musicians and gospel music publishers of our time, was a pioneer in sponsoring gospel quartets on local radio stations. He was a man who did much through the Stamps-Baxter Music School to encourage young people to study gospel music. One of his most popular songs is "Try Jesus."

GEORGE BENNARD
(1873–1958)

Converted to Christianity at an early age while attending a meeting of the Salvation Army, he had a strong desire to be a gospel minister but, because of financial problems, found higher education to be beyond his reach. Thus, he studied through association with other ministers and through his own private study and reading. For several years he was a brigade leader of the Salvation Army and later became an evangelist for the Methodist Episcopal Church in the United States and Canada. Composer of over 300 gospel songs, his most widely known song is the beloved "Old Rugged Cross."

ALBERT E. BRUMLEY
(1905–1977)

He is known and loved as one of the greatest gospel songwriters of all time, having written such standards as "I'll Fly Away," "I'll Meet You In The Morning," "Jesus Hold My Hand," "There's A Little Pine Log Cabin" and "If We Never Meet Again." His hit gospel songs are too numerous to name as he wrote hundreds and they were all hits. He was a friend and associate of such gospel greats as V.O. and Frank Stamps, E. M. Bartlett and J. R. Baxter Jr. Together with his sons, he owned and operated two gospel music publishing firms, Albert E. Brumley & Sons and Hartford Music Company. His humility and "down-to-earth" manner endeared him to all he met.

FANNY CROSBY
(1820–1915)

Francis Jane Crosby was born to John and Mercy Crosby at Southeast, New York, March 24, 1820. Blind from birth, she entered the Institute for the Blind in New York City at the age of fifteen. While preparing herself for a successful teaching career she published the first of many books of poetry. Not until 1864, shortly after her marriage to Alexander Van Alstyne, did she write her first hymn and find her vocation. Fanny Crosby (Van Alstyne) is credited with writing over six thousand songs, among them "Pass Me Not" and "Blessed Assurance." On one occasion she thanked God for blindness, because she looked forward to the day when the first face she would behold would be that of her blessed Redeemer. Fanny was granted her vision on February 12, 1915 at the age of ninety-five.

DENVER CRUMPLER
(1914–1957)

Denver Crumpler was born in Arkansas in 1914 and died in Decatur, Georgia in April, 1957. During his comparatively short life span of 43 years, his contribution to gospel music and the happiness of his fellow man, in every walk of life, reached a scope that only eternity will reveal. He sang with a group known as The Melody Boys in the early thirties, was with The Rangers Quartet from 1938 until 1953 and then sang with The Statesmen Quartet until his death in 1957. Denver gave gospel music dignity, the performance of a true professional and one of the highest lyric tenor voices ever known. He gave to gospel music all any man can give—his entire life.

JOHN DANIEL
(1906–1961)

John Daniel was born near Boaz, Alabama. With his brother, Troy, he organized The John Daniel Quartet. After representing several publishing companies, John made a decision many people thought showed more courage than reason. His became the first quartet to sing gospel songs full time and was the first gospel group to appear regularly on WSM's Grand Ole Opry. The concerts were family entertainment at its best. Daniel's life story can best be told by saying he loved to sing.

MAHALIA JACKSON
(See Pictorial Encyclopedia.)

ADGER M. PACE
(1882–1959)

Adger M. Pace was born in Pelzer, South Carolina. A lifetime student of harmony and counterpoint, he was a leading authority and was considered one of the foremost harmonists of the South. He wrote and contributed to more than 3,500 gospel songs. In November, 1958, at a convention of singers at Birmingham, Alabama, he was awarded the honorary degree of Doctor of Music. He traveled several years with The Vaughan Radio Quartet and later was made editor of the Vaughan Publishing House in Lawrenceburg, Tennessee. The song most closely associated with him is "That Glad Reunion Day."

HOMER RODEHEAVER
(1880–1955)

Rodeheaver was born in Union Furnace, Ohio. From 1909 until 1931 he was music director of the Billy Sunday Evangelistic Campaigns. He served in the Spanish-American War as a trombonist with the Fourth Tennessee Regimental Band and with the Y.M.C.A. in France from August to December 1918. He toured the world with Evangelist W. R. Biederwolf in 1923-24, and in 1936 toured the African Mission Field in the Belgian Congo. He was president of the Rodeheaver, Hall-Mack Company and founder of the Rodeheaver Boys' Ranch in Palatka, Florida. His motto was: "Every cloud will wear a rainbow if your heart keeps right."

A. J. SHOWALTER
(1858–1924)

Anthony Johnson Showalter, author, composer, editor, publisher and teacher; born in Rockingham County, Virginia. He began the study of music in singing schools and private classes taught by his father. At twenty-two, he had his first book published; his *Harmony and Composition,* the first work of its kind by a southern author, was published when he was twenty-three. Went abroad in 1895 to study the methods of teachers and conductors in England, France, Germany, and other European countries. He was president of the A. J. Showalter Company, Dalton, Georgia, and the Showalter-Patton Company in Dallas.

TOM ("DAD") SPEER
(1891–1966)

His first musical memory was a gospel song his mother sang. His first musical effort was a melody inspired by the lyrical sounds of Brushy Creek in his native Cullman County, Alabama. From earliest childhood, Tom Speer felt compelled toward a life of service in gospel music. He wrote songs constantly, sang at every opportunity, and became a devoted and respected teacher in music schools throughout the South. His influence on the lives of others was immeasurable. Rupert Cravens, a young, unschooled Missouri farm lad, learned harmony, theory and Christian love from "Dad" Speer at the Vaughan Singing School in Lawrenceburg, Tennessee. Rupert became a minister and one of gospel music's most prolific songwriters. Mosie Lister was another of "Dad" Speer's successes. He turned away from a promising career as a country singer to devote his life to writing gospel music. "Dad" Speer's life touched thousands and everyone who knew him, no matter how briefly, caught a glimpse of the meaning of "Heaven's Jubilee."

LENA BROCK ("MOM") SPEER (1900–1967)

Lena Brock was born to a gospel music heritage. Her father, one of the South's leading musicians and teachers, taught his children to sing almost before they could talk. In 1920 Lena married Tom Speer. Their four children, Brock, Rosa Nell, Mary Tom and Ben, followed their parents' footsteps and became outstanding professional musicians in their own right. Every day of their lives together was a song. They thrilled audiences throughout the United States and Canada with their sincere, skillful performances. Together they recorded more than a dozen gospel albums which included classics such as "Heaven Will Surely Be Worth It All," "Time Has Made A Change," and "Mom" and "Dad's" theme song, "Won't We Be So Happy?". Even when illness took "Dad" from her side, "Mom" Speer never stopped singing and only her final, fatal sickness ever stilled the sound of her powerful musical witness. The gospel music heritage lives today in the lives of the Speer children and grandchildren, who are carrying on the proud legacy of gospel music left behind by "Mom" and "Dad."

FRANK STAMPS (1898–1965)

Frank Stamps was a born leader. Life to him was giving his time and talent to help make the world a better place in which to live. Stamps and The Stamps Quartet were the first gospel group to be recorded by a major record label, RCA Victor. Two gospel songs by the group, "Give the World a Smile" and "Love Leads the Way," sold one million copies. The song he made famous, "I Have My Hand in the Hand of the Lord," was not just a song to sing, it was his way of life.

VIRGIL OLIVER STAMPS (1892–1940)

V. O. Stamps began his career in 1914 as a singing-school teacher. He founded the V. O. Stamps Music Company in 1924, later known as the Stamps-Baxter Company. Though he was a noted singer, writer, publisher and pioneer recording artist, his greatest accomplishment was spreading gospel music through the medium of radio, then relatively new. For several years, he had many salaried quartets on national radio stations. His name became a household word, and it can be truly said that V. O. Stamps was the first to introduce southern-style gospel singing to total America.

GLENN KIEFFER VAUGHAN (1893–1969)

Born in Cisco, Texas, he moved to Lawrenceburg, Tennessee, in 1902. Vaughan entered the Vaughan Music Company in 1918, and became its president and co-owner in 1941. He organized and toured with The Original Vaughan Quartet, which became the first gospel group to engage in regular broadcast activity. In 1923 he was active in the establishment of Radio Station WOAN in Lawrenceburg. He taught voice at the Vaughan normal schools and composed many gospel songs.

During World War II Vaughan issued

a proclamation, "The Pause For Prayer," for the men and women in service. Each morning at 9 o'clock a recording of the Liberty Bell sounded over Lawrenceburg's local radio station; this recording was joined by the bells of every church and school in town.

He served four successful, progressive years as mayor of Lawrenceburg, having been elected to office without opposition in 1947. In 1949 he was elected president of the National Singing Convention.

Kieffer Vaughan loved horses and the very qualities he admired in them he possessed himself: good conformation, admirable performance, gentle manners and high intelligence.

JAMES D. VAUGHAN
(1864–1941)

James D. Vaughan, at the turn of the century, founded the James D. Vaughan Music Publishing Company, which through the years grew into one of the largest publishers of gospel music in the United States. He also founded and developed the Vaughan School of Music, which produced some of gospel music's most outstanding exponents, performers and musicians. The *Vaughan Family Visitor,* one of gospel music's oldest publications of information about the world of gospel music, still thrives under the banner of The Church of God, Cleveland, Tennessee. Vaughan was also gospel music's broadcast pioneer, having owned and operated the first radio station in Tennessee, WOAN in Lawrenceburg, presently WREC, Memphis. He is considered by many to be the rock on which much of today's gospel music was built.

JAMES PARKS WAITES
(1899–1973)

He was known the world over as "Big Jim," the dean of gospel bass singers. Jim's rich bass voice has been heard by millions via radio, television, recordings and personal appearances. His artistry is loved by everyone. His God-given talent has been used to bless mankind the world over under every conceivable circumstance. Jim's innumerable achievements were accomplished while working with the following groups: The Morros-Henson Quartet, The Electrical Workers Quartet, The Vaughan Radio Quartet, The Stamps Quartet, The John Daniel Quartet, The LeFevres, The Homeland Harmony Quartet, and The Rebels Quartet.

WILLIAM BURTON WALBERT
(1886–1959)

He was born in Barren County, Kentucky, and was a student of the State Normal College at Bowling Green, a graduate of Dana's Musical Institute of Warren, Ohio and of the Vaughan School of Music, Lawrenceburg, Tennessee. Walbert became affiliated with The Vaughan Quartet and traveled extensively in every part of the United States and Canada for twenty-five years. He was head of the Vaughan School of Music after the death of James D. Vaughan in 1941. Of Walbert, his son writes: "I have been unusually fortunate in being blessed with a wonderful father. He was the sweetest and kindest man I have ever known."

ROBERT E. WINSETT
(1876–1952)

Robert E. Winsett, gospel music composer and publisher, was born in Bledsoe County, Tennessee. A music teacher for forty-two years, he wrote his first gospel song when he was seven years old. In 1908, Winsett published *Pentecostal Power Complete,* which sold one million copies. Probably his greatest honor was posthumously awarded in 1969, when his song "Jesus is Coming Soon" won the Dove Award as Gospel Song of the Year. It would seem that from the very beginning God placed His hand on His servant in the ministry of gospel song.

JAMES S. WETHERINGTON
(1922–1973)

James S. ("Big Chief") Wetherington was a native of Ty Ty, Georgia. He resided in Atlanta for approximately 25 years. He was a member of the Assembly of God Tabernacle in Atlanta and directed the choir when not on tour with The Statesmen Quartet. "Big Chief," of Indian extraction, received his education in the Georgia Public School system. He was a veteran of World War II, serving in the U.S. Navy.

"Big Chief" Wetherington was a highly respected quartet man, serving as a very competent bass singer with The Statesmen at the time of his death. He died just a few days before his 51st birthday, having suffered a heart attack in his motel room in Nashville where he was appearing in the National Quartet Convention. He had sung with The Statesmen for 25 years and was well known in gospel quartet circles.

He was a partner with Hovie Lister and Doy Ott in the Faith and J. M. Henson Publishing Companies and The Statesmen Quartet. He was sole owner of the Lodo Music Company. "Big Chief" Wetherington will be long remembered for his genial manner, ready smile, his encouragement of new talent and his deep love for gospel music. He was instrumental in helping J. D. Sumner in the formation of the National Quartet Convention.

Radio Stations

ALABAMA

WABT Box 666, Tuskeegee
WACT/1420 Tuscaloosa
WAGC/1560 Centre
WAMI/860 Opp
WANA/1490 Anniston
WANL/1540 Lineville
WAVU/630, WOSB Albertville
WAYD/104.9 Ozark
WBHP/1230 Huntsville
WBIB/1110 Centerville
WBSA/1300 Boaz
WBTS/1480 Bridgeport
WCRL/1570 Oneonta
WCTA/920 Andalusia
WDJC/93.7 Birmingham
WEBJ/1240 Brewton
WEIS/990 Centre
WELB AM/1350 Elba
WELR AM-FM/1360 Roanoke
WENN AM/1230 FM/107.7
   Birmingham
WERH AM-FM/370 Hamilton
WETU/1250 Wetumpka
WFEB Sylacauga
WFHK/1430 Pell City
WFPA/1400 Ft. Wayne
WIPH Birmingham
WJAM/1310 Marion
WJBY/930 Gadsden
WJHO/1400 Opelika
WJLD Birmingham
WJOH/1400 Opelika
WJMW/730 Athens
WJOF FM/104.3 Athens
WKLD/97.7 Oneonta
WKLF/980 Clanton
WLAY/1450 Sheffield
WLPH/1450 Birmingham
WMFC/1360 Monroeville
WMGY Montgomery
WMOO/1560 Mobile

WMSL Decatur
WNDA/95.1 Huntsville
WNUZ/1230 Talledega
WPID/1280 Piedmont
WRAG/590 Carrollton
WRCK/1410 Tuscumbia
WRFS AM-FM/1050 Alenander City
WROS/1330 Scottsboro
WRSA/96.9 Lacey's Spring
WSHF/1290 Sheffield
WTUB/105.5 Troy
WULA AM-FM/1240 Eufaula
WVSA/1380 Vernon
WVSM/1500 Rainsville
WWWB/1360 Jasper
WWWF/990 Fayette
WWWR/920 Russellville
WYAM/1450 Bessemer
WYLS/1350 York

ALASKA

KICY/350 Nome
KJNP/1170 North Pole

ARIZONA

KFMM FM/99.5 Tucson
KHCS/1010 Phoenix
KHEP/101.5 Phoenix

ARKANSAS

KAMD/910 Camden
KAMO/1390 Rogers
KAMS FM Mammoth Springs
KBHC/1260 Nashville
KBIB/1560 Monette
KBJT/1570 Fordyce
KBRS/1340 Springdale
KCCB/1260 Corning
KCCL Paris
KDDA/1560 Dumas

(Arkansas cont.)

KDEW/1470 DeWitt
KDQN/1390 DeQueen
KDRS/1490 Paragould
KENA/1450 Mena
KFDF/1580 Van Buren
KGMR/1500 Jacksonville
KJBU/600 Siloam
KPBA/1590 Pine Bluff
KSOH/1050 Little Rock
KSUD/730 West Memphis
KWCK FM/1300 Searcy
KWAK/1240 Stuttgart
KWCB Searcy
KXOW/106.3 Hot Springs

CALIFORNIA

KAVR/960 Apple Valley
KBBL/99.1 Riverside
KCHJ/101.9 Bakersfield
KCNR/1090 Fortuna
KCHV/970 Indio
KDNO/98.5 Delano
KECR/93.3 El Cajon
KERS Sacramento
KEST/1450 San Francisco
KEWQ/930 Paradise
KGER/1390 Long Beach
KLBS/1330 Los Banos
KLRO/94.9 San Diego
KMAX FM/107.1 Pasadena
KMGO/1000 Vista
KNGS/620 Hanford
KOAD/1240 Lemoore
KPRL/1230 Paso Robles
KQLH FM/95.1 San Bernardino
KREL/1370 Corona
KRDU/1130 Dinubia
KSOM/1510 Ontario
KUCR/88.1 UC Riverside

KVIP AM-FM/540 Redding
KWCR/98.1 Santa Barbara
KYMS/106.3 Santa Ana

COLORADO

KAAT/1090 Denver
KPIK/1580 Colorado Springs
KPOF Westminster
KQXL/1550 Arvada
KRKS/990 Denver
KWYD Security

CONNECTICUT

WIHS FM/104.9 Middletown

DELAWARE

WKEN/1600 Hartly

FLORIDA

WAPG/1480 Arcadia
WAPR/1390 Avon
WAUG Wauchula
WBIX/1010 Jacksonville
WCNU/1010 Crestview
WCOF Immokalee
WEBY Pensacola
WFIV/1080 Orlando
WFIY Kissimmee
WGLY Coral Gables
WGNB AM-FM/1520 St. Petersburg
WIII Homestead
WINQ/1010 Seffner
WJOE/1080 Pensacola
WJSB/1050 Crestview
WKMK/1000 Blountstown
WNER/1250 Live Oak
WOMA Tallahassee
WOON/1230 Lakeland
WPAS Zephyrhills

WPCV FM Winter Haven
WPLA/910 Plant City
WPRV Wauchula
WQDI Homestead
WRBD/1470 Ft. Lauderdale
WRTM/102.3 Blountstown
WSBP/740 Chattahoochee
WSOR/95.3 Ft. Myers
WSWN/900 Belle Glade
WTBJ/1090 Apopka
WTMF Tampa
WTMT Tallahassee
WTWB/1570 Auburndale
WTYS/1340 Marianna
WVCF/1480 Windemere
WWAB/1330 Lakeland
WWBC/1510 Cocoa
WWQS Orlando
WWSD Monticello
WXBM/102.3 Pensacola
WYRL/102.3 Melbourne
WZEP/1460 De Funiak Springs

GEORGIA

WACL/570 Waycross
WACX/1600 Austell
WAFT/101.1 Valdosta
WAUG Augusta
WBBK/1260 Blakely
WBHB/1240 Fitzgerald
WBIT/1470 Adel
WBMK West Point
WCHK/1290 Canton
WCQS Alma
WDGL Douglasville
WDMG/860 Douglas
WDUN/1240 Gainesville
WDYX/1460 Buford
WEHK AM-FM Canton
WGFS/1430 Covington
WGHG Clayton
WGRA/790 Pelham

WGSR/1570 Millen
WGTA/950 Summerville
WGUN/1010 Decatur
WGUS/1380 Augusta
WHIE/1320 Griffin
WHYD/1270 Columbus
WISK/1390 Americus
WJEM/1150 Valdosta
WKIG/1580 Glennville
WKUN Monroe
WLET/1420 Toccoa
WLOP/1370 Jesup
WLOR/730 Thomasville
WLYB Albany
WMAH Ft. Benning
WMES/1570 Ashburn
WMGA/1130 Moultrie
WMGR/930 Bainbridge
WMTM AM-FM/1300 Moultrie
WNEA/1300 Newman
WNEG/630 Tocca
WNGA Nashville
WOKA AM-FM/1310 Douglas
WOWE/105.5 Rossville
WPEH/1420 Louisville
WRIP/980 Rossville
WRLD/1490 West Point
WRWH Cleveland
WSEM/1500 Donaldsonville
WSIZ/1380 Ocilla
WSNE AM/1170 Cumming
WSOJ FM/98.3 Jesup
WSYL/1490 Sylvania
WTGA/1590 Thomaston
WTIF/1340 East Point
WTJH/1260 East Point
WTTI/1530 Dalton
WTWA Thomson
WUFE/1260 Baxley
WUFF/710 Eastman
WVLF Alma
WVMG FM/1440 Cochran
WVMG AM/1440 Cochran

(*Georgia cont.*)
WWCC/1440 Bremen
WWGA Waynesboro
WYNX/1550 Smyrna

HAWAII

KAIM/870 Honolulu

IDAHO

KBGN/1060 Caldwell
KCRH Northwest Nazarene College,
  Nampa
KGEM/1140 Boise

ILLINOIS

WBBA/158.0 Pittsfield
WDDD/107.3 Marion
WDLM/960 East Moline
WEIC FM Charleston
WETN/88.1 Wheaton
WFIW/1390 Fairfield
WHOW/1520 Clinton
WJBM/1480 Jerseyville
WLCC/88.9 Lincoln
WLNR/106.3 Lansing
WMBI AM-FM/1110 Chicago
WMOK/920 Metropolis
WPEO/1020 Peoria
WPOK AM-FM Pontiac
WRFM Chicago
WTAQ/1300 LaGrange

INDIANA

WBAT/1400 Marion
WBNL/1540 Boonville
WCNB Connersville
WHME FM South Bend
WHON/930 Richmond
WIFF FM/105.5 Auburn

WMPJ Scottsburg
WQLK/96.1 Richmond
WRIN/1560 Rensselaer
WSBT/960 South Bend
WSLM Salem
WSVL FM Shelbyville
WTLC/105 Indianapolis
WVAK/1560 Paoli
WVHI/105.3 Evansville
WVTL Monticello
WWVR/105.5 Terre Haute
WXUS/92.7 Lafayette
WYCA/92.3 Hammond

IOWA

KDMI/97.3 Des Moines
KFGQ/99.3 Boone
KNWS/1090 Waterloo
KSAY/96.1 Clinton
KSMN/1010 Mason City
KTAV Knoxville
KTOF/104.5 Cedar Rapids
KWKY/1015 Des Moines
WMT/600 Cedar Rapids

KANSAS

KCLO/1410 Leavenworth
KFDI Wichita
KFLA/1310 Scott City
KJRS Newton
KSKG Salina
WNIC Winfield

KENTUCKY

WABD Ft. Campbell
WAIN/1270 Columbia
WANY/1390 Albany
WCTT/680 Corbin
WDOC/1310 Prestonburg
WEKG/810 Jackson

WFIA/900 Louisville
WFKY/1490 Frankfort
WFSL Stanford
WFTM/1240 Maysville
WGOH/1370 Grayson
WGRK Greenburg
WHKK/100.9 Erlanger
WIXI Lancaster
WJKY/1060 Jamestown
WJMM/100.9 Lexington
WJRS/104.9 Jamestown
WKAY Glagow
WKDO/1560 Liberty
WKDZ Cadiz
WKIC/1390 Hazard
WKKS/1570 Vanceburg
WKWY FM Frankfort
WKXO/1500 Berea
WLBJ/1410 Bowling Green
WLCK/1250 Scottsville
WLJC/102.3 Beattyville
WLKS/1450 West Liberty
WLLS/1600 Beaver Dam
WMIK/560 Middlesboro
WMTL/1580 Leitchfield
WPDE AM-FM Paris
WPHN Liberty
WRVK/1460 Renfro Valley
WSIP/1490 Paintsville
WSOF Madisonville
WTKY/1370 Tompkinsville
WVHI/105.3 Henderson
WYWY/950 Barbourville

LOUISIANA

KAJN Cromley
KCIJ/980 Shreveport
KDLA/1010 DeRidder
KDXI/1360 Mansfield
KLUV/1580 Haynesville
KMAR AM/1570 Winnsboro
KMRC/1430 Morgan City

KNCB Vivian
KREB/106.1 Monroe
KTDL/1470 Farmersville
KTOC AM-FM/920 Jonesboro
KTRY/730 Bastrop
KWCL/1280 Shreveport
WBFS Slidell
WBOX Bogalusa
WFCG Franklin
WLUX/1550 Baton Rouge
WVOG/600 New Orleans
WYLD/940 New Orleans

MAINE

WDHP FM/96.9 Caribou

MARYLAND

WASA/1330 Havre De Grace
WBMD/750 Baltimore
WHDG/103.7 Havre de Grace
WOLC/102.5 Princess Anne
WRBS/95.1 Baltimore
WSID Baltimore
WTHV Thurmont

MASSACHUSETTS

WRYT/95.0 Boston

MICHIGAN

WANG FM Coldwater
WAOP/980 Otsego
WBFG/98.7 Detroit
WCBF Claire
WCZN Flint
WGPR/107.5 Detroit
WJLB Detroit
WKPR/1420 Kalamazoo
WLQB Flint
WMPC/1230 Lapeer

(*Michigan cont.*)
WMPR Flint
WMUZ/103.5 Detroit
WSAE/89.3 Spring Arbor
WUFN/96.7 Albion
WUGN/99.7 Midland
WUNN/1110 Mason
WVOC Battle Creek
WYFC/1520 Ypsilanti
WYNZ Ypsilanti
WZND/99.3 Zeeland

MINNESOTA

KNOF/95.3 St. Paul
KTIS/900 Northwestern College Radio,
    Rossville
WWJC/850 Duluth
WWJO/98.1 St. Cloud

MISSISSIPPI

WABU Waynesboro
WACR Columbus
WAML/1340 Laurel
WBFN/1500 Quitman
WBKH/950 Hattiesburg
WBKN/1410 Newton
WCPC/940 Houston
WCSA/1260 Ripley
WECP/1480 Forest
WEPA/710 Eupora
WESY/1580 Leland
WFFF AM-FM/1360 Columbia
WFTO/1330 Fulton
WGOT/1063 Newton
WGVM Greenville
WHOC/1490 Philadelphia
WIGG/1420 Wiggins
WJFR/96.3 Jackson
WJXN/1450 Jackson
WKCU/1350 Corinth
WKPO/1510 Prentiss

WLSM/1270 Louisville
WMAG/860 Forest
WMBC/1400 Columbus
WMLC/1270 Monticello
WNAU/1470 New Albany
WORV/1580 Hattiesburg
WOSM/103.1 Ocean Springs
WOSM FM Ocean Springs
WRKN Brandon
WASO Seratbbia
WSEL/1440 Pontotoc
WSJC/810 Magee
WTUP/1490 Tupelo
WTYL/1290 Tylertown
WVYL/1320 Water Valley
WVOM/1270 Luka
WWHO Jackson
WXTN/1000 Lexington

MISSOURI

KALM/1290 Thayer
KBFL/90.3 Buffalo
KBOA AM-FM/830 Kennett
KBTC/1250 Houston
KCBC Springfield
KCHI/1010 Chillicothe
KECC Springfield
KFTW/1450 Fredericktown
KLFJ/1550 Springfield
KLTI/1560 Macon
KAMA Butler
KOBC/90.7 Joplin
KODE/1230 Joplin
KPCG FM/102.5 Joplin
KPRS Kansas City
KPWB/1140 Piedmont
KRMS/1150 Osage Beach
KSIM Sikeston
KSOA AVA
KSWM/940 Aurora
KTCB/1470 Malden
KTSR/90.1 Kansas City

KTUI/1560 Sullivan
KWFC/97.3 Springfield
KWPM/1450 West Plains
KWTO AM-FM/560 Springfield
KXEN/1590 St. Louis
KXLW/1320 St. Louis
KYMO/1080 East Prairie

MONTANA

KGVW/630 Belgrade
KIVE Glendive

NEBRASKA

KBHL/95.3 Lincoln
KGBI/100.7 Omaha
KJLT/970 N. Platte
KJSK Columbia
WJAG Norfolk
KOWH/660 Omaha

NEVADA

KNIS/94.7 Carson City

NEW JERSEY

WAWZ/1380 Alma White College,
   Zarephath
WBNX Carlstadt
WFME FM/94.7 West Orange
WKDN FM/106.9 Camden
WLCR Trenton
WLUP Franklin
WNNN/101.1 Salem
WRLB Metuchen
WWDJ AM/970 Hackensack

NEW MEXICO

KAVE/1240 Carlsbad
KCHS/1400 Truth or Consequences
KDAZ/730 Albuquerque

KENM Portales
KKIM/1000 Albuquerque
KWEW/1480 Hobbs

NEW YORK

CBN Ithaca
WBAB Babylon
WBIV FM/107.7 Buffalo
WCBA/1350 Corning
WGNR FM Oneonta
WHAZ/1330 Troy
WIZR AM/930 FM/104.9 Johnstown
WKOV/101.9 Albany
WJSL Houghton
WKOP/1360 Binghamton
WMIV/95.1 Rochester
WOIV/105.1 Syracuse
WOUR FM/96.9 Ithaca
WYRD/1540 Syracuse

NORTH CAROLINA

WABZ/1010 Albemarle
WADA/1390 Shelby
WADE Wadesboro
WAGY/1320 Forrest City
WAKS/1460 Varina
WATA/1450 Boone
WBHN/1590 Bryson City
WBLA Elizabethtown
WBMA/1350 Black Mountain
WBTE/990 Windsor
WCAB/590 Rutherfordton
WCEC/810 Rocky Mount
WCOK/1060 Sparta
WCSL Cherryville
WDBM/550 Statesville
WDSL/1520 Mocksville
WEGO Concord
WELS/1010 Kinston
WFCM Winston-Salem
WFGW/1010 Black Mountain

(*North Carolina cont.*)
WFMA/100.7 Rocky Mount
WFSC/1050 Franklin
WGPL Winston-Salem
WGWR FM/1260 Asheboro
WHIT/1450 New Bern
WHKY AM-FM/1290 Hickory
WHPE/1070 High Point
WHRY Hickory
WHVL/1600 Hendersonville
WIFM/1540 Elkin
WJRM/1390 Troy
WKBC/810 N. Wilkesboro
WKDX/1250 Hamlet
WKGX/1080 Lenoir
WKYK/1540 Burnsville
WLLE/570 Raleigh
WLOE/1490 Eden
WLTC/1370 Gastonia
WMDE Greensboro
WMMH/1460 Marshall
WMNC/92.1 Morgantown
WMNG F. Morgantown
WMSJ Sylva
WNOS High Point
WPEG FM/97.9 Concord
WPET/950 Greensoro
WPGD/1550 Winston-Salem
WPTL/920 Canton
WPYB/1130 Benson
WQWX Mebane
WRCM/92.1 Jacksonville
WRKB Kamapolis
WRNC/1240 Raleigh
WRRZ/880 Clinton
WSAT Salisbury
WSJS/600 Winston-Salem
WSKY/1230 Asheville
WSTH/860 Taylorsville
WSVM/1490 Valdese
WTIK/1310 Durham
WTLK/1570 Taylorsville

WTNC/790 Thomasville
WTOE/1470 Spruce Pine
WTSB/1340 Lumberton
WVCB/1410 Shallotte
WVOE/1590 Chadbourn
WWIT Canton
WWMO/102. Reidsville
WXNC FM Henderson
WXRC Hickory
WYDK/1480 Yadkinville

NORTH DAKOTA

KBOM/1270 Bismarck
KFNW/1170 Fargo
KHRT/1320 Monot

OHIO

WALR Akron
WAKW/93.3 Cincinnati
WBEX/1490 Chillicothe
WBZI/95.3 Xenia
WCNW/1560 Fairfield
WCHI Chillicothe
WCOL FM Columbus
WDMT Cleveland
WCRF/103.3 Cleveland
WEEC/100.7 Springfield
WELM Cleveland
WELW Cleveland
WGIC Xenia
WGGN/97.7 Castalia
WIBO/920 Waverly
WIRO/1230 Ironton
WLRO/1380 Lorain
WLYK/107.1 Milford
WMGS Bowling Green
WMNI/920 Columbus
WMOH/1450 Hamilton
WOKZ Alton
WOMP/100.5 Bellaire
WPAY/104. Portsmouth
WPBF Middletown

WPKO/1380 Waverly
WPOS/102.3 Holland
WQMS/96.5 Hamilton
WRMZ/91.1 Alliance
WSLR/1350 Akron
WSUM/1000 Cleveland
WTGN/97.7 Lima
WTOF/98.1 Canton
WZIP AM/1050 Cincinnati

OKLAHOMA

KBJH Tulsa
KEBC/94.7 Oklahoma City
KELR/1460 El Reno
KFJL Oklahoma City
KFMJ/1050 Tulsa
KGOY Oklahoma City
KJHN Antlers
KKMA Owasso
KLCO/1280 Poteau
KORV Tulsa
KTJS/1420 Hobart
KTLQ/1350 Tahlequah
KVYL/1370 Holdenville
KWSH Wewoka

OREGON

KBMC FM/94.5 Eugene
KOHU/1360 Hermiston
KORE/1050 Springfield
KWIL/790 Albany

PENNSYLVANIA

WAVL/910 Apollo
WAYZ Waynesboro
WBYO/107.5 Boyerton
WDAC/94.5 Lancaster
WDAS Philadelphia
WDBA/ 107.3 Dubois
WFMZ/100.7 Allentown

WGCB/1440 Red Lion
WHGM FM/103.9 Altoona
WHYP/1530 Northeast
WISR/680 Butler
WJSM/1110 Martinsburg
WKPS/88.9 New Wilmington
WLBR/1270 Lebanon
WMSP/94.9 Harrisburg
WPEL/1250 Montrose
WPGM/1570 Danville
WKE FM Everett
WTLN FM/95.3 Philadelphia
WXVR Media

SOUTH CAROLINA

WAGI FM/105.3 Gaffney
WAGS/1380 Bishopville
WAGY FM/1320 Gaffney
WAIM/1230 Anderson
WANS/1280 Anderson
WATP Marion
WAZS/980 Summerville
WBBR/1580 Travelers Rest
WBCY/1460 Union
WBUG/1430 Ridgeland
WCAY/620 Cayce
WCKI/1300 Greer
WCMJ Chester
WCPL Pageland
WDKD/1310 Kingstree
WDSC/800 Dillon
WEAC Gaffney
WEAC FM Gaffney
WELP/1360 Easley
WESC/660 Greenville
WFIS/1600 Fountain Inn
WJOT/1260 Lake City
WKDK/1240 Newberry
WKHJ/1440 Holly Hill
WKKR/1540 Pickens
WKMG/1520 Newberry
WLBG/860 Laurens

(South Carolina cont.)
WLCM Lancaster
WLOW/1300 Aiken
WOIC/1320 Columbia
WOLS/1230 Florence
WORO Spartenburg
WPCC Clinton
WQIZ/810 Orangeburg
WQXL/1470 Columbia
WRHI/1340 Rock Hill
WSJW/1510 Woodruff
WWMC FM Moncks Corner
WYCL/980 York

SOUTH DAKOTA

KNWC/1270 Sioux Falls
KVSR FM/97.9 Rapid City

TENNESSEE

WAAN/1480 Waynesboro
WAEW/1330 Crossville
WAGG Franklin
WAMG/1130 Gallatin
WBFJ Woodbury
WBLC Lenoir City
WBOL/1560 Bolivar
WCMT/1410 Martin
WCOR Lebanon
WDBL/1590 Springfield
WDOD/96.5 Chattanooga
WDSG/1450 Dyersburg
WDTM/1330 Selmer
WDXE/1370 Lawrenceburg
WDXI/1310 Jackson
WDXL/1490 Lexington
WEAG/1470 Alcoa
WEEN/1460 LaFayette
WEKR/1240 Fayetteville
WENR/1090 Englewood
WFWL/1220 Camden
WGRV/1340 Greenville

WHAL AM-FM/1400 Shelbyville
WHBT Harriman
WHDM/1440 McKenzie
WHLP/1570 Centerville
WIDD/1520 Elizabethton
WIRJ Humboldt
WJFC/1480 Jefferson City
WJKM Hartsville
WJLE/1480 Smithville
WKBJ/1600 Milan
WKBL Covington
WKPT FM/1400 Kingsport
WKTA/106.9 McKenzie
WKXV/900 Knoxville
WLAF/1450 LaFollette
WLAR Athens
WLIJ/1580 Shelbyville
WLIL/730 Lenoir City
WLIV/920 Livingston
WLSB/1400 Copperhill
WMCH Church Hill
WMCT/1390 Mountain City
WMLR/1540 Hohenwald
WMOC/1450 Chattanooga
WNAH/1360 Nashville
WNTT/1250 Tazewell
WOFE/580 Rockwood
WPHC/1060 Waverly
WPJD/1550 Daisy
WRFN/88.1 Nashville
WRGS/1570 Rogersville
WRIP/980 Chattanooga
WOWE FM/105.5 Chattanooga
WSEV/930 Smithville
WSKT/1580 Knoxville
WSLV/1110 Ardmore
WSMG/1450 Greenville
WTCV/102.9 Memphis
WTNE/1500 Trenton
WTNN/1380 Millington
WTRB/1570 Ripley
WVRC Sparta

WWGM/1560 Nashville
WYSH/1380 Clinton
WYXI/1390 Athens

TEXAS

KBBB/1600 Borger
KBUC/1310 San Antonio
KBUK Baytown
KBUY Fort Worth
KBWD/1380 Brownwood
KBYP/1580 Shamrock
KCAN/1550 Canyon
KCAS Slaton
KCHU/90.9 Dallas
KCLR/1530 Ralls
KCOM/1550 Comanche
KCTA/1030 Corpus Christi
KCYL/1450 Lampasas
KDOX Marshall
KDRY/1110 San Antonio
KDTX FM Dallas
KEES/1430 Longview
KFMK/97.9 Houston
KFRO/1370 Longview
KGBC Galveston
KHCB/105.1 Houston
KHEM/1270 Big Spring
KHYM/1060 Gilmer
KIMP/960 Mt. Pleasant
KIKZ/1250 Seminole
KISO El Paso
KIVY/1290 Crockett
KIZZ El Paso
KKAS/1300 Silsbee
KKKK/99.1 Midland
KLBK/1340 Lubbock
KLIS Palestine
KLKZ Seminole
KLUF Lufkin
KLUL Houston
KMHT/1450 Marshall
KMIL/1330 Cameron

KMOO Mineola
KNOK/970 Fort Worth
KOLJ/1150 Quanah
KPBC/1040 Dallas
KPDN/1340 Pampa
KPLT Paris
KRBA/1340 Pampa
KRBA/1340 Lufkin
KSKY/660 Dallas
KSTA/1000 Coleman
KTAL FM Texarkana
KTBB/600 Tyler
KTRM/95.1 Beaumont
KVLL/1220 Woodville
KWBA Baytown
KWFA/1500 Merkle
KWGO/99.5 Lubbock
KZAK Tyler
KZOL/1570 Farwell

VIRGINIA

WABH/1150 Deerfield
WBBI/1230 Abington
WBDY Bluefield
WBZI/95.3 Blackburg
WDYL FM/92.1 Richmond
WEMC/91.7 Harrisonburg
WEOO Smithfield
WESR Tasley
WFAX/1220 Falls Church
WFHG/980 Bristol
WFIC/1530 Collinsville
WHBG/1360 Harrisonburg
WHEO/1270 Stuart
WHHV Hillsville
WIKI/1410 Richmond
WIVE/1430 Ashland
WJJJ/1260 Christian
WJJS FM/101.7 Lynchburg
WJLM/93.5 Roanoke
WKBA/1550 Roanoke
WKBY Chatham

(Virginia cont.)
WKCW/1420 Warrenton
WKDE/1000 Altavista
WKJC Bluefield
WLCM Lynchburg
WLSD/1220 Big Stone Gap
WPCE Portsmouth
WRAA/1330 Luray
WRIS/1410 Roanoke
WSIG/790 Mt. Jackson
WSLS Roanoke
WSVA/550 Harrisburg
WSWV/1570 Pennington Gap
WTZE/1470 Tazewell
WWOD/100.1 Lynchburg
WXGI/950 Richmond
WXRI/105.3 Chesapeake
WYAL AM/1280 Richmond
WYTI/1570 Rocky Mount

WASHINGTON

KAYE Puyallup
KARI/550 Blaine
KBLE/1050 Seattle
KLYN FM/106.5 Lynden
KMO/1360 Tacoma
KNCC Kirkland
KOQT/1550 Bellingham
KTEL/1490 Walla Walla
KTW Seattle
KVDY Spokane
KYAC/1250 Seattle

WASHINGTON, D.C.

WPLK

WEST VIRGINIA

WBKW FM/95.5 Beckley
WCST/1010 Berkley Springs

WELD/690 Fisher
WETZ New Martinsville
WHJC/1360 Matewan
WKJC Welch
WKLC/1300 St. Albans
WMOV/1360 Ravenswood
WMUL FM/88.1 Huntington
WOAY/860 Oak Hill
WOVE Welch
WPAR/1450 Parkersburg
WPNS Hurricane
WRDS Charleston
WSCW/1410 Clarksburg
WSGB/1490 Sutton
WVAF/99.9 Charleston
WVAR/600 Richwood
WWHY/1470 Huntington
WWNR/620 Beckley
WWVA/1170 Wheeling

WISCONSIN

WAWA/1590 Elm Grove
WDMW FM/92.1 Menomonie
WGEZ/1490 Beloit
WNOV Milwaukee
WRVM/102.7 Suring
WWIB/103.7 Cornell

CANADA

CHLO St. Thomas, Ont.
CJSN and CKWS Swift Current, Sask.
CKTB St. Catharines, Ont.
CKWS Kingston, Ontario
VOAR St. Johns, Newfoundland

PUERTO RICO

WCGB/1050 Juana Diaz
WIVV/1370 San Juan

Television Stations

ARIZONA

KTVE-TV
Harold Grimmett
"Rise & Shine"
El Dorado

COLORADO

KKTV-TV
First Assembly of God
"A New Song"
Colorado Springs

FLORIDA

WFLA-TV
Harold Johnson
"Soulful Outreach"
Tampa

WJXS-TV
Herbert Gold
"A.M. Talk Show"
Jacksonville

WLCY-TV
Mike Klausmeier
"Reflections"
St. Petersburg

GEORGIA

WCTV-TV
Roy LaMere
"Farm Report"
Thomasville

WHAE-TV
Lynwood Maddox
"Countdown To A Miracle"
Atlanta

WHAE-TV
Paul Dubois
"The Living Word"
Roswell

WHAE-TV
Low Evans
"Hi Folks"
Forest Park

WHAE-TV
Rev. & Mrs. James Swilley
"Something Special"
Atlanta

WJBF-TV
Steve Manderson
"The Lewis Family Show"
Augusta

IOWA

KCRG-TV
Rev. Dan Cox
"The Hour Of Hope"
Waterloo

KANSAS

KARD-TV
Elmer Childress
"Elmer Childress Show"
Wichita

LOUISIANA

KNOW-TV
Ansel Smith
"Jubilettes Gospel Sing"
Monroe

MASSACHUSETTS

WWLP-TV
Thomas Lamaeche
"The Chalice of Salvation"
Springfield

NEBRASKA

KOLN-TV
Sara Murdock
"Morning Show"
Lincoln

NEW YORK

WNBC-TV
Dr. Russell Bareber
"The First Estate"
New York

NORTH CAROLINA

WATR-TV
Jim Moss
"PTL Club"
Charlotte

WXII-TV
Bill Neubach
"Gospel Song"
Winston-Salem

OHIO

WDTN-TV
Sammy Stevens
"Valley Gospel Showcase"
Dayton

WTRF-TV
Rev. Stan Scott
"Spiritual Awakening"
Winterville

SOUTH CAROLINA

WSPA-TV
Bill Bailey
"Gospel Challengers"
Spartenburg

TENNESEE

WTVF-TV
Merle Emery
"Singing Convention"
Nashville

VIRGINIA

WTVR-TV
John V. Shand
"Focus on Black Religious Life"
Richmond

"In Concert"—
A Photo Album

ANDRAE CROUCH: *"I have one question when I write a new song: 'Does it reach you?'"*

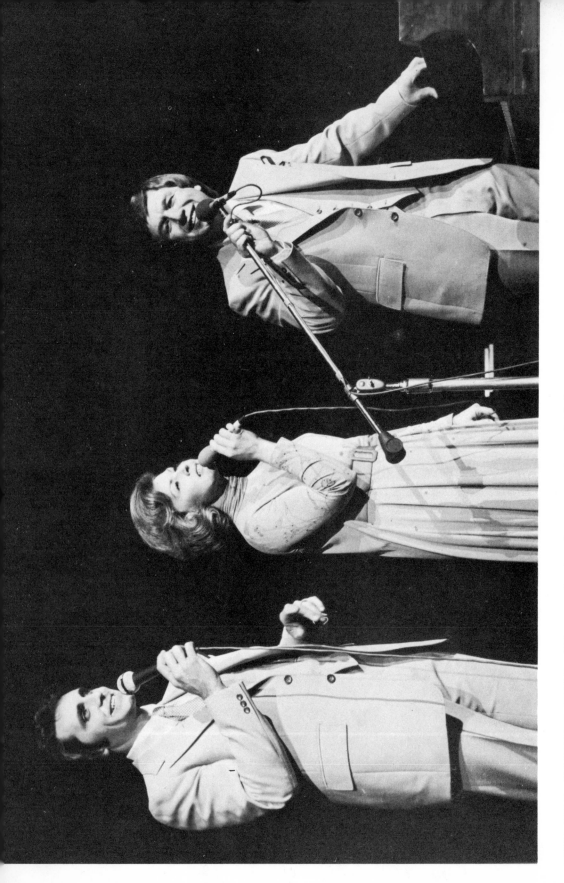

THE BILL GAITHER TRIO: *"Communicating the resurrection principle in daily life"*

CHUCK GIRARD'S LOVE SONG: *A soft blend of beautiful harmony*

TAMI CHERÉ: *"A burning desire to share her Christian experience"*

NORMA ZIMMER: *"The most gracious and charming lady on television"*

BARRY McGUIRE: *"I sing to people because I love 'em"*

THE HAPPY GOODMAN FAMILY: *Recipients of many gospel music awards*

B.J. THOMAS: *"The birth of another vision"*

THE BOONES: *A family tradition of superlative performing*

234

THE HEMPHILLS: *Deep South gospel music in a downhome country style*

WALTER HAWKINS: *"Soul gospel at its peak of perfection"*

TRAMAINE HAWKINS: *Walter's talented wife and lead singer*

EDWIN HAWKINS: *Walter's brother gained nationwide fame for "Oh Happy Day"*

TIM SHEPPARD: *"I wish to share His life and love with everyone I meet"*

HENRY SLAUGHTER: *Combines strong faith and an excellent musical presentation*

THE IMPERIALS: *Traditional roots and new directions*

THE WALL BROS. BAND: *Becoming one of the most popular Christian bands*

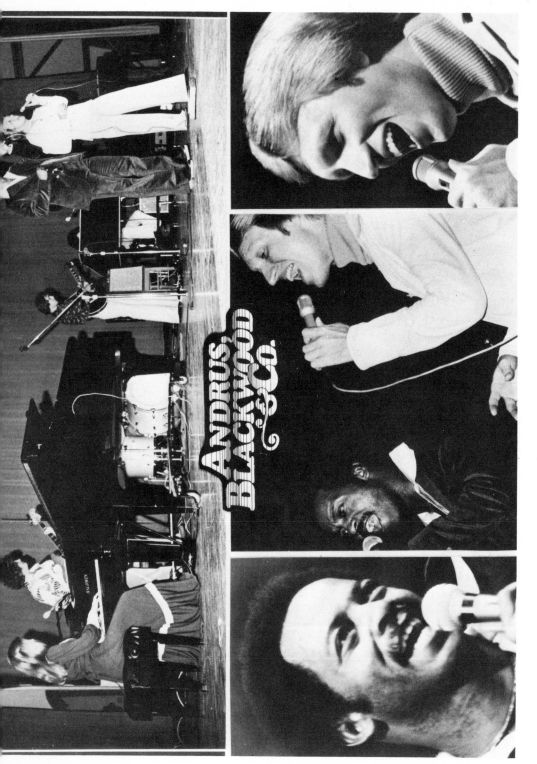

ANDRUS, BLACKWOOD & CO.: *Their debut prophesied an exciting future*

DINO AND DEBBY: *He received a Dove and Grammy award in 1978*

THE LANNY WOLFE TRIO: *Unforgettable music and message*

THE STATESMEN'S HOVIE LISTER: *Pacesetter of gospel music*

BILLY PRESTON: *Humble servant of God through music*

SHARALEE:
Enchants all
who come in
contact with her

THE KINGSMEN: *A style of excitement*

JIMMY SWAGGART: *Genuine concern for people*

THE RAMBOS: *Give all the credit to the Lord*

REBA: *A deep desire to spread the gospel*

THE SPEER FAMILY: *Inspirational entertainment in its highest form*

A Sampling of
Christian Music

The first part of the 1900's brought the innovation of quartet singing into gospel music. The solo quartet, using traditional hymns performed by four harmonizing voices singing in parts, quickly overtook choir and solo singing as America's most popular gospel form. The groups, frequently known as Stamps-Baxter Quartets, based on the early Stamps Quartet and the Stamps-Baxter publishing company, were mobile enough to tour the country, singing at churches and revivals. The quartet began to find its center in Nashville, along with slowly developing family groups, such as The Carter Family.

During the Second World War, the record industry began to mushroom across America. A group like The Carter Family was easily able to place on a small disc what before had been communicable only by live performance. Gospel record companies such as Word Inc., in Waco, Texas, built their foundations on one of America's most rapidly growing fields of music.

Today, gospel music can be divided roughly into four categories: black spirituals, including performers like the early Aretha Franklin and the late Mahalia Jackson, singing traditional psalms and hymns in a rhythmic, bluesy way; Southern gospel, including quartets like The Florida Boys, singing traditional hymns in an easy, structured, harmonic style; middle-of-the-road gospel, referring mostly to solo or choir performances of standard church music (often sung by personalities like Dale Evans or Burl Ives); and Jesus rock, the newest and most exploratory gospel style popularized by such celebrities as B. J. Thomas, and showing a blend between contemporary rock and traditional faith.

Each branch of today's gospel appeals to a particular group of gospel music lovers, and each serves its own purpose. Whereas the calm, ordered, lyrical singing of The Happy Goodman Family might move a crowd to tears at a Birmingham revival, only the hard-driving gospel rock of Andrae

Crouch and The Disciples will get a teenage crowd in Los Angeles jumping up and down in the aisles.

But all kinds of gospel music have the same basis and motive—to preach the gospel through music. However it's done, by a church choir in Tucson, or by Babe Stovall, standing in the New Orleans shadows like a moonstruck disciple, it still derives its energy from a firm belief in God.

AMAZING GRACE

JOHN NEWTON

Folk Hymn Tune

Play R.H. an octave higher on second verse.

1. A - maz - ing grace! how sweet the sound,
2. 'Twas grace that taught my heart to fear,
3. Thru' man - y dan - gers, toils, and snares,

That saved a wretch like me!
And grace my fears re - lieved;
I have al - read - y come;

I once was lost, but now am found,
How pre - cious did that grace ap - pear
'Tis grace hath brought me safe thus far,

Was blind, but now I see.
The hour I first be - lieved!
And grace will lead me home.

(THE CROSS IS MY)
STATUE OF LIBERTY

Words and Music by
NEIL ENLOE

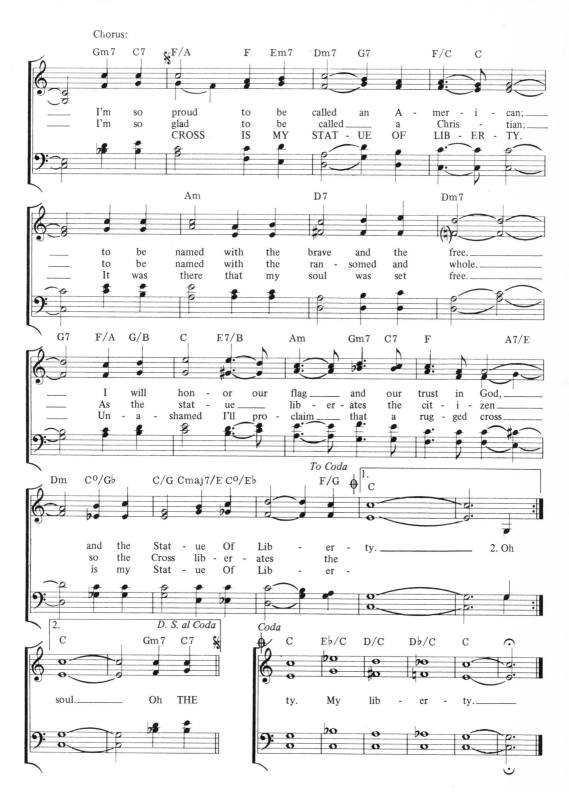

BLESSED ASSURANCE

GO TELL IT ON THE MOUNTAIN

SPIRITUAL

GO, TELL IT ON THE MOUN-TAIN, O-ver the hills and ev-ery-where.

Go, tell it on the moun - tain that Je - sus Christ is born.

1. When I was a sin-ner, I prayed both night and day; I
2. When I was a seek-er, I sought both night and day; I

asked the Lord to help me, and He showed me the way.
asked the Lord to help me, and He taught me to pray.

BRINGING THE SHEAVES

KNOWLES SHAW

GEORGE A. MINOR

1. Sow-ing in the morn-ing, sow-ing seeds of kind-ness, Sow-ing in the
2. Sow-ing in the sun-shine, sow-ing in the shad-ows, Fear-ing nei-ther
3. Go-ing forth with weep-ing, sow-ing for the Mas-ter, Tho' the loss sus-

noon-tide and the dew-y eve; Wait-ing for the har-vest,
clouds nor win-ter's chill-ing breeze; By and by the har-vest,
tained our spir-it oft-en grieves; When our weep-ing's o-ver,

and the time of reap-ing, We shall come re-joic-ing, bring-ing in the sheaves.
and the la-bor end-ed, We shall come re-joic-ing, bring-ing in the sheaves.
He will bid us wel-come, We shall come re-joic-ing, bring-ing in the sheaves.

CHORUS

Bring-ing in the sheaves, bring-ing in the sheaves, We shall come re-joic-
Bring-ing in the sheaves, bring-ing in the sheaves, We shall come re-joic-

ing, bring-ing in the sheaves; ing, bring-ing in the sheaves.

NOBODY KNOWS

Spiritual

O NO-BOD-Y KNOWS the trou-ble I've seen, No-bod-y knows my sor-rows,

No-bod-y knows the trou-ble I've seen, Glo-ry, hal-le-lu-jah!

Some-times I'm up, some-times I'm down: O yes, Lord;
Al-though you see me go-in' slow O yes, Lord;
What makes old Sa-tan hate me so? O yes, Lord;

Some-times I'm al-most to the ground, O yes, Lord.
I have my tri-als here be-low, O yes, Lord.
He had me once and let me go, O yes, Lord.

DOWN BY THE RIVERSIDE

Arr. by Claude Mac Arthur

Goin' t' lay down my bur - den,
Goin' t' lay down my sword and shield, Down by the riv-er-side,
Goin' t' try on my long white robe,
Goin' t' try on my star-ry crown,

Down by the river-side, Down by the river-side, Goin' t' lay down my bur - den,
Goin' t' lay down my sword and shield,
Goin' t' try on my long white robe
Goin' t' try on my star-ry crown,

Down by the riv-er-side, Goin' to stud-y war no more, ain't goin t'

stud-y war no more, Ain't goin t' stud-y war no more, ain't goin t'

stud-y war no more. Ain't goin t' stud y' war no more.

5. Goin' t' meet my dear old mother.   7. Goin' t' meet dem Hebrew children.
6. Goin' t' meet my dear old father.   8. Goin' t' meet my loving Jesus.

ROCK OF AGES

Augustus M. Toplady

Thomas Hastings

1. Rock of A - ges, cleft for me, Let me hide my - self in Thee;
2. Could my tears for - ev - er flow, Could my zeal no lan-guor know,
3. While I draw this fleet - ing breath, When my eyes shall close in death,

Let the wa - ter and the blood, From Thy wound - ed side which flowed,
These for sin could not a - tone; Thou must save, and Thou a - lone:
When I rise to worlds unknown, And be - hold Thee on Thy throne,

Be of sin the dou - ble cure, Save from wrath and make me pure.
In my hand no price I bring, Sim - ply to Thy cross I cling.
Rock ot A - ges, cleft for me, Let me hide my - self in Thee.

I LOVE TO TELL THE STORY

KATHERINE HANKEY

WILLIAM G. FISCHER

1. I love to tell the sto - ry Of un - seen things a - bove, Of Je - sus
2. I love to tell the sto - ry; More won - der - ful it seems Than all the
3. I love to tell the sto - ry; 'Tis pleas-ant to re - peat What seems each
4. I love to tell the sto - ry; For those who know it best Seem hun - ger -

and His glo - ry, Of Je - sus and His love, I love to tell the sto - ry,
gold - en fan-cies Of all our golden dreams. I love to tell the sto - ry,
time I tell it, More won-der-ful-ly sweet. I love to tell the sto - ry;
ing and thirsting To hear it like the rest. And when, in scenes of glo - ry,

Because I know 'tis true, It sat - is - fies my longings, As nothing else can do.
It did so much for me; And that is just the rea-son I tell it now to thee
For some have never heard The message of salvation From God's own holy word.
I sing the new, new song, 'Twill be the old, old story, That I have loved so long.

CHORUS

I love to tell the sto - ry! 'Twill be my theme in glo - ry

To tell the old, old sto - ry Of Je - sus and His love.

SWING LOW, SWEET CHARIOT

Arr. by Claude Mac Arthur

Swing low, sweet char-i-ot, Com-ing for to car-ry me home, Swing low, sweet char-i-ot, com-ing for to car-ry me home.

I looked o-ver Jor-dan, and what did I see,
If you get there be-fore I do,
I'm some-times up, I'm some-times down,

com-ing for to car-ry me home? A band of an-gels
com-ing for to car-ry me home; Tell all my friends I'm
com-ing for to car-ry me home; But still my soul feels

com-ing af-ter me, com-ing for to car-ry me home.
com-ing too. com-ing for to car-ry me home.
heav-en-ly bound, com-ing for to car-ry me home.

D. C.

IN THE SWEET BY AND BY

ARE YOU WASHED IN THE BLOOD?

E. A. H.   E. A. Hoffman

1. Have you been to Je - sus for the cleansing pow'r? Are you washed in the
2. Are you walk-ing dai - ly by the Sav-ior's side? Are you washed in the
3. When the Bridegroom cometh will your robes be white, Pure and white in the
4. Lay a - side the gar-ments that are stained with sin, And be washed in the

blood of the Lamb? Are you ful - ly trust-ing in His grace this hour? Are you
blood of the Lamb? Do you rest each mo-ment in the Cru - ci - fied? Are you
blood of the Lamb? Will your soul be read - y for the mansions bright, And be
blood of the Lamb; There's a fountain flowing for the soul un-clean: O be

CHORUS

washed in the blood of the Lamb? Are you washed in the blood,
Are you washed in the blood,

In the soul-cleans-ing blood of the Lamb? Are your gar-ments
of the Lamb?

spot-less? Are they white as snow? Are you washed in the blood of the Lamb?

265

SHALL WE GATHER AT THE RIVER?

Robert Lowry   Robert Lowry

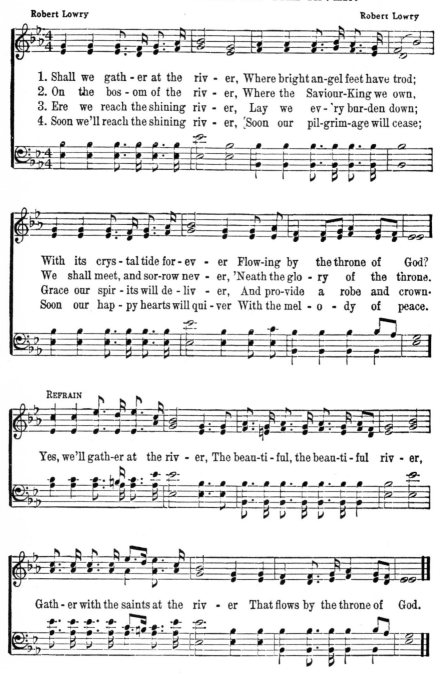

1. Shall we gath - er at the riv - er, Where bright an-gel feet have trod;
2. On the bos - om of the riv - er, Where the Saviour-King we own,
3. Ere we reach the shining riv - er, Lay we ev - 'ry bur-den down;
4. Soon we'll reach the shining riv - er, Soon our pil-grim-age will cease;

With its crys - tal tide for-ev - er Flow-ing by the throne of God?
We shall meet, and sor-row nev - er, 'Neath the glo - ry of the throne.
Grace our spir - its will de - liv - er, And pro-vide a robe and crown·
Soon our hap - py hearts will qui - ver With the mel - o - dy of peace.

REFRAIN

Yes, we'll gath-er at the riv - er, The beau-ti - ful, the beau-ti - ful riv - er,

Gath - er with the saints at the riv - er That flows by the throne of God.

In the Garden

C. A. M.

C. AUSTIN MILES
Arr. W. R. F.

1. I come to the gar - den a - lone, _____ While the dew is still on the ros - es, And the voice I hear fall-ing on my ear The Son of God dis - clos - es.

2. speaks, and the sound of His voice _____ Is so sweet the birds hush their sing - ing, And the mel - o - dy, That He gave to me With - in my heart is ring - ing.

3. stay in the gar - den with Him _____ Tho' the night a - round me be fall - ing, But He bids me go; Thro' the voice of woe His voice to me is call - ing.

The Old Rugged Cross

Rev. GEORGE BENNARD

On a hill far a-way stood an old rug-ged cross,The em-blem of suf-f'ring and shame;_And I love that old cross where the dear-est and best For a world of lost sin-ners was slain.__ So I'll cher-ish the old rug-ged cross,_ Till my tro-phies at last I lay down.__ I will

Major Recording Discography

The discography offers you a list of album titles that are representative of each artist's work. It does not contain listings that have been dropped from manufacturers' catalogs, nor does it contain each and every album on which the artists contained in this encyclopedia performed.

ARTIST AND ALBUM TITLE	*RECORD NO.*	*LABEL*
ANDRUS, BLACKWOOD & CO.		
Following You	R3515(D)	Greentree
Grand Opening	R3467(C)	Greentree
THE ARCHERS		
Keep Singin' That Love Song	R3224(C)	Impact
The Archers/Life In Jesus	R3213(C)	Impact
In The Beginning	R3503	Impact
Fresh Surrender	LS5707	Light
The Archers . . . Things We Deeply Feel	LS5679	Light
Stand Up!		Light
AYALA, BOB		
Joy By Surprise	MSB 6577	Myrrh
Wood Between The Worlds	MSB 6608	Myrrh
BAGWELL, WENDY		
This, That & The Other	CAS 9679	Canaan
Bust Out Laffin'	CAS 9765	Canaan
The Spirit in '76	CAS 9780	Canaan
We're Not Getting Older— Just Closer To Heaven!	CAS 9794	Canaan
Plain Georgia Gospel	CAS 9810	Canaan
Appearing Tonight	CAS 9831	Canaan
Live From Hiram	CAS 9845	Canaan

ARTIST AND ALBUM TITLE	*RECORD NO.*	*LABEL*
BANKS, BISHOP JEFF (**THE BANKS BROTHERS**)		
By And By	14264	Savoy
Do Not Pass Me	14168	Savoy
Holy Spirit	14248	Savoy
It Took A Miracle	14102	Savoy
Jesus Knows	14216	Savoy
My Rock	14184	Savoy
Revival Time	14329	Savoy
Silver Anniversary Album	14399	Savoy
Stand By Me	14146	Savoy
There's Power	14300	Savoy
Wondrous Cross	14082	Savoy
BETHLEHEM		
Bethlehem	MM0040A	Maranatha!
BETHLEHEM GOSPEL SINGERS		
My God Can See You	1406	HSE Records
THE BLACKWOOD BROTHERS		
The Amazing Blackwood Brothers	CAS 2504	Camden
Beautiful Isle	ACL-0831	Camden
The Best of the Blackwood Brothers	ANL 1-1091	RCA
Father's Prayer	6134	Sky.
Featuring Cecil Blackwood	6137	Sky.
Hallelujah Meetin'	6155	Sky.
Hallelujah To The King	6138	Sky.
How Great Thou Art	CAS-2601	Camden
Hymns of Gold	6158	Sky.

ARTIST AND ALBUM TITLE	RECORD NO.	LABEL
It's Worth It All	6139	Sky.
Learning To Lean	6161	Sky.
Live From Nashville	6173	Sky.
Lord We Praise You	6166	Sky.
Blackwood Brothers On Tour	ACL-0428	Camden
Put Your Hand In The Hand	CXS-9011	Camden
Release Me (From My Sin)	6124	Sky.
Sheltered In Arms Of God	CAS-2446	Camden
Blackwood Brothers Sing Bill Gaither	6175	Sky.
There He Goes	6142	Sky.
Touch Of Country	6156	Sky.
What A Beautiful Day	6147	Sky.

THE BOONES

Born Again Soundtrack	LL1041	Lamb/Lion
First Class	LL1038	Lamb/Lion
Glass Castles	LL1022	Lamb/Lion

BOONE, DEBBY

You Light Up My Life	BS 3118	Warner/Curb
Midstream	BSK 3530	Warner/Curb
Debby Boone	BSK 3301	Warner/Curb

BOONE, PAT

Pat Boone Sings The New Songs Of The Jesus People	LL1002	Lamb/Lion
Pat Boone And The First Nashville Jesus Band	LL1004	Lamb/Lion
The Family Who Prays	LL1006	Lamb/Lion
Born Again	LL1007	Lamb/Lion
S-A-V-E-D	LL1013	Lamb/Lion
Songs From The Inner Court (With Paul Johnson)	LL1016	Lamb/Lion

ARTIST AND ALBUM TITLE	RECORD NO.	LABEL
(*Boone, Pat, cont.*)		
Something Supernatural	LL1017	Lamb/Lion
Miracle Merry-Go-Round	LL1029	Lamb/Lion
Just The Way I Am	LL1039	Lamb/Lion

BRIDGE

Bridge	R3461(C)	Impact
Peace In The Midst Of The Storm	R3492(C)	Impact
Bridge With Bob Benson, Live	R3519(C)	Impact

BROWN, SCOTT WESLEY

I Am A Christian	NP 33009	Newpax
Scott Wesley Brown	——	Sparrow
I'm Not Religious, I Just Love The Lord	——	Sparrow

BURGESS, DAN

Thank You Lord	LS 5662	Light
With Songs You'll Want To Sing	LS 5730	Light
Celebrate His Love	——	Light

BURTON, WENDELL

Wendell	LL 1036	Lamb/Lion

BYRON, JON

Portrait of Love	LS 5758	Light

ARTIST AND ALBUM TITLE	RECORD NO.	LABEL
CAESAR, SHIRLEY		
The Best Of Shirley Caesar	14202	Savoy
CAMP, STEVE		
Sayin' It With Love	MSB-6604	Myrrh
CARSON, MARTHA		
Martha Carson Sings	CAS-906	Camden
Satisfied	T-1507	Capitol
Talk With The Lord	T-1607	Capitol
CASH, JOHNNY		
America/A 200-Year Salute	KC-31645	Columbia
Any Old Wind That Blows	KC-32091	Columbia
At Folsom Prison	CS-9639	Columbia
At San Quentin	CS-9827	Columbia
Ballads Of The True West	C2S-838	Columbia
Bitter Tears/Ballads Of The American Indian	CS-9048	Columbia
Blood, Sweat And Tears	CS-8730	Columbia
Carryin' On With J. Cash and June Carter	CS-9528	Columbia
Christmas	KC-31754	Columbia
The Christmas Spirit	CS-8917	Columbia
Everybody Loves A Nut	CS-9292	Columbia
Give My Love To Rose	KH-31256	Harmony
The Gospel Road	KG-32253	Columbia
Greatest Hits, Vol. 1	CS-9478	Columbia
Greatest Hits, Vol. 2	KC-30887	Columbia
The Holy Land	CS-9726	Columbia
Hymns By Johnny Cash	CS-8125	Columbia
Hymns From The Heart	CS-8522	Columbia

ARTIST AND ALBUM TITLE	RECORD NO.	LABEL
(Cash, Johnny, cont.)		
I Can See Clearly Now	NE-31607	Epic
I Walk The Line	CS-8990	Columbia
The Johnny Cash Show	KC-30100	Columbia
The Johnny Cash Songbook	KH-31602	Harmony
Man In Black	C-30550	Columbia
Mean As Hell/Ballads From The True West	CS-9246	Columbia
Orange Blossom Special	CS-9109	Columbia
Ride This Train	CS-8255	Columbia
Ring Of Fire	CS-8853	Columbia
A Thing Called Love	KC-31332	Columbia
This Is Johnny Cash	HS-11342	Columbia
Understand Your Man	KH-30916	Harmony
The Walls Of A Prison	KH-30138	Harmony
The World Of Johnny Cash	GP-29	Columbia

THE CATHEDRAL QUARTET

The Last Sunday	CAS 9733	Canaan
Our Statue Of Liberty	CAS 9761	Canaan
For Keeps	CAS 9776	Canaan
Easy On The Ears—Heavy On The Heart	CAS 9791	Canaan
Then . . . And Now	CAS 9807	Canaan
Sunshine And Roses	CAS 9821	Canaan
You Ain't Heard Nothing Yet	CAS 9842	Canaan

CHERÉ, TAMI

Keep Singin' That Love Song	LS 5732	Light
He's Everything To Me	LS 5754	Light

CHILDREN OF THE DAY

Never Felt So Free	LS 5712	Light
Come To The Waters	LS 5713	Light

ARTIST AND ALBUM TITLE	RECORD NO.	LABEL
With All Our Love	LS 5714	Light
Where Else Would I Go	LS 5715	Light
Christmas Album	LS 5716	Light

CHRISTIAN, CHRIS

Chris Christian	MSA 6569	Myrrh
Chance	MSB 6600	Myrrh

CLARK, TERRY

Welcome	GNR 8107	Good News

CLAWSON, CYNTHIA

In The Garden	TR 101	Triangle
The Way I Feel	TR 112	Triangle
It Was His Love	TR 116	Triangle

CLEVELAND, THE REVEREND JAMES

All You Need	14346	Savoy
At The Cross	14205	Savoy
Bread Of Heaven	14171	Savoy
Christ Is The Answer	14059	Savoy
Down Memory Lane	14311	Savoy
Free At Last	14211	Savoy
Give Me My Flowers	14117	Savoy
God's Promises	14220	Savoy
Grace Of God	14134	Savoy
Greatest Love Story	14286	Savoy
Hark The Voice	14252	Savoy
Heaven Is Good Enough	14103	Savoy

ARTIST AND ALBUM TITLE	RECORD NO.	LABEL
(Cleveland, The Reverend James, cont.)		
His Name Is Wonderful	14206	Savoy
How Great Thou Art	14063	Savoy
I Stood On The Banks	14096	Savoy
I'm One Of Them	14236	Savoy
It's Real	14125	Savoy
Live At Carnegie Hall	7014	Savoy
Lord Help Me	14319	Savoy
99½ Won't Do	14265	Savoy
No Failure In God	14052	Savoy
Out On A Hill	14045	Savoy
Peace Be Still	14076	Savoy
Pilgrim On Sorrow	14176	Savoy
Somebody Knows	14167	Savoy
Soul Of James Cleveland	14068	Savoy
Stood On Banks	14096	Savoy
Sun Will Shine	14085	Savoy
Trust In God	14302	Savoy
Where Can I Go	14230	Savoy
With Gospel Star Parade	14375	Savoy
Without A Song	14375	Savoy
You'll Never Walk Alone	14159	Savoy

CONTINENTAL SINGERS AND ORCHESTRA

Continental Orchestra	R3426(C)	Jim

THE COURIERS

Town And Country	7037	Tempo
Gospel Favorites	7044	Tempo
The Couriers Sing Folk	7059	Tempo
Statue Of Liberty	7081	Tempo
Sing With Us	7096	Tempo
Kinda Country	7112	Tempo
Mighty Power	7119	Tempo

ARTIST AND ALBUM TITLE	RECORD NO.	LABEL
Ovation	7134	Tempo
Comfort, Strength & Happiness	7176	Tempo
We're Peculiar People	4850	——

COURTNEY, RAGAN

Bright New Wings	TR 109	Triangle
Angels	TR 115	Triangle
Beginnings	TR 107	Triangle
Acts	TR 122	Triangle

CROUCH, ANDRAE, AND
THE DISCIPLES

Take The Message Everywhere	LS 5504	Light
Keep On Singin'	LS 5546	Light
Soulfully	LS 5581	Light
Just Andrae	LS 5598	Light
Live At Carnegie Hall	LS 5602	Light
Take Me Back	LS 5637	Light
The Best Of Andrae	LS 5678	Light
This Is Another Day	LS 5683	Light
Live In London	LSX 5717	Light

CULVERWELL, ANDREW

Take Another Look	DST 4005	DaySpring

DALTON, LARRY

The Great Praise Meeting	LS 5697	Light
Living Sound	LS 5601	Light
Living Sound Sings Around The World	LS 5652	Light
Brass, Strings And Ivory	LS 5741	Light

ARTIST AND ALBUM TITLE	RECORD NO.	LABEL
DANNIEBELLE		
Danniebelle	LS 5638	Light
This Moment	LS 5675	Light
He Is King	LS 5702	Light
DAVIS, JIMMIE		
Lord, Let Me Be There	CAS 9751	Canaan
Christ Is My Sunshine	CAS 9760	Canaan
Living By Faith	CAS 9773	Canaan
The Singing Governor: A Live Album!	CAS 9786	Canaan
Put Jesus First	CAS 9804	Canaan
Songs Of The Spirit	CAS 9817	Canaan
Walking In The Sunshine	CAS 9839	Canaan
DINO AND DEBBY (KARTSONAKIS)		
Dino Plays Folk Musical Themes	LS 5635	Light
My Tribute	LS 5661	Light
Dino-Patriotic	LS 5685	Light
Dino On Tour . . . With Debby	LS 5700	Light
Miracle (w/David Rose)	LS 5720	Light
Alleluia	LS 5721	Light
He Touched Me	LS 5723	Light
Playing Your Favorite Christmas Carols	LS 5724	Light
Classic Country	LS 5727	Light
Love Song	LSB 5742	Light
Debby Sings Alleluia	LS 5718	Light
DIXIE ECHOES		
Turn Your Radio On	SS33001	Supreme
I Want To See Jesus	SS33002	Supreme
Live—The Dixie Echoes	SS33008	Supreme

ARTIST AND ALBUM TITLE	*RECORD NO.*	*LABEL*
My Real Home	SS33011	Supreme
The Dixie Echoes Today	SS33015	Supreme
Get On Board	SS33018	Supreme
Come On In	SS33020	Supreme
Heavenly Echoes	SS33024	Supreme
The Best Of The Dixie Echoes	SS33028	Supreme
Coast To Coast	SS33029	Supreme

THE DIXIE MELODY BOYS

Are You Ready	365	QCIA

DIXON, JESSY

It's All Right Now	LS 5719	Light

DOGWOOD

After The Flood, Before The Fire	LL 1020	Lamb/Lion
Love Note	LL 1026	Lamb/Lion
Out In The Open	LL 1035	Lamb/Lion

DOUGLAS, THE REVEREND ISAAC

Faith Will Survive	3027	Creed
A Little Higher	3036	Creed
Rev. Isaac Douglas, with the Birmingham Choir	3045	Creed
You've Got A Friend	3047	Creed
The Harvest Is Plentiful	3056	Creed
Do You Know Him	3059	Creed
By The Grace Of God	3064	Creed
In Times Like These	3071	Creed

ARTIST AND ALBUM TITLE	RECORD NO.	LABEL
(Douglas, The Reverend Isaac, cont.)		
Beautiful Zion	3072	Creed
You Really Ought To Get To Know Him	3075	Creed
Stand Up For Jesus	2-3076	Creed
Special Appearance	3081	Creed
You Light Up My Life	3090	Creed

FARRELL & FARRELL

Farrell & Farrell	NP 33050	Newpax

FIELD, FRED

Fred Field And Friends	MM0031A	Maranatha!

FIREWORKS

Fireworks	MSB 6587	Myrrh

FISCHER, JOHN

Still Life	LS 5645	Light
New Covenant	LS 5658	Light
Naphtali	LS 5693	Light
Inside	LS 5711	Light
Johnny's Cafe	LS 5757	Light

THE FLORIDA BOYS

What A Difference Jesus Makes	CAS 9739	Canaan
True Gospel	CAS 9752	Canaan

ARTIST AND ALBUM TITLE	RECORD NO.	LABEL
First Class Gospel	CAS 9768	Canaan
Here They Come	CAS 9799	Canaan
He Loves You	CAS 9799	Canaan
In Concert . . . Live	CAS 9814	Canaan
Vintage Gospel	CAS 9818	Canaan
The Best Of The Florida Boys	CAS 9834	Canaan
Sing About A New Day	CAS 9837	Canaan

FONG, ODEN

Mustard Seed Faith	018	Maranatha!
Come For The Children	MM051A	A&S

FORD, DAVID

Peace Like A River	TR 117	Triangle
Words Of Life	TR 110	Triangle

FORD, TENNESSEE ERNIE

He Touched Me	WSA 8764	Word
Swing Wide Your Golden Gate	WSB 8798	Word
Holy, Holy, Holy	ST-334	Capitol
America the Beautiful	STAO-412	Capitol
Tennessee Ernie Ford	STBB-506	Capitol
Everything Is Beautiful	ST-583	Capitol
Abide with Me	ST-730	Capitol
Tennessee Ernie Ford Hymns	ST-756	Capitol
Tennessee Ernie Ford Spirituals	ST-818	Capitol
C-h-r-i-s-t-m-a-s	ST-831	Capitol
The Folk Album	ST-833	Capitol
Near the Cross	ST-1005	Capitol
A Friend We Have	ST-1272	Capitol
Sixteen Tons	DT-1380	Capitol
Sing a Hymn with Me	ST-1679	Capitol

ARTIST AND ALBUM TITLE	RECORD NO.	LABEL
(Ford, Tennessee Ernie, cont.)		
Book of Favorite Hymns	ST-1794	Capitol
God Lives!	ST-2618	Capitol
Tennessee Ernie Ford Deluxe Set	STCL-2942	Capitol
Mr. Words and Music	ST-11001	Capitol
It's Tennessee Ernie Ford	ST-11092	Capitol

FOUND FREE

Closer Than Ever	R3530	Greentree

FRANCISCO, DON

Brother Of The Son	NP 33010	Newpax
Forgiven	NP 33042	Newpax

THE BILL GAITHER TRIO

It's A Miracle	WST 8686	Word
The Very Best Of The Very Best	WSB 8804	Word
Pilgrim's Progress	R3495(C)	Impact
Moments For Forever	R3457(D)	Impact
My Heart Can Sing	R3445(C)	Impact
Praise	R3408(C)	Impact
Jesus, We Just Want To Thank You	R3379(C)	Impact
In Retrospect	R3367(D)	Impact
I'm A Promise	R3344(C)	Impact
Something Beautiful/An Evening with The Bill Gaither Trio	R3337(D)	Impact
Thanks For Sunshine	R3295(C)	Impact
Especially For Children	R3214(C)	Impact
Let's Just Praise The Lord	R3209(C)	Impact
Christmas . . . Back Home In Indiana	R3197(Y)	Impact
Live (2-record set)	R3178(D)	Impact
My Faith Still Holds	R3161(C)	Impact

ARTIST AND ALBUM TITLE	*RECORD NO.*	*LABEL*
Because He Lives	R3130(C)	Impact
The King Is Coming	R3083(C)	Impact
Sings Warm	R3051(C)	Impact
He Touched Me	R3017	Impact
I'm Free	R1989(C)	Impact
Happiness	R1974(C)	Impact

GAITHER, DANNY

Singing To The World	R3527(C)	Impact
It Is Well With My Soul	R3432(C)	Impact
Sing A Song Of Love	R3278(C)	Impact
Sweet And High	R3166(C)	Impact

GILBERT, JIM

I Love You With The Love Of The Lord	LS 5753	Light

GIRARD, CHUCK

Chuck Girard	GNR 8102	Good News
Glow In The Dark	GNR 8103	Good News
Written On The Wind	GNR 8106	Good News

THE HAPPY GOODMAN FAMILY

The Best Of The Happy Goodmans	CAS 9614	Canaan
What A Happy Time!	CAS 9628	Canaan
Good 'N' Happy	CAS 9636	Canaan
The Happy Gospel Of The Happy Goodmans	CAS 9644	Canaan
Portrait of Excitement	CAS 9655	Canaan

ARTIST AND ALBUM TITLE	RECORD NO.	LABEL
(The Happy Goodman Family, cont.)		
This Happy House	CAS 9663	Canaan
Good Times With The Happy Goodmans	CAS 9682	Canaan
Wanted Live	CAS 9705	Canaan
Leave Your Sorrows And Come Along	CAS 9706	Canaan
Legendary	CAS 9736	Canaan
Covered In Warmth	CAS 9772	Canaan
Happy Goodman Family Hour	CAS 9755	Canaan
$99^{44}/_{100}\%$ Goodmans	CAS 9789	Canaan
In Concert . . . Live	CAX 9816	Canaan
Refreshing	CAS 9828	Canaan

GOSPEL SEED

Growing	MSB 6594	Myrrh

GRANDQUIST, NANCY

Somebody Special	NP33064	Newpax

GRANT, AMY

Amy Grant	MSB 6586	Myrrh

GREEN, KEITH

For Him Who Has Ears To Hear	SPR 1015	Sparrow
No Compromise	SPR 1024	Sparrow

ARTIST AND ALBUM TITLE	*RECORD NO.*	*LABEL*
GREEN, LILLY		
Especially For You	MSB 6570	Myrrh
I Am Blessed	MSB 6618	Myrrh
GRINE, JANNY		
Free Indeed	SPR 1005	Sparrow
Covenant Woman	SPR 1011	Sparrow
He Made Me Worthy	SPR 1021	Sparrow
Think On These Things	SPR 1028	Sparrow
HALE (ROBERT) & WILDER (DEAN)		
Joy To The World	WST 8745	Word
Devotion And Praise	WST 8753	Word
Rise Up, O Men Of God	WST 8774	Word
Lord Make Me An Instrument	WST 8574	Word
Now Praise God And Sing	WST 8771	Word
Break Forth And Sing	WSB 8778	Word
Shenandoah	WSB 8789	Word
HARRIS, LARNELLE		
Tell It To Jesus	WST 8669	Word
Larnelle . . . More	WST 8731	Word
Free	WSB 8795	Word
HAWKINS, WALTER		
Love Alive	LS 5686	Light
Jesus Christ Is The Way	LS 5705	Light
Love Alive II	LS 5735	Light

ARTIST AND ALBUM TITLE	RECORD NO.	LABEL
THE HEMPHILLS		
In God's Sunshine	R3455(C)	HeartWarming
Without A Doubt	R3406(C)	HeartWarming
One Live Family (2-record set)	R3352(D)	HeartWarming
Home Cookin'	——	Heart Warming
HIBBARD, BRUCE		
A Light Within	PSR 006	Seed
THE HINSONS		
The Hinsons Sing About The Lighthouse	5056	Calvary
He Pilots My Ship	5074	Calvary
We Promised You Gospel	5088	Calvary
Touch Of Hinsons, Depths Of Glory	5110	Calvary
Harvest Of Hits	5116	Calvary
Live And On Stage	5121	Calvary
High Voltage	5130	Calvary
The Group That God Built	5142	Calvary
On The Road	5159	Calvary
Prime	5162	Calvary
HOLM, DALLAS		
Tell 'Em Again	R3480(C)	Greentree
Dallas Holm & Praise/Live	R3441(C)	Greentree
Just Right	R3391(C)	Greentree
Nothing But Praise	R3354(C)	Greentree
Peace, Joy And Love	R3257(C)	Greentree
Didn't He Shine	R3198(C)	Greentree
Looking Back	R3139(C)	Greentree

ARTIST AND ALBUM TITLE	RECORD NO.	LABEL
HONEYTREE		
Honeytree	MSA 6523	Myrrh
The Way I Feel	MSA 6530	Myrrh
Evergreen	MSA 6553	Myrrh
Me And My Old Guitar	MSB 6584	Myrrh
The Melodies In Me	MSB 6591	Myrrh
HOWARD, TOM		
View From The Bridge	SRA 2003	Solid Rock
HUFFAM, TEDDY, & THE GEMS		
That All May Be One	CAS 9809	Canaan
Cookin'	CAS 9825	Canaan
Live	CAS 9829	Canaan
THE IMPERIALS		
Best Of The Imperials	R3465(C)	Impact
1968–1972 (2-record set)	R3424(D)	Impact
Just Because	R3390(C)	Impact
No Shortage	R3288(C)	Impact
Follow The Man With The Music	R3227(C)	Impact
Imperials . . . Live (2-record set)	R3215(C)	Impact
Imperials	R3165(C)	Impact
Time To Get It Together	R3082(C)	Impact
Gospel's Alive And Well	R3045(C)	Impact
Love Is The Thing	R3029(C)	Impact
Now!	R1990(C)	Impact
Sail On	DST 4006	DaySpring
Live	DST 4007	DaySpring
Heed The Call	DST 4011	DaySpring

ARTIST AND ALBUM TITLE	RECORD NO.	LABEL

INGLES, DAVID

I Want To Stroll Over Heaven With You	R3489(C)	Impact
There's A Whole Lot Of People Going Home	R3505(C)	Impact
Oasis Of Love	R3521(C)	Impact
Satan Has Been Paralyzed	R3494(C)	Impact
The Seed Of Abraham	R3470(C)	Impact

THE INSPIRATIONS

Our Inspiration	CAS 9704	Canaan
Wake Up In Glory	CAS 9707	Canaan
Old Time Singin'	CAS 9718	Canaan
We Shall Rise	CAS 9725	Canaan
Touring The City	CAS 9740	Canaan
When I Wake Up To Sleep No More	CAS 9747	Canaan
More To Go To Heaven For	CAS 9758	Canaan
I'm Taking A Flight	CAS 9769	Canaan
Golden Street Parade	CAS 9779	Canaan
Inspirations Live	CAS 9792	Canaan
A Night of Inspiration	CAS 9803	Canaan
On Heaven's Bright Shore	CAS 9806	Canaan
When I Get Home	CAS 9819	Canaan
Looking for You	CAS 9838	Canaan

JACKSON, MAHALIA

Bless This House	CS-8761	Columbia
Garden Of Prayer	CS-9346	Columbia
Great Gettin' Up	CS-8153	Columbia
Greatest Hits	CS-8804	Columbia
How I Got Over	C-34073E	Columbia
Hymns Of Dr. King	CS-9686E	Columbia
I Believe	CS-8349	Columbia
In Concert	CS-9490	Columbia
Mighty Fortress	CS-9659	Columbia

ARTIST AND ALBUM TITLE	RECORD NO.	LABEL
My Faith	CS-9405	Columbia
Power And The Glory	CS-8264	Columbia
Recorded In Europe	CS-8526	Columbia
Right Out Of The Church	CS-9813	Columbia
What The World Needs Now	CS-9950	Columbia

JEREMIAH PEOPLE

Let Love Live	LS 5614	Light
Building For The Very Third Time	LS 5636	Light
First Love	LS 5669	Light
Where Your Heart Is	LS 5710	Light
Reflections and Images	LS 5756	Light

JERRY AND THE SINGING GOFFS

Say I Do	QC 323	QCA
This Is Love	QC 331	QCA

JOHNSON, MIKE

The Artist/The Riddle	NP 33011	Newpax
More Than Just An Act	NP 33043	Newpax

JOHNSON, PHIL

Somebody Like You	R3507(C)	Greentree

KEAGGY, PHIL

What A Day	NS 001	New Song
Love Broke Thru	NS 002	New Song

ARTIST AND ALBUM TITLE	*RECORD NO.*	*LABEL*
(*Keaggy, Phil, cont.*)		
Emerging	NS 004	New Song
The Master And The Musician	NS 006	New Song

THE KINGSMEN

Big And Live	CAS 9749	Canaan
24 Carat Gospel	CAS 9774	Canaan
It Made News In Heaven	CAS 9788	Canaan
Just In Time	CAS 9801	Canaan
The Best Of The Kingsmen	CAS 9835	Canaan
Upper Window	R3518(C)	HeartWarming
Chattanooga Live	R3477(C)	HeartWarming
Just A Little Closer Home	R3452(C)	HeartWarming

KLAUDT INDIAN FAMILY

Coast To Coast Television	KF900	Klaudt Family
Traveling On	KF901	Klaudt Family
Gospel Favorites	KF902	Klaudt Family
Whispering Hope	KF903	Klaudt Family
At The End Of The Trail	KF904	Klaudt Family
The Klaudt Indian Family	KF905	Klaudt Family
The Highest Hill	KF906	Klaudt Family
Where He Leads Me	KF907	Klaudt Family
Christmas Peace On Earth	KF908	Klaudt Family
Mom Klaudt Sings Peace Like A River	KF909	Klaudt Family
Gospel War Hoops	KF910	Klaudt Family
Gospel Moods of Ralph Seibel	KF911	Klaudt Family

LAFFERTY, KAREN

Sweet Communion	MM0037A	Maranatha!
Bird In A Golden Sky	MM0017A	Maranatha!

ARTIST AND ALBUM TITLE	RECORD NO.	LABEL
LAWRENCE, DOUG		
Doug Lawrence	LS 5671	Light
LEE, J.J.		
J.J.	NP33065	Newpax
THE LEFEVRES		
(Now The Rex Nelon Singers)		
Experience	CAS 9777	Canaan
Stepping On The Clouds	CAS 9757	Canaan
The LeFevres Salute Gospel Music—USA!	CAS 9790	Canaan
Singing 'Til He Comes	CAS 9805	Canaan
THE LEWIS FAMILY		
Country Sunday	CAS 9730	Canaan
Absolutely Lewis!	CAS 9764	Canaan
Style Gospel	CAS 9782	Canaan
The Lewis Family Just Keeps On Praising His Name	CAS 9795	Canaan
Alive And Pickin'	CAS 9798	Canaan
Country Faith	CAS 9820	Canaan
Wrapped With Grace And Tied With Love	CAS 9836	Canaan
LIMPIC & RAYBURN		
Limpic & Rayburn	MSA 6575	Myrrh
Caught In The Crossfire	MSB 6595	Myrrh

ARTIST AND ALBUM TITLE	RECORD NO.	LABEL
MANN, JOHNNY		
The Church's One Foundation	LS 5656	Light
The Four Freedoms	LS 5682	Light
The Johnny Mann Singers		
Sing Andrae Crouch	LS 5748	Light
MANN, LYNN		
God's Quiet Love	LS 5692	Light
McGUIRE, BARRY		
Seeds	MSA 6519	Myrrh
Lighten Up	MSA 6531	Myrrh
THE McKEITHENS		
The McKeithens	3076	Harvest
My Second Home	1843	Harvest
Memories	1881	Harvest
Keep On Praising	1921	Harvest
McSPADDEN, GARY		
Higher Purpose	PR 33054	Paragon
McVAY, LEWIS		
Spirit of St. Lewis	MM0041A	Maranatha!

ARTIST AND ALBUM TITLE	RECORD NO.	LABEL
MEECE, DAVID		
David	MSA 6562	Myrrh
I Just Call On You	MSB 6578	Myrrh
Everybody Needs A Little Help	MSB 6620	Myrrh
THE MERCY RIVER BOYS		
Good Times A Comin'	CAS 9783	Canaan
The Promise	CAS 9797	Canaan
Something For Everyone	CAS 9813	Canaan
Refresh Our Spirit	CAS 9827	Canaan
MIGHTY CLOUDS OF JOY		
Family Circle	114	Peacock Records
A Bright Side	121	Peacock Records
Live At The Music Hall	134	Peacock Records
Golden Gems Of Gospel	140	Peacock Records
Presenting The Untouchable Mighty Clouds Of Joy	151	Peacock Records
Songs Of Reverend Julius Cheeks	163	Peacock Records
The Super Groups	166	Peacock Records
Live At The Apollo	173	Peacock Records
Best Of The Mighty Clouds Of Joy	183	Peacock Records
A Holiday Gift Just For You	235	Peacock Records
Mother's Favorite Songs	240	Peacock Records
The Best Of The Mighty Clouds Of Joy	59136	ABC Records
God Bless America	59170	ABC Records
Gospel At Its Best	59200	ABC Records
It's Time	50177	ABC Records
Kickin'	899	ABC Records
Truth Is The Power	986	ABC Records
Live And Direct	1038	ABC Records
The Very Best Of The Mighty Clouds Of Joy	1091-2	ABC Records
Changing Times	JEA 35971	Citylights/Epic

ARTIST AND ALBUM TITLE	RECORD NO.	LABEL
NELON SINGERS, REX (Formerly the LeFevres)		
The Sun's Coming Up	CAS 9823	Canaan
Live	CAS 9830	Canaan
More Than Conquerors	CAS 9841	Canaan
NELSON, ERICK		
Flow River Flow	MM0028A	Maranatha!
NETHERTON, TOM		
What A Friend . . . We Have In Jesus	WST 8667	Word
Just As I Am	WST 8690	Word
Hem Of His Garment	WSB 8759	Word
NIELSON AND YOUNG		
Nielson and Young	PR 33049	Paragon
THE NORMAN BROTHERS		
All Of My Hard Times	1523	HSE Records
NORMAN, LARRY		
Upon This Rock	R3121(C)	Impact
In Another Land	SRA 2001	Solid Rock

ARTIST AND ALBUM TITLE	RECORD NO.	LABEL
NUTSHELL		
Begin Again	MSB 6513	Myrrh
Flyaway	MST 6592	Myrrh
THE OAK RIDGE BOYS		
Super Gospel—Four Sides Of		
Gospel Excitement	R3320(C)	HeartWarming
Gospel Gold	R3294(C)	HeartWarming
Street Gospel	R3200(C)	HeartWarming
Best Of Oak Ridge Boys	KC 35202	Columbia
Sky High	C 33057	Columbia
Oak Ridge Boys	KC 32742	Columbia
Old Fashioned Music	C 33935	Columbia
OLDHAM, DOUG		
Gold Treasury of Hymns (2-record set)	R3496(D)	Impact
I Am . . . Because	R3430(C)	Impact
Doug Oldham And Friends	R3393(C)	Impact
Doug/Warm	R3345(C)	Impact
Dog Oldham And The Speers—Live		
I Just Feel Like Something Good		
Is About To Happen (2-record set)	R3353(D)	Impact
The Church Triumphant . . .		
Alive And Well!	R3324(C)	Impact
Doug Oldham Sings More Songs Of		
Bill Gaither	R3272(C)	Impact
To God Be The Glory	R3240(C)	Impact
Live (2-record set)	R3211(D)	Impact
Christmas With . . .	R3193(Y)	Impact
Get All Excited		
Go Tell Everybody!	R3183(C)	Impact
Through It All	R3156(C)	Impact
Doug Oldham Sings The Best Of		
Bill Gaither	R3143(C)	Impact
The King Is Coming	R3087(C)	Impact

ARTIST AND ALBUM TITLE	RECORD NO.	LABEL
OMARTIAN, MICHAEL		
White Horse	MSA 6564	Myrrh
Adam Again	MSA 6576	Myrrh
Seasons Of The Soul	MSB 6606	Myrrh
ONE TRUTH		
Gospel Truth	R3469(C)	Greentree
OWENS-COLLINS, JAMIE		
Laughter In Your Soul	LS 5631	Light
Growing Pains	LS 5684	Light
Love Eyes	LS 5736	Light
PANTANO/SALSBURY		
Hit The Switch	SRA 2008	Solid Rock
PANTRY, JOHN		
Empty Handed	MM0044A	Maranatha!
PATILLO, LEON		
Dance, Children, Dance	MM0049A	Maranatha!

ARTIST AND ALBUM TITLE	RECORD NO.	LABEL
PAXTON, GARY S.		
Gary S. Paxton	NP 33005	Newpax
More From Gary S. Paxton	NP 33033	Newpax
The Gospel According to Gary S. Paxton		
(Gary S. Paxton Singers)	PR 33048	Paragon
POPE, DAVE		
Face To Face	MSA 6572	Myrrh
POWELL, SARA JORDAN		
God Loved	14301	Savoy
I Find No Fault	14394	Savoy
Songs Of Faith	14278	Savoy
Touch Somebody's	14347	Savoy
When Jesus Comes To Stay	14465	Savoy
PRESLEY, ELVIS		
Elvis Presley	LSP-1254	RCA
Elvis	LSP-1382	RCA
Loving You	LSP-1515	RCA
Elvis' Golden Records	LSP-1707	RCA
King Creole	LSP-1884	RCA
For LP Fans Only	LSP-1990	RCA
A Date With Elvis	LSP-2011	RCA
50,000,000 Elvis Fans Can't Be Wrong—		
Elvis' Gold Records, Vol. 2	LSP-2075	RCA
Elvis Is Back!	LSP-2231	RCA
G. I. Blues	LSP-2256	RCA
His Hand In Mine	LSP-2328	RCA
Something For Everybody	LSP-2370	RCA

ARTIST AND ALBUM TITLE	RECORD NO.	LABEL
(Presley, Elvis, cont.)		
Blue Hawaii	LSP-2426	RCA
Pot Luck	LSP-2523	RCA
Girls! Girls! Girls!	LSP-2621	RCA
"Fun In Acapulco"	LSP-2756	RCA
Elvis' Golden Records, Vol. 3	LSP-2765	RCA
"Kissin' Cousins"	LSP-2894	RCA
Roustabout	LSP-2999	RCA
Girl Happy	LSP-3338	RCA
Elvis For Everyone!	LSP-3450	RCA
Paradise Hawaiian Style	LSP-3643	RCA
How Great Thou Art	LSP-3758	RCA
Elvis' Gold Records, Vol. 4	LSP-3921	RCA
Speedway	LSP-3989	RCA
Elvis—TV Special	LPM-4088	RCA
From Elvis In Memphis	LSP-4155	RCA
On Stage (February 1970)	LSP-4362	RCA
Elvis In Person At The International Hotel, Las Vegas, Nevada	LSP-4428	RCA
Elvis Back In Memphis	LSP-4429	RCA
Elvis—That's The Way It Is	LSP-4445	RCA
Elvis Country	LSP-4460	RCA
Love Letters From Elvis	LSP-4530	RCA
Elvis Sings The Wonderful World Of Christmas	LSP-4579	RCA
Elvis Now	LSP-4671	RCA
He Touched Me	LSP-4690	RCA
Elvis As Recorded Live At Madison Square Garden	LSP-4776	RCA
Elvis	APL-1-0283	RCA
From Memphis To Vegas/ From Vegas To Memphis	LSP-6020	RCA
Elvis' Worldwide Fifty Gold Award Hits, Vol. 1	LPM-6401	RCA
Elvis—Aloha From Hawaii Via Satellite	VPSX-6089	RCA
Separate Ways	2611	RCA

PRESTON, BILLY

Behold	MSB 6605	Myrrh

ARTIST AND ALBUM TITLE	*RECORD NO.*	*LABEL*
PRICE, FLO		
Back Home	LS 5593	Light
Our House	LS 5608	Light
I Like The Sound Of America	LS 5633	Light
And That's The Truth	LS 5659	Light
The Best You Can Be	LS 5694	Light
THE RAMBOS		
Queen Of Paradise	R3499(C)	HeartWarming
Naturally	R3459(C)	HeartWarming
Rambo Country (2-record set)	R3429(D)	HeartWarming
The Son Is Shining	R3398(C)	HeartWarming
These Three Are One	R3366(C)	HeartWarming
There Has To Be A Song	R3359(C)	HeartWarming
Alive . . . And Live At Soul's Harbor (2-record set)	R3347(D)	HeartWarming
Best of The Rambos	R3187(C)	HeartWarming
Soul In The Family	R3173(C)	HeartWarming
The Singing Rambos . . . Live (2-record set)	R3116(D)	HeartWarming
This Is My Valley	R3032(C)	HeartWarming
RAMBO, DOTTIE		
Love Letters	R3454(C)	HeartWarming
Down By The Creek Bank (recording plus workbook)	R3484(D)	HeartWarming
REBA (RAMBO)		
The Lady Is A Child	R3486(C)	Greentree
Lady	R3419(C)	Greentree
The Prodigal	R3543(C)	Greentree

ARTIST AND ALBUM TITLE	RECORD NO.	LABEL
RETTINO, ERNIE & DEBBIE		
Joseph	W 101/2	Windchime
Friends	MM0009	Maranatha!
More Than Friends	MM0035	Maranatha!
Joy In The Morning	MM0019	Maranatha!
Changing	MM0043	Maranatha!
Come Walk With Me		
(solo album by Debbie Rettino)	MM0004	Maranatha!
RILEY, JEANNIE C.		
Give Myself A Party	4805	MGM
Down To Earth	4849	MGM
When Love Has Gone Away	SE-4891	MGM
Wings To Fly	R3539(C)	Benson
ROGERS, ROY AND DALE EVANS		
The Country Side of Roy Rogers	ST-594	Capitol
A Man From Duck Run	ST-785	Capitol
The Bible Tells Me So	ST-1745	Capitol
Take A Little Love	ST-1120	Capitol
In The Sweet By And By	WST 8589	Word
The Good Life	WSA 8761	Word
SANDQUIST, TED		
The Courts Of The King	NS 003	New Song
THE SCENICLAND BOYS		
Songs From The Heart	1564	Scenicland Boys
At Home	——	Scenicland Boys

ARTIST AND ALBUM TITLE	RECORD NO.	LABEL
The Best Of The Scenicland Boys	——	Scenicland Boys
Especially For You	——	Scenicland Boys
Back Home	——	Scenicland Boys
I Cried Out To Jesus	——	Scenicland Boys
Nothing But Good Gospel	——	Scenicland Boys
I Know Jesus Will Always Be There	——	Scenicland Boys
He Kept On Loving Me	——	Scenicland Boys

THE 2ND CHAPTER OF ACTS

With Footnotes	MSA 6526	Myrrh
In The Volume Of The Book	MSA 6542	Myrrh
To The Bride	MSX 6548	Myrrh
How The West Was One	MSY 6598	Myrrh

SEGO BROTHERS AND NAOMI

It Will Be Different The Next Time	R3433(C)	HeartWarming
Down Home Singin'	R3336(C)	HeartWarming
Live At Hallelujah Square	R3321(C)	HeartWarming
What A Happy Time/Live	R3279(C)	HeartWarming
The Dearest Friend I Ever Had	R3206(C)	HeartWarming
Sorry, I Never Knew You	R3186(C)	HeartWarming

THE SENSATIONAL FRIENDLY FOUR

Live So God Can Use You	1525	HSE Records

THE SENSATIONAL GOSPELAIRES

Give God A Chance	1526	HSE Records
In Times Like These	1500	HSE Records

ARTIST AND ALBUM TITLE	RECORD NO.	LABEL
SHARALEE		
Daughter of Music	R3520	Greentree
THE SHARRETTS		
A Song For The Heart	DST 4003	DaySpring
You Turn Me Around	DST 4013	DaySpring
SHEA, GEORGE BEVERLY		
The Longer I Serve Him	WST 8671	Word
Angels Shall Keep Thee	WST 8719	Word
The Old Rugged Cross	WSB 8796	Word
SHEPPARD, TIM		
Inside My Room	R3451(C)	Greentree
Diary	R3394(C)	Greentree
THE SINGING CHRISTIANS (See The Mercy River Boys)		
SLAUGHTER, HENRY AND HAZEL		
Rejoice	R3453(C)	HeartWarming
Thanks . . . I Think I'll Play One	R3439(C)	HeartWarming
In Retrospect (2-record set)	R3423(D)	HeartWarming
The Sweetest Hallelujah	R3395	HeartWarming
HENRY PLAYS SONGS FROM "ALLELUJA!"	R3307(C)	HeartWarming
ALL IN THE NAME OF JESUS	R3293(C)	HeartWarming
The Joyous Excitement of Henry and Hazel Slaughter (2-record set)	R3338(D)	HeartWarming
Blessed Assurance	R3255(C)	HeartWarming
Tribute	R3208(C)	HeartWarming
Slaughter On Church Street	R3199(C)	HeartWarming

ARTIST AND ALBUM TITLE	RECORD NO.	LABEL
Live	R3179	HeartWarming
We've Come This Far By Faith	R1945	HeartWarming
Artist At Work	R1816(C)	HeartWarming

SMITH, CONNIE

Connie Smith Sings Great Sacred Songs	LSP-3589	RCA
The Best Of Connie Smith	LSP-3848	RCA
Sunday Morning With Nat Stuckey and Connie Smith	LSP-4300	RCA
The Best Of Connie Smith, Vol. 2	LSP-4324	RCA
I Never Once Stopped Loving You	LSP-4394	RCA
Where Is My Castle?	LSP-4474	RCA
Just One Time	LSP-4534	RCA
Come Along and Walk With Me	LSP-4598	RCA
Ain't We Havin' Us A Good Time	LSP-4694	RCA
"If It Ain't Love" and Other Great Dallas Frazier Songs	LSP-4748	RCA
Love Is The Look You're Looking For	LSP-4840	RCA
Dream Painter	APL-1-0188	RCA
A Lady Named Smith	KC-32185	Columbia

SNELL, ADRIAN

Listen To The Peace	MM0045A	Maranatha!

THE SOUL STIRRERS

The Best Of The Soul Stirrers	10015	Checker
Christ Is All	10091	Checker
Glory	10066	Checker
Going Back To The Lord Again	2150	Spec.
Golden Gospel	10038	Checker
Gospel Music Vol. 1	94007	Imper.
Gospel Truth	10027	Checker

ARTIST AND ALBUM TITLE	RECORD NO.	LABEL
(*The Soul Stirrers, cont.*)		
He's A Friend	10071	Checker
Judgement	10058	Checker
Resting Easy	10021	Checker
Soul Stirrers Vol. 1	0086	Jewel
Soul Stirrers Featuring Sam Cooke	2106E	Spec.
Soul's In . . . But Gospel's Out Of Sight	10056	Checker
Strength, Power And Love	0084	Jewel
That's Heaven With Sam Cooke	2146E	Spec.
Thrilling—In Concert	10051	Checker
Tribute To Sam Cooke	10063	Checker
Original Soul Stirrers With Sam Cooke	2137E	Spec.

THE SPEER FAMILY

	RECORD NO.	LABEL
Promises To Keep	R3526(C)	HeartWarming
The Songs Live On (The Best Of) (2-record set)	R3512(D)	HeartWarming
Between The Cross And Heaven (There's A Whole Lotta Livin' Goin' On)	R3388(C)	HeartWarming
Doug Oldham And The Speers—Live I Just Feel Like Something Good Is About To Happen (2-record set)	R3353(D)	HeartWarming
Something Good Is About To Happen	R3328(C)	HeartWarming
A Tribute To Bill and Gloria Gaither (2-record set)	R3349(D)	HeartWarming
In Concert (2-record set)	R3180(D)	HeartWarming

THE STATESMEN

	RECORD NO.	LABEL
Get Away Jordan	6180	Sky.

STONEHILL, RANDY

	RECORD NO.	LABEL
Welcome To Paradise	SRA 2002	Solid Rock

ARTIST AND ALBUM TITLE	RECORD NO.	LABEL
STOOKEY, NOEL PAUL		
Something New And Fresh	NWS 0376	New World
Real To Reel	NWS 0477	New World
Paul And . . .	NWS 0171	New World
One Night Stand	NWS 0272	New World
Band And Bodyworks	NWS 1379	New World
SUMNER, J.D. AND THE STAMPS		
Live At Murray State University		
(2-record set)	R3365(D)	HeartWarming
What A Happy Time	R3302(C)	HeartWarming
Elvis' Favorite Gospel	362	QCA
Golden Gospel	6150	Sky.
Gospel's Best	715	Power
Green Green Grass Of Home	6193	Pick.
J.D. Sumner & The Stamps	714	Power
Memories Of Our Friend Elvis	373	QCA
Old Rugged Cross	707	Power
Old Time Religion	705	Power
16 Greats	3007	Star.
Street Corner Preacher	359	QCA
Vintage Gospel	6144	Sky.
What A Day	706	Power
What A Saviour	985	Star.
SUTTER, LYNN		
Everlasting Kind Of Love	DST 4010	DaySpring
SWAGGART, JIMMY		
Somewhere Listenin'	R3628	Jim
We'll Talk It Over	R3627(C)	Jim

ARTIST AND ALBUM TITLE	RECORD NO.	LABEL
(*Swaggart, Jimmy, cont.*)		
Jimmy Swaggart Live From Nashville (2-record set)	R3626(D)	Jim
Heaven's Sounding Sweeter All The Time	R3625(C)	Jim
God's Gonna' Bless His Children	R3624(C)	Jim
Only Jesus	R3623(C)	Jim
The Name Of Jesus	R3622(C)	Jim
When I Say Jesus	R3621(C)	Jim
Hallelujah	R3620(C)	Jim
Touching Jesus	R3619(C)	Jim
Holy	R3618(C)	Jim
Songs From Mama's Songbook	R3617(C)	Jim
Jesus Is The Sweetest Name I Know	R3616(C)	Jim
Jesus Will Outshine Them All	R3615(C)	Jim
There Is A River	R3614(C)	Jim
Campmeeting Organ—Instrumental	R3613(C)	Jim
Campmeeting Piano—Instrumental	R3612(C)	Jim
This Is Just What Heaven Means To Me	R3611(C)	Jim
Down The Sawdust Trail	R3610(C)	Jim
You Don't Need To Understand	R3609(C)	Jim
Someone To Care	R3608(C)	Jim
The Golden Gospel Piano (Instrumental)	R3607(C)	Jim
At An Altar Of Prayer	R3606(C)	Jim
I'm Nearer Home	R3605(C)	Jim
I've Got Nothing To Lose	R3604(C)	Jim
In The Shelter Of His Arms	R3603(C)	Jim
God Took Away My Yesterdays	R3602(C)	Jim
Some Golden Daybreak	R3601(C)	Jim

THE SWEET COMFORT BAND

Breaking The Ice	LS 5751	Light

TAYLOR, DANNY

I'm Not Just A One-Man Show	NP 33026	Newpax

ARTIST AND ALBUM TITLE	RECORD NO.	LABEL
THE TELESTIALS		
Experience The Telestials Live	5158	Calvary
Free Indeed	5146	Calvary
One Way Flight	5125	Calvary
Sing About The Bride	5111	Calvary
THOMAS, B.J.		
Home Where I Belong	MSB 6574	Myrrh
Happy Man	MSB 6593	Myrrh
You Gave Me Love		
(When Nobody Gave Me A Prayer)	MSB 6633	Myrrh
THE THRASHER BROTHERS		
One Day At A Time	CAS 9748	Canaan
Heart To Heart	CAS 9770	Canaan
In The Spirit Of The Dove	CAS 9808	Canaan
TORNQUIST, EVIE		
Evie	WST 8628	Word
Evie Again	WST 8642	Word
Gentle Moments	WST 8714	Word
Du Skulle Vara Med I Sangen	WST 8724	Word
Mirror	WSB 8735	Word
TURNER, NORRIS		
I Want To Be Ready	1506	HSE Records
Stop And Get Religion	HS 1360	HSE Records
Give God A Chance	1383	HSE Records

ARTIST AND ALBUM TITLE	RECORD NO.	LABEL
THE VOICES OF NASHVILLE		
Let It Be Me	1465	HSE Records
WALKER, ALBERTINA		
Albertina Walker And Caravans	0057	Jewel
WALL, ALWYN BAND		
The Prize	MSB 6596	Myrrh
THE WALL BROTHERS BAND		
Start All Over Again	R3485(C)	Greentree
At The Door	R3418(C)	Greentree
Wall Brothers	R3409(C)	Greentree
WARD, CLARA (Ward Singers)		
Soul And Inspiration	3251	Pick.
Gospel Concert With Clara Ward	14046	Savoy
I Feet The Spirit	14026	Savoy
Just Over The Horizon	14060	Savoy
Lord Touch Me	14006	Savoy
Meeting Tonight	14015	Savoy
Memorial Album	14308	Savoy
Newport Spiritual All-Stars	14013	Savoy
Packing Up	14020	Savoy
Surely God Is Able	14001	Savoy
That Old Landmark	14034	Savoy
Whole World In His Hands	14027	Savoy

ARTIST AND ALBUM TITLE	RECORD NO.	LABEL
WILDER, DEAN (See **HALE & WILDER**)		
WILKIN, MARIJOHN		
Lord, Let Me Leave A Song	DST 4008	DaySpring
I Have Returned	MSA 6537	Myrrh
Where I'm Going	MSA 6549	Myrrh
Reach Up And Touch God's Hand	MSA 6559	Myrrh
WILLARD, KELLY		
Blame It On The One I Love	MM0047T	Maranatha!
WOLFE, LANNY TRIO		
Have A Nice Day	R3482(C)	Impact
An Evening With The Lanny Wolfe Trio (2-record set)	R3434(D)	Impact
A Brand New Touch	R3407(C)	Impact
Shout It . . . Jesus Is Coming	R3356(C)	Impact
The Lanny Wolfe Trio . . . Rejoicing/ Live! (2-record set)	R3346(D)	Impact
Come On, Let's Praise Him	R3301(C)	Impact
Let's Sing A Song About Jesus	R3222(C)	Impact
There's Something In The Air	R3177(C)	Impact
ZIMMER, NORMA		
Reach Out And Touch	WST 8538	Word
Bless This House	WST 8568	Word
In The Garden	WST 8641	Word

Gospel Music Association

BOARD OF DIRECTORS

OFFICERS

President
W. F. Myers
New York, N.Y.

Executive V-P
Hal Spencer
Burbank, CA.

Secretary
Norman Odlum
New York, N.Y.

Treasurer
Herman Harper
Nashville, TN.

Chairman of the Board
Frances Preston
Nashville, TN.

Vice-Presidents
James Bullard
Hollywood, CA.

Ron Coker
Nashville, TN.

Lou Hildreth
Nashville, TN.

Charlie Monk
Nashville, TN.

Stan Moser
Waco, TX.

Ed Shea
Nashville, TN.

Carroll Stout
Flora, IND.

Joe Talbot
Nashville, TN.

J. G. Whitfield
Pensacola, FL.

Bud Wingard
Nashville, TN.

Trustees
Les Beasley
Cantonment, FL.

John T. Benson, III
Nashville, TN.

Marvin Norcross
Waco, TX.

Brock Speer
Nashville, TN.

Executive Director
Don Butler
Nashville, TN.

Legal Advisor
R. David Ludwick
Nashville, TN.

Index

(The index does not include people listed in the alphabetical encyclopedia section since they are readily located in the book.)

A & S Records, 285
ABC Records, 133, 297
Abernathy, Lee Roy, 199
Abilene Christian College, 45
Act One Company, 51
Agape Force Prep School, 40
Alethians, 140
American Bandstand, 45
American Bible Society, 152
American Federation of Television
    and Radio Artists, 183
American Legion, 118, 152
American Song Festival, 160
America Sings, 105, 179
Amplified Version, 92
Anderson, Bill, 164
Anna Tuell Holy Hour Singers, The,
    151
Apollo Theater, 63
Arbor, Brush, 67
Arthur, Brooks, 33
Arthur Godfrey Talent Scout Show,
    29, 33
Autry, Gene, 58

Babb, Dr. Morgan, 182
Bacharach, Burt, 177
Back Home Choir, 27
Banks, The Reverend Charles, 27
Bartlett, E. M., 200, 201
Baxter, J. R., Jr., 200, 201
Beatles, The, 141
Bennard, George, 200
Benson Company, The, 22, 75, 80, 99,
    106, 133, 134, 151, 162, 173, 188,
    304
Bernstein, Leonard, 186
Bethany Nazarene College, 89
Biederwolf, W. R., 202
Billboard, 24, 32, 49, 133, 138, 164
Billy Sunday Evangelistic Campaigns,
    202
Bivens Specials, 107
Blackwood, James, Sr., 28, 29-30,
    170, 199
Bradford, Shorty, 199

Broadman Press, 188
Brumely, Albert E., 200-201
Buckhorn Music, 186
Buzz, 130
Byrdett Singers, The, 27

Calvary Chapel, 82, 83, 113, 149
Calvary Records, 290, 311
Camden Records, 274, 275, 277
The Camp-Meeting Hour, 173
Campus Crusade, 134
Campus Life, 96, 116
Campus Life, 65
Campus Life Singers, The, 39
Canaanland Music, 114
Canaan Records, 43, 70, 83, 98, 115,
    125, 273, 278, 282, 284, 285, 287,
    288, 291, 292, 294, 295, 297, 298, 311
Capitol Records, 277, 285, 286, 304
Caravans, The, 39, 92
Carmichael, Ralph, 24, 43, 44, 56
    Orchestra and Chorus, 114, 142
Carnegie Hall, 25, 27, 49, 54, 63, 103,
    175, 180
Carter, President Jimmy, 28
Cashbox, 91, 133, 164
Charisma Records, 24
Charity Singers, The, 39
Checker Records, 307, 308
Children of Faith, 46
Christian Broadcasting Network, 48,
    106, 133
Christianity Today, 96
Christian Life Center, 85
Chuck Wagon Gang, The, 58
Cincinnati Conservatory of Music, 72
Clark, Paul, 93, 108
Cogics, 141
Cole, Bill, 90
Columbia Records, 105, 277, 278, 292,
    293, 299, 307
Concert For Bangladesh, 141
Contemporary Christian Music, 145
Continental Ministries, 103
Cooke, Sam, 165
Country Music Association, 131

Country Music Hall of Fame, 58
Cox, Ida, 102
Cravens, Rupert, 202
Creed Records, 283, 284
Crosby, Fanny, 201
Crumpler, Denver, 201

Daniel, John, 201
David, Hal, 177
DaySpring Records, 55, 99, 160, 173, 281, 291, 306, 309, 313
Dean, Jimmy, 99, 167
Derricks, The Reverend Clevant, 103
Diadem Records, 60
Dillard, Ernest, 157
Discovery Art Guild, 68
Dorsey, Professor Thomas A., 48, 52
Dot Records, 33
Dove, 66
Dragon, Carmen, 190

Eastern New York Mass Choir, 151
Ebony, 39, 49
Electrical Workers Quartet, The, 204
Epic Records, 278, 297
Evangelical Film Foundation, The, 133, 143
Excursions, 105
Expo '72, 24

Fairfield Four, The, 182
Faith Publishing Company, 205
Family Affair, 182
Foley, Red, 30
Ford, President Gerald, 74
Foster, Paul, 165
Franklin, Aretha, 48, 92
Fuller Seminary, 38

Garden of Prayer Cathedral Choir, 152
Gentle Faith, 67
Giovanni, Nikki, 65
GMA Fan Award, 29
Golden Stars of Greenwood, The, 180
Good News, 126
Good News Records, 46, 47, 279, 287
Gospel Keytones, The, 124
Gospel Music Association, 58, 70, 105, 125, 160, 199, 200
Gospel Music Hall of Fame, 70, 125, 160, 199-205
Gospel Music Workshop of America, 49
Gospel Singing Caravan, 105, 114

Gospel Singing Jubilee, The, 63, 70, 83, 95, 125, 153, 177
Gospel West, 190
Graham, Billy, 54, 128, 160, 169
  Association, 28
  Crusade, 105, 116, 160, 189
Grammy Awards, 29, 39, 49, 54, 60, 63, 76, 83, 91, 99, 117, 133, 139, 143, 167, 178, 179, 180
Grand Ole Gospel, 177, 199
Grand Ole Opry, 54, 164, 199, 201
Great Circle Records, 151
Greentree Records, 22, 75, 95, 134, 159, 162, 184, 273, 286, 290, 293, 300, 303, 306, 312

Hall-Moody Institute, 200
Happy Two, The, 199
Harmon, Nancy, 125
Harmony Records, 277, 278
Harris, R. H., 165
Hartford Music Company, 200, 201
Harvest Records, 296
HeartWarming Records, 92, 145, 162, 290, 294, 299, 303, 305, 306, 307, 308, 309
Henson Publishing Company, 205
Hildebrandt, Ray, 67
Hollywood Bowl, 114, 190
Hollywood Free Theater, 37
Homeland Harmony Quartet, 125, 199, 204
Hope of Glory, 66
Hour of Power, The, 189
HSE Records, 158, 180, 274, 298, 305, 311, 312
Huffman, Joe, 80, 133
Hurok, Sol, 114

I Believe in Miracles, 60
Impact Books, 133
Impact Records, 24, 51, 133, 273, 276, 286, 287, 291, 292, 298, 299, 313
Imperial Records, 307
International Orphans, Inc., 152
Inter-Varsity Christian Fellowship, 105

JC Power Outlet, 137
J. C. White Singers, 102
Jesus '73, 175
Jewel Records, 308, 312
Jim Records, 173, 280, 309, 310
Johnson Ensemble, The, 65

Johnson, Paul, 117, 118
Johnson Publishing Company, 183
Juilliard School of Music, The, 60

Kennedy, President John F., 103
Klaudt Family Records, 294
Kuhlman, Kathryn, 60

Lamb/Lion Records, 37, 275, 276, 283
Lawrence Welk Show, The, 127, 189
Lee, Danny, 43
LeFevre, Eva Mae, 199
Lexicon Music, 37, 56, 142
Liberation Suite, 46
Light Records, 24, 37, 38, 43, 44, 45,
    51, 54, 56, 60, 63, 68, 81, 90, 103,
    114, 118, 136, 142, 173, 174, 273,
    276, 278, 279, 281, 282, 283, 284,
    287, 289, 293, 295, 296, 300, 303, 310
Lister, Mosie, 199, 202
Living Sound, 81, 82
Lodo Music Company, 205
Logos, 116
Love Inn Community, 153
Love Inn Company, 153
Love Song, 66, 67, 82, 83, 108

MacKenzie, Bob, 43, 78
Madison Square Garden, 27, 54, 63,
    175
Madora Festival, 127
Malcolm & Alwyn, 130
Manna Records, 55
Maranatha! Music, 67, 71, 113, 121,
    126, 138, 139, 149, 174, 187, 274,
    284, 285, 294, 296, 298, 300, 304,
    307, 313
Mary Johnson Davis Singers, The, 27
Matthews, Randy, 106
McGuire, Dony, 23
Melody Boys, The, 201
Memphis Crusade, 28
Metromedia Records, 175
MGM Records, 304
Midnight Special, 45
Mighty Flyers, The, 183
Millenium, 66
Miracle Men, 199
Morros-Henson Quartet, The, 204
Movement for World Evangelization,
    138
Museum of Modern Art, 65
Music Hall America, 45
Mustard Seed Faith, 70, 121

Myrrh Records, 24, 46, 66, 67, 85, 96,
    116, 137, 141, 178, 273, 277, 279,
    284, 288, 289, 291, 295, 296, 297,
    299, 300, 301, 302, 305, 311, 312,
    313

Nashboro Records, 65
Nashville Gospel, 164
Nashville Songwriters Association
    Hall of Fame, 186
National Academy of Recording Arts
    and Sciences, 29, 167
National Association of Negro
    Musicians, 49
National Association of Television
    and Radio Announcers (NATRA),
    49, 101
National Council of Negro Women,
    183
National Quartet Convention, 29, 98,
    170, 199, 205
National Singing Convention, 204
New Christy Minstrels, The, 119
New England Conservatory of Music,
    89
New Life Records, 51
Neworld Productions, 169, 309
Newpax Records, 66, 75, 85, 106, 114,
    175, 276, 284, 286, 288, 293, 295,
    301, 310
Newport Jazz Festival, 27, 103
New Song Records, 293, 294, 304
Newton-John, Olivia, 45
Newton, Wayne, 45
New York City Opera, 89, 185
New York Community Choir, The, 65
Noah, 66
Norcross, Marvin, 98

Ole Time Gospel Hour, 177
Opryland Dixieland Band, 45
Oral Roberts and You, 56
Oral Roberts Presents, 56
Oral Roberts University, 55, 60, 81
Original Famous Ward Singers, The,
    185
Osmonds, The, 30, 32, 45
Ott, Doy, 205
Outlaw, Jimmy, 165
Owens, Jimmy, 134, 135, 169

Pace, Adger M., 201-202
Parable, 67

Paragon Records, 129, 175, 188, 296, 298, 301
Pat Terry Group, 66
Peabody Conservatory of Music, 123
Peacock Records, 123, 297
Peninsula Bible Church, 68
Petra, 40
Pickwick Records, 309, 312
Pinewood Studio, 78
Power Records, 309
Presidential Prayer Breakfast, 28
PTL Club, The, 48, 85, 125, 151, 177
PUSH, 182, 183

QCA Records, 63, 283, 293, 309

Radio & Records, 133
Radio and Television Commission of the Southern Baptist Convention, 48
Rangers, The, 199, 201
RCA Records, 167, 203, 274, 301, 302, 307
Record World, 133, 157, 178, 180
Red, Buryl, 47, 52
Redman, Mike, 118
Reed, Jerry, 45
Religious Heritage of America, 152
Richard, Cliff, 140
Robert Paterson Singers, The, 151
Roberts, Oral,
    crusades, 55
    television shows, 56, 83
Roberts, Richard and Patti, 55
Robinson, James, 48
Rodeheaver, Homer, 202
Ross, Nedra, 153
Ross, Scott, 153
Round Table International, 152
Rubinstein, Arthur, 60

Sacred Festival of Music, 190
Salt Company, 24
Santana, 54, 139
Savoy Records, 48, 63, 107, 274, 277, 279, 280, 301, 312
Schuller, Dr. Robert, 189
Seed Records, 93, 290
Selahs, The, 126, 180
700 Club, The, 48, 85, 106, 151, 159, 177
Shaw, Robert, 186
Shekinah Fellowship, 87
Showalter, A. J., 202

Silverdome, 153
Silverton Gospel Singers, The, 129
Sinatra, Frank, 117
Singing News, 30, 43, 70, 83, 95, 98, 109, 199
Skylite Records, 200, 274, 275, 308, 309
Smith, Bessie, 102
Snow, Jimmy, 177
Solid Rock Foundation, The, 87
Solid Rock Records, 130, 291, 298, 300, 308
Songwriters Hall of Fame, 185
Sonlight, 92
Soul, 65
Southeastern Bible College, 159
Southern Baptist Theological Seminary, 71
Sparrow Records, 36, 87, 88, 119, 157, 169, 276, 288, 289
Specialty Records, 307, 308
Speer, Jack Brock, 165, 167, 200
Speer, Lena Brock "Mom," 165, 167, 203
Speer, Tom "Dad," 165, 167, 202, 203
Spurrlows, 114
SRP Records, 155, 304, 305
Stallings, John, 151
Stamps, Frank, 170, 201, 203
Stamps, Virgil Oliver, 201, 203
Stand Up And Cheer, 117, 118, 158
Starday Records, 309
Stone, Cliff, 72
Sun Records, 40, 141
Supreme Records, 63, 282, 283

Taylor, Johnnie, 165
TEAR Fund Concerts, 140
Ted Mack Amateur Hour, 33, 179
Temple Bible College, 49
Tempo Records, 175, 280, 281
Texas Baptist Convention, 52
Thomas Road Baptist Church, 133
Travis, Merle, 72
Triangle Records, 48, 52, 72, 279, 281, 285
Truth, 162
Tyndale House, 190

United Artists, 65
Up With People, 116

Vanderbilt Divinity School, 200
Van Hook, Jim, 35, 75

Variety, 30
Vaughan Family Visitor, 204
Vaughan, Glenn Kieffer, 203-204
Vaughan, James D., 204
Vaughan Music Publishing Company,
 201, 204
Vaughan Radio Quartet, The, 202,
 203, 204
Vaughan School of Music, 202, 204
Venture Recording Company, 107
Voices of Tabernacle, The, 48

Waddy, Henrietta, 185
Waites, James Parks, 204
Walbert, William Burton, 204
Warner/Curb, 32, 275
Warren Roberts Program, 153
Welk, Lawrence, 127, 189-190
Wetherington, James S., 205

Wide World of Entertainment, 45
Wild, Malcolm, 183
Williams, Hank, 177
Williams, Marion, 185
Windchime Records, 304
Winsett, Robert E., 205
Wood, Randy, 33
Word, Inc., 27, 51, 55, 70, 75, 76, 83,
 98, 99, 128, 137, 141, 142, 160, 180,
 285, 286, 289, 298, 304, 306, 311,
 313
World Action & Television Singers, 60
World Records, 152
Wright Special, The, 92

Young Life, 96
Youth For Christ, 85, 116, 121

Ziegler, J. T., 158

PICTURE CREDITS

The editors and publishers wish to thank the following people and organizations for pictures which they supplied for this book:

A&M Records; ABC Records; Dill Beaty; Cecil Blackwood; Bridge; Bob Bronson Photography; Russ Busby; Bruno of Hollywood; Canaan Records; Century II Promotions, Inc.; Citylights; Continental Ministries; Cooga Mooga, Inc.; Windy Drum Commercial Photography; Epic; Fonville; Great Circle Representation; Greentree Records; HeartWarming Records; His'n Her Creative Consultants; HOB; Impact; L'Abri Management; Lamb and Lion; Light Records; Don Light Talent, Inc.; Linda Miller and Associates Personal Management; New Direction Artist Guild; One Truth; David J. Pavol; Rosina Management Corp.; Sharing Christ Ministries; Spring House Associates; Fay Sims; Splendor Productions, Inc.; Supreme Records; Frank Valeri; The Wayne Coombs Agency, Inc.

a group of five young men, including his two sons.

Dixie Echoes can be seen throughout the United States on the *The Gospel Singing Jubilee* TV show. Since 1960 they have made over twenty albums. They now record exclusively for Supreme Records.

THE DIXIE MELODY BOYS

Ed O'Neal—Bass
Henry Daniels—Baritone
David Kimbrell—Lead
Jamey Ragle—1st Tenor
Greg Simpkins—Piano
Allen O'Neal—Guitar
Reb Lancaster—Bass
Ron Well—Steel Guitar

The Dixie Melody Boys have been singing their praises to God since 1960 at fairs, churches and revivals. Made up of four singers and a four-piece band, The Dixie Melody Boys have also appeared as guests on many local and national TV programs. They record for QCA records in Cincinnati, and have had national hits from each of their albums. One of their latest and most notable releases was *Lord Don't Move That Mountain.*

DIXON, JESSY

"My singing was anointed, but I wasn't," says Jessy Dixon. Ever since his boyhood in San Antonio, Texas, Jessy had attended church. He is the first to admit, however, that as he grew older he attended for the music rather than the faith. Later he went to St. Mary's College as a music major. It was there that Jessy caught the ear of gospel vocalist James Cleveland.

Dixon relocated to Chicago as a vocalist, accompanist and composer for Cleveland's Gospel Chimes singers. His career moved ahead quickly. He organized his own group, The Jessy Dixon Singers, with a recording contract on the Savoy label. Success continued with twelve hit albums including Grammy nominee *He Ain't Heavy* and three singles—"Sit At His Feet and Be Blessed," "These Old Heavy Burdens," and "God Never Fails."

Jessy confesses it was frustrating working in the gospel world without really accepting Christ as his Lord and Savior. "I was making a living singing," he says. "It was all I knew how to do because it was all I had ever done."

Soon things happened that quickly changed his life. A close friend explained the difference that finding Jesus had made. Dixon attended a Bible study discussion on the book of Romans and a few days later heard a radio preacher teaching the same message. Dixon had found a new life.

Since his conversion in 1972, Dixon has appeared at numerous college concerts as well as such major music centers as Carnegie Hall, Madison Square Garden and Harlem's Apollo Theater.

Dixon's most recent album on Light Records, entitled *It's All Right Now,* as well as his work with co-producer Andrae Crouch, reflects his own joy in the Lord and his artistic maturation.

63

JESSY DIXON: *Reflects his own joy in the Lord*

DOGWOOD

Ron Elder
Steve Chapman

Dogwood is a team of two cheerful young men, friends from their teens who traveled many hard roads before committing themselves to a life in Jesus and sharing the truths they found through their music.

From similar backgrounds in West Virginia, Ron Elder and Steve Chapman are both sons of ministers. In addition to this common bond, they also shared the same interest in music—gospel and country.

Their paths parted when Steve joined the Navy and Ron went off to college. Separated from one another and their families for a short time, they temporarily fell away from the Lord. They met again, discovered that music was an important link between them and traveled together around the country. During their travels they renewed their commitment to Christ, entering into a positive musical ministry. They had found a direction and, in 1974, Dogwood was born.

After The Flood, Before The Fire was their first album and introduced them to the Jesus music audience. *Love Note* was the duo's second album and enhanced their growing reputation in contemporary Christian music. *Free Love* magazine called *Love Note* "a real progression for the group . . . an album that rises above the commonplace country gospel/Jesus music genre to provide a real ministry." *Campus Life* described the album as "clean as spring water" featuring "crystal clear acoustics and vocals." Both The Imperials and The Boones have included Dogwood songs on their albums.

DOUGLAS, THE REVEREND ISAAC

The Reverend Isaac Douglas is a young man whose singing resounds with gruff, passionate vocal stylings. He knows how to drive any audience to its feet in an outburst of spontaneous, joyful participation. And he's done so in this country and abroad, before church and college audiences, in theaters and concert halls.

Many feel that Isaac is the latest in the long line of great male solo personalities that includes such gospel luminaries as The Reverend James Cleveland. As a boy, Isaac heard all the great gospel pioneers and he sees himself as a guardian of the traditions represented by his original vocal inspirations. While he's one of the most "progressive" of gospel stylists, he never forgets his roots.

Born in Philadelphia, Isaac moved to New York in the mid-sixties and formed his own all-male gospel group, The Isaac Douglas Singers. Their United Artists release, *Lord Have Mercy,* helped establish him as a young star. He next helped found The New York Community Choir. With this group, he helped provide the vocal background for Nikki Giovanni's best-selling album *Truth Is On The Way.* With his participation in a hit album, and frequent appearances at New York's Museum of Modern Art and on the TV program *Soul,* Douglas became a genuine gospel celebrity.

In the early seventies, Douglas underwent a change of direction. Inspired by the great James Cleveland, he moved to Los Angeles and joined the ministry. About this time, he also began recording for Nashboro Records, first with his group, then with The New York Community Choir. To fortify his ties with Nashboro, Douglas then moved to Nashville. Isaac has now recorded with choirs from all over the country; recently, with The Johnson Ensemble, he recorded the plaintive "The Harvest Is Plentiful."

F

FARRELL & FARRELL

Bob and Jayne Farrell are a husband-and-wife team who have been traveling and ministering through their music for several years. Before becoming true Christians both were involved in secular music—Bob played with several rock bands and Jayne spent some time singing on the nightclub circuit.

After accepting the Lord, each of them became involved in several individual ministries before uniting as husband and wife. For several years, in addition to her counseling work with young women in the areas of marriage and dating, Jayne was a featured soloist in crusades. Bob got his start in Jesus music in 1970 as co-founder of the group Millennium. In 1972, he joined one of the early pioneer Christian bands, Dove, a group which released an album on Myrrh in the early 1970s.

As a music team, both Bob and Jayne share the vocalizing and lyric-writing responsibilities, but Bob does most of the composing. One of his most popular songs, "Lifesaver," became a big hit for Hope of Glory, while another of his tunes, "Restored," was recorded by the Pat Terry Group.

The duo's first album for NewPax Records, entitled *Farrell & Farrell,* highlights the pair's versatile songs ranging from soft country to light rock and easy ballads.

FIELD, FRED

Fred Field surrendered his life to the Lord Jesus Christ, and almost simultaneously three of his friends, all roommates and comrades in music, also received the blessing of a personal relationship with Jesus Christ. Together the four—Fred Field, Chuck Girard, Tom Coomes and Jay Truax—formed the group Love Song, pioneering a new kind of music. This exciting "new wave" in music, reflecting and embodying their musical and cultural roots, lyrically spoke of their new-found Meaning of Life.

In 1972, two years after coming into a personal relationship with the Lord, Fred traveled with a group called Noah to the Munich Olympics. For the ensuing two years Noah gave concerts across the expanse of the European continent and the Middle East, and recorded in Germany and Israel. Based in Amsterdam, but resident part of the time in Tel Aviv, the group did extensive work at United States military bases in Germany on behalf of military chaplains and their drug-prevention programs.